The Power of PenPoint™

The Power of PenPoint™

Robert Carr
Dan Shafer

Addison-Wesley Publishing Company, Inc.
Reading, Massachusetts • Menlo Park, California • New York
Don Mills, Ontario • Wokingham, England • Amsterdam
Bonn • Sydney • Singapore • Tokyo • Madrid • San Juan
Paris • Seoul • Milan • Mexico City • Taipei

ISBN 0-201-57763-1

Sponsoring Editor, Carole McClendon
Cover design by Jean Seal
Set in 11-point Helvetica Light by Don Huntington

1 2 3 4 5 6 7 8 9 -MW- 9594939291
First printing, February, 1991

This book is dedicated to my wife Andrea, and my son Ian.

R.C.

This one's for Alicia, whose generation will look back on what we've considered so fantastic...and agree!

D.S.

Contents

viii
. . . .

The Power of PenPoint

Preface

. . . .

This book presents an architectural overview of PenPoint, a new, object-oriented, preemptive multitasking operating system specifically optimized for pen-based computing.

Who Should Read This Book?

As we wrote this book, we had in mind three audiences.

First, we wanted to appeal to technical and engineering managers, who have to make decisions about where to concentrate their companies' software development efforts during the next two or three years. This book contains enough technical detail and information about development techniques, environments, and strategies to make it possible for such managers to factor PenPoint into their thinking.

Second, we knew that as soon as PenPoint was officially announced, there would be significant interest from programmers wanting to know what this new operating system is and how it might affect their work. This book provides a foundation from which such readers can determine their levels of interest in creating software for the pen-based computers of the 1990s. It also gives these programmers a technical base from which to delve into the thousands of pages of documentation about the Software Developer's Kit (SDK) by pointing out the important concepts, data structures, classes, and messages on which

xviii

- -

The Power of PenPoint

to focus. (This SDK documentation, incidentally, is being published by Addison-Wesley in its GO Technical Library series.)

Finally, we are well aware of a vast group of people who are simply technically curious; we belong to that group. For this group of people who begin their exposure to PenPoint with no particular thought to using it or programming in it, we have used examples and comparisons with older operating systems as a way of differentiating PenPoint from those systems. We have also included a number of commentaries explaining the rationale behind PenPoint's design features, which will help such readers understand it better.

What's the Purpose of This Book?

Keeping in mind the three audiences discussed previously, we set ourselves several goals in writing this book and making it available early in PenPoint's history.

We wanted to convey something of how it feels to work with a pen-based computer and to program applications for this new paradigm. It is important to us that readers of this book gain an appreciation for the gestalt of pen-based computing and what makes it different for both the user and the application designer from all forms of computing that have preceded it. A book that accomplished only that purpose would, we felt, be useful and interesting.

But we wanted to go beyond the gestalt and look under the hood of Pen-Point. We wanted to take a look at how PenPoint accomplishes the behavior that makes it a unique operating system. How does its object-oriented nature influence its design, and vice versa? How are its various pieces organized, and how do they interact?

Finally, we wanted to give prospective PenPoint programmers a sense of what programming for PenPoint is like, as well as a way of knowing how to make best use of the SDK documentation with which they will deal as they develop PenPoint applications.

It is important to note what this book is not. It is not a programming manual; you will not find, in fact, a single line of sample code in its pages. It is not a complete reference guide to PenPoint; such a book occupies many more pages than this volume. Finally, it is not an end-user manual or even a comprehensive overview of the PenPoint user interface.

How Is This Book Organized?

This book has sixteen chapters, three appendices, and a Glossary.

Chapter 1 is an introduction to PenPoint. It begins with a discussion of the development of pen-based computing and includes a rationale for the development of a new operating system to support the new paradigm. It also provides a top-level view of PenPoint and its organization.

Chapter 2 focuses on the user interface to PenPoint, examining the operating system from the user's perspective. It focuses on the two important new ideas the user sees on a PenPoint-based system: the pen and the notebook metaphor.

Chapter 3 describes the development tools, environment, and approach to PenPoint programming. It begins with a brief discussion of the reasons you should consider undertaking PenPoint development, moves to explaining the learning process you should follow to master the environment, and offers some design hints. It also talks specifically about software support and the development process.

Chapter 4 begins the technical examination of PenPoint that occupies the rest of the book. It focuses on the kernel layer of the operating system, that layer closest to the hardware of a PenPoint-based system.

Chapter 5 concentrates on the Class Manager, a significant element of PenPoint in which the object-oriented behavior of the operating system is concentrated. Here, you'll learn how to create new classes and subclass existing ones.

Chapter 6 explains the use of the Application Framework, the portion of PenPoint with which you will become most familiar as you build your programs. This collection of classes defines the protocols that make up a PenPoint application. It is also a complete implementation of a generic PenPoint application.

Chapter 7 describes the windowing subsystem in PenPoint. Here, you'll see that PenPoint windows are designed to be memory-efficient, or lightweight, objects so that you can afford to define a great many of them in an application. You'll see how to create and manage the windows that provide the framework for your application's interface.

xx

. . . .

The Power of PenPoint

Chapter 8 discusses an important new concept in PenPoint: recursive live embedding. PenPoint users can open new documents from within existing documents even when the new document is created and managed by a different application from that of the host document. This process can continue to a theoretically unlimited number of levels of embedding. But this capability presents special problems for an operating system. You'll see in this chapter how PenPoint implements this feature and deals with the problem, as well as how your applications are affected.

Chapter 9 discusses ImagePoint, the graphics subsystem in PenPoint. This is the part of the system that produces the actual images on the screen in the windows discussed in Chapter 7. You will learn how windows work, how to create and manage them, and how multiple overlapping windows from multiple applications interact with each other.

Chapter 10 describes the User Interface Toolkit, a collection of classes that makes it easy for you to give your PenPoint applications the look and feel users will come to expect from pen-based programs. You'll learn about the various controls, decorations, and other components of the user interface.

Chapter 11 provides an in-depth look at the PenPoint file system. This is a key component of PenPoint; much of the special functionality of the system (such as installable objects and PenPoint's unique connectivity) are based on the file system. You'll see how the system works, how it cooperates with existing file systems, and how to use it in your applications.

Chapter 12 explains the concept of resources and how they are used in PenPoint. You'll learn that you can use the system's Resource Manager to help you manage your data and objects in such a way that you don't have to spend time designing file formats, or worrying about where files are located in the hierarchy when your application runs or the precise location of elements within a file. The Resource Manager can take care of all of those details for you.

Chapter 13 concentrates on the input subsystem. This is where you learn about the pen and how it works from a programming perspective. You'll also gain an understanding of how handwriting translation works and how it affects your application.

Chapter 14 presents the key ideas behind the text-editing capabilities of PenPoint. You'll see how PenPoint's text editor is built on the view-data model and how to make use of this editing capability in your application.

Chapter 15 outlines the Service Manager, a unique collection of routines that permit PenPoint to install and deinstall, connect and disconnect, activate and deactivate a variety of device drivers and background services. You'll see that PenPoint is unique in allowing the user to install, deinstall, and configure services on the fly without shutting down the system or interfering with other operations.

Chapter 16 describes how a PenPoint-based system's built-in connectivity is implemented. Networking takes center stage, but other issues such as electronic mail, facsimile transmission, and the unique concept of deferred I/O are also discussed.

Appendix A is a chapter-by-chapter collection of programming information about the important elements of PenPoint discussed in chapters 4–15. The important data structures and their key fields are discussed. Tables summarize the most-often-used classes and the messages they define, with which you will want to become most familiar.

Appendix B offers some design and programming hints for programmers and in the process gives you a different slant on the gestalt of PenPoint development.

Appendix C provides insight into how to evaluate pen-based computers and handwriting recognition technology.

Glossary is a glossary of terms used in this book and in describing PenPoint.

What Are Those Gray Boxes?

Scattered throughout the book, you'll find sections printed on a gray background. These special boxes contain information of two types.

First, there are notes. These generally point out an important exception or clarification of information in the main text. They are always labeled NOTE.

Second, there are asides and insights. These gray boxes have longer, more explanatory headings and provide the perspective of PenPoint architect Robert Carr with regard to such issues as why he and his team decided to take a certain approach to design, the advantages of a particular design element, or the trade-offs involved in the decision-making process. These should give you valuable insight into the minds of the people who designed PenPoint.

Becoming a Developer

GO Corporation has an active program underway to train and support qualified application developers. Excellent documentation, developer tools, and courses are available. If you are interested in developing software for PenPoint and would like more information, please call or write:

Developer Marketing, GO Corporation, 950 Tower Lane, Suite 1400, Foster City, Calif. 94404; (415) 345-7400.

Contacting the Authors

We enjoy hearing from people who have read this book and have insights, questions, compliments, complaints, or other communication to share with us. We can both be reached on MCI Mail, as RCARR and DSHAFER, respectively. Or you can write to Robert at GO Corporation, 950 Tower Lane, Suite 1400, Foster City, Calif. 94404. Dan is also accessible via CompuServe (71246,402), CONNECT (DSHAFER), and AppleLink (DSHAFER).

Acknowledgments

PenPoint is the result of a team effort by more than 70 dedicated individuals. To the degree PenPoint's design and implementation are successful and excellent, and to the degree PenPoint is well-received by the market, all credit and acknowledgment must go to this entire team. I believe PenPoint will be more than merely successful.

Software engineers, documentation professionals, product marketing personnel, user interface design experts, testers, software quality assurance people, and, yes, management and financial backers: every role and every individual made invaluable contributions. PenPoint is a good product because of the inspiration, patience, and particularly the hard work of these individuals.

I particularly want to thank those who joined the PenPoint team early, when we had only our imaginations. It is a rare individual who can confront the challenge of invention. But as hard as truly original imagining is, building a working version proved to be ten times harder.

R.C.

Like PenPoint, this book is a collaboration among a number of people. We wish to express appreciation to Alex Brown, John Zussman, Patty Zussman, Carol Broadbent, and many other GO Corporation staffers who assisted with the design, development, and production of this book. Carole McClendon, Joanne Clapp Fullagar, Rachel Guichard, and Mary Cavaliere of Addison-

xxiv

. . . .

The Power of PenPoint

Wesley believed in the book, nurtured it through its development and publication, and share in the credit for the finished product. Don and Rae Huntington of Production Services did their usual wonderful job of being the last ones in the chain of production and of performing admirably under pressure.

R.C. & D.S.

1

Introduction

....

PenPoint is a new operating system designed and built from the ground up by GO Corporation for the unique requirements of mobile, pen-based computers. It is a 32-bit, object-oriented, multitasking operating system that packs the power of workstation-class operating systems into a compact implementation that does not require a hard disk.

Shrinking hardware sizes and the addition of a pen make possible a dramatic change in the way computers are used. Instead of controlling the computer through a combination of mouse and keyboard, PenPoint proposes the use of a single, simple pen. Instead of using computers only at desks or tables, PenPoint proposes mobile usage throughout the day, wherever the user is: in meetings, standing, walking, at a desk, in the car, even on the couch at home.

PenPoint computers are powerful, tabletlike devices that behave much more like a notebook than traditional computers. Users control PenPoint computers with special pens that are sensed by the screen. The user writes directly on the screen, combining the convenience of a notebook with the power of a computer. Data is entered by handwriting, which PenPoint translates into standard text. Commands are issued by pointing and by gestures such as circling and scratching out.

In the early 1980s, the desktop personal computer market was only able to flourish after the arrival of a standard operating system that allowed many hardware companies to build systems that all could run the same application software. In the 1990s, there is a need for a new, general-purpose, mobile, pen-based operating system to play a similar role in catalyzing the opportunities in the high-growth markets for mobile, pen-based computing. PenPoint is designed to be that catalyst.

Our Friend the Pen

Under PenPoint, the pen is the primary input device. The pen is used for pointing (by touching the screen), data entry (through handwriting), and commands (through gestures).

Using a pen, it is easy to make a simple gesture that specifies both what you want to do (the operation) and what you want to do it to (the operand). This results in a more natural, direct feel when using the computer. Take the example of deleting a word. In a mouse-driven interface, you must double-click the mouse to select the word, then choose Delete from a menu or the keyboard. In PenPoint, you simply draw an "X" over the word, and it is deleted. Gesture commands are difficult (at best) with a mouse. In contrast, the pen is a single unified tool that combines the functions of a mouse and keyboard and adds the new function of gesture commands.

The pen is the most natural and ergonomic computer input device. Humans are capable of incredible precision and deftness with penlike devices: Walk into any museum and view the artwork created with pencil, pen, and brush. This deftness is possible because the pen allows the eyes and hand to coordinate closely. Furthermore, the pen does not require an on-screen cursor, since the pen tip itself indicates the pen's location on the screen. Users are freed from learning about the concept of cursors, which accelerates learning and improves efficiency in using the system.

It is also important to recognize how comfortable meeting attendees are when other people are writing with pens and how uncomfortable and distracted they are by typing on keyboard-based computers. In other words, the pen is socially acceptable in a wide variety of meeting situations. Furthermore, pen-based computers can be used while standing and walking, while keyboards always require a table or desk.

Mobile Pen-Based Computing: An Untapped Market

In recent years, the growth rate of sales of desktop computers has slowed dramatically. Even with a graphical user interface (GUI), computers remain difficult for most people to learn and, because they are *desktop* systems, they cannot meet the needs of the millions of American workers who spend most of their day *away* from a desk. Despite the high sales rate of personal computers throughout the 1980s, today only about one-third of the 78 million white-collar workers in the United States use desktop systems.

Of those who do not use PCs, there are between 25 million and 35 million who spend much of their time away from their desk. These users need mobile, pen-based computers. Examples of these professionals include sales person-nel, lawyers, doctors, journalists, scientists, lab technicians, managers, execu-tives, estimators, inspectors, and field engineers. In addition, there are signifi-cant numbers of blue-collar clipboard users and government workers who are not served by desktop PC technology.

At the heart of these markets that will benefit from PenPoint is a new set of tasks — that don't belong at a desk or can't be performed there — as well as new users. Recognizing that there are new tasks makes it easier to answer the often-asked question: "Will brand-new customers or users of existing comput-ers use mobile, pen-based computers?" It will be both. While the dominant new market opportunity consists of the more than 25 million new users who spend most of their time away from their desk (if they indeed have one), there are many users of existing PC technology who will benefit from these devices as well.

Because they are used for new tasks, and often by new users, pen-based computing needs new application software suited for these new markets. Entire new categories of applications such as meeting-aid software, note-taking, and group document markup and revision will emerge. Applications that are limited in the current PC market because they are deskbound (for example, calendars, personal-information managers, and forms-completion systems) will flourish in the mobile, pen-based market. They are all hampered in their market success so long as they must be run on a desktop PC or laptop computer.

Pen-based computers will come in a variety of sizes and shapes. The pen naturally scales to any paper size, so a variety of screen sizes makes sense. Contrast this situation with the keyboard, which cannot be shrunk smaller than typewriter size and still be usable. Depending on the task, users will buy shirt-pocket, steno pad, notebook (page-sized screens), and desktop visual tablet configurations of pen-based computers. Users interested in ultimate portability for lightweight electronic mail, calendering, and personal-information management would choose a pocket-sized device. Steno pads might be most appropriate for on-screen forms completion. Users interested in serious document processing will typically want page-sized screens. Lastly, graphic artists and CAD/CAM users will probably prefer using a pen on a live screen in the visual tablet configuration at their desk or drawing table.

The Laptop Isn't a Solution

A common question is "Why aren't laptops an appropriate solution for the mobile market?" They aren't because they are actually desktop devices, not mobile devices. Laptops are evolutionary personal computers. Their very premise is that they are 100 percent compatible with desktop computers (that is, they must run the same software). They are therefore reduced-sized desktop computers optimized for transportability (to move from desk to desk), not mobility.

Like their desktop-based predecessors, laptop computers command the user's full attention during their operation. They simply cannot be made unobtrusive the way a mobile, pen-based system can. When a laptop is placed on a table or desk, the laptop computer must be opened up with the screen folding up into the air. This intrudes into interpersonal space. Typing on a laptop keyboard is intrusive in many group situations and therefore rarely done. And, of course, keyboard computers cannot be used while standing or walking.

The real need is not for mobile, pen-based computers to run the same software as desktop computers, but for them to have access to data files stored on existing desktop computers and networks. Desktop operating systems do a poor job of providing access to each other's data files. In contrast, PenPoint excels at providing access to a variety of desktop operating systems' data files.

Why Build a New Operating System?

GO Corporation was founded in 1987 to pioneer mobile, pen-based computing. Early in its development, GO Corporation determined that there were three major alternative approaches to developing system software for this market. The first alternative is to assemble a unique collection from standard pieces. This is essentially what NeXT, Inc., has done: It took a version of UNIX and Display PostScript and surrounded them with a variety of less standard pieces. This alternative has the disadvantage that it does not bring along an installed base of applications and that existing standard pieces were developed for the desktop and perform poorly in a pen-based, mobile computing environment.

The second alternative is to add a "pen compatibility box" to an existing standard operating system such as OS/2 or Microsoft Windows. The pen compatibility box would attempt to run existing mouse-based software by using the pen to emulate the keyboard and mouse. While technically possible, this approach misses the point of the pen: The pen can be much simpler to use than the mouse and keyboard. When the pen is layered above a mouse-based GUI, a more complex system results, not a simpler one. The user of such a system must ultimately be fully aware of the underlying keyboard and mouse system and the mapping between it and the pen.

The third alternative is to design and build a new operating system from the ground up for the unique requirements of the mobile, pen-based market. This is the approach that GO Corporation took. Today, PenPoint is available for applications and hardware development activities.

Key Requirements

There are a number of key requirements for an operating system for the mobile, pen-based computer market.

The first key requirement is for a user interface designed to require only a fraction of the user's concentration; it must not presume the user's full attention will be focused on running the computer system, as desktop user interfaces do. The user interface must also provide support for the pen through gestures and handwriting translation.

6
· ·

The Power of PenPoint

In addition, applications on the pen-based system must be rewritten so they can, wherever possible, supply context for handwriting translation. Only an application can understand the meaning (semantics) of various regions of its screen display. Therefore, when the pen is touched to the screen, the application should be able to control the translation and meaning of the pen ink. For example, only an application can specify whether certain fields it displays are alpha or numeric. This simple information is vital in performing high-accuracy handwriting translations.

Mobility brings a number of key requirements, including deferred data transfer, detachable networking, and low memory and power consumption.

Deferred data transfer refers to users' need to issue data transfer commands on their schedule, not the computer's. With laptop computers, users must wait until they have an actual connection to a network, telephone line, or printer before they can give an electronic-mail, print, or facsimile command. Users must therefore perform the clerical work of keeping lists of file names to send or print when the appropriate facilities become available. This is burdensome. It is much more efficient to allow users to "address" the electronic-mail message when they've finished composing it; the user can then be free to move on to the next task, and the computer can perform the clerical task of tracking pending operations. An operating system for the mobile, pen-based market must provide mechanisms for deferred data transfer.

Detachable networking refers to the need for users to be able to make and break networking connections at will. In addition, the operating system must support multiple network protocol stacks so that the same pen-based machine can talk to many types of computers and networks (including wireless) in the course of a single day. When a connection is temporarily broken, the system should gracefully suspend the connection and be ready to resume it again when the connection is remade.

An operating system for the mobile, pen-based markets must excel at data compatibility with many existing personal computer and networking standards. Interestingly, a new operating system can actually do a better job at this than an existing one. Existing operating systems tend to be compatible only with themselves, creating islands of data without bridges. A new operating system can be designed to be promiscuously compatible and connectable.

Memory and power consumption needs must be minimized, not maximized, by an operating system. Desktop operating systems and applications are rapidly growing to fill all space available on large hard disks. These large hard disks are not always small enough or durable enough for small, pen-based computers that can get knocked about in use. Therefore, pen-based computers require a system that can minimize total memory requirements, including disk space. Also, the operating system must include sophisticated power management because batteries are a significant portion of the weight of pen-based computers.

Any successful operating system must provide a rich development environment. While existing systems have a head start on building a collection of tools and trained programmers, a modern, object-oriented operating system can do the best job of this. This is because it can provide the most-productive coding environment for the applications developer, since its application programming interfaces (APIs) will be consistent, coherent, and provide the right functionality for the new market. In contrast, traditional desktop operating systems are increasingly burdened with the complexity that stems from piling layer upon layer of software.

Finally, since the mobile, pen-based computer market is new, any operating system choice must provide a strong foundation upon which an entire new market can be built. The operating system must incorporate proven, robust technology choices such as 32-bit addressing, flat-memory model portability, and object orientation.

What Is PenPoint?

To understand PenPoint, you must grasp the significance of three adjectives: general-purpose, mobile, and pen-based. A general-purpose operating system is essential because computer markets naturally seek out general-purpose system software; no one wants to buy a vertically integrated solution that ties hardware, system software, and applications together into a single-vendor solution. Mobility is vital for the markets of people who spend most of their time away from the desk. Pen-based operation means that applications and system user interfaces are extensively rewritten to take advantage of the pen.

General Purpose versus Special Purpose

New technology markets are usually first served by special-purpose solutions. In the computer business, these take the form of vertically integrated hardware/system software/application combinations such as the dedicated word processors from the early years of microcomputers. On the inside, they were personal computers, but they lacked a general-purpose operating system. Instead, they incorporated special-purpose system software.

MS-DOS and the IBM PC put a nearly complete halt to dedicated word processors.

Markets naturally loathe special-purpose solutions and favor those based on general-purpose operating systems, because customers would always rather spend a little more money and gain freedom of choice of applications and freedom of choice of hardware vendors.

PenPoint is designed to be a general-purpose operating system available to the market on many different hardware platforms. Any PenPoint application will run unchanged on all PenPoint hardware.

Notebook User Interface

PenPoint was designed to be driven primarily by a pen. Because of this, PenPoint includes many new elements not found in traditional GUIs. Three of the most important are the notebook metaphor, gestures, and powerful handwriting translation. Together, these constitute the Notebook User Interface (NUI).

The notebook metaphor in PenPoint provides the user with a simple-to-operate, on-screen Notebook (see Figure 1-1). The user's information is organized as a collection of pages and sections. Tabs appear at the right-hand side of the screen, and there is a Table of Contents at the front of the Notebook. At the bottom of the screen is the Bookshelf, a repository for systemwide objects and resources such as In Box, Out Box, and on-line Help. (Chapter 2 describes the notebook metaphor and other aspects of the NUI in detail.)

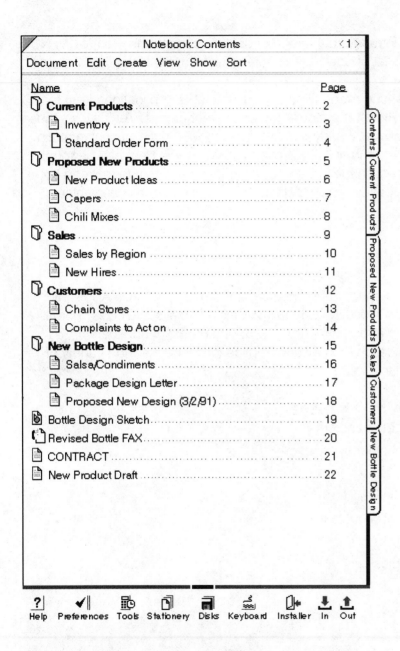

? ✓‖ 🗟 🗋 🖫 ⌨ 🚪◂ ⬇ ⬆
Help   Preferences   Tools   Stationery   Disks   Keyboard   Installer   In   Out

Figure 1-1   The Notebook Table of Contents

We have already introduced the idea of gesture commands. PenPoint's NUI builds in a standard set of powerful gestures that work consistently across all applications.

PenPoint's handwriting recognition system insulates applications from the need to develop any form of pattern-recognition techniques. Yet it allows those programs full control over the translation process, which is essential in attaining true pen-based user interfaces. While the user writes, PenPoint performs the recognition process in the background, so that the resulting text can be displayed immediately after the user signals that all of the text has been entered.

Application Framework

All applications written for PenPoint must adhere to PenPoint's Application Framework (discussed in detail in Chapter 6), which is a set of protocols rigorously defining the structure and common behavior of a PenPoint application.

Through the Application Framework, applications inherit a wide variety of standard behaviors, including

- gesture recognition and response
- copy and move data transfers
- live embedding of other applications
- view-data model
- installation and configuration
- creation of application instances
- on-line help
- document properties
- spell-checking
- search and replace
- printing
- import/exporting file formats
- application life cycle

New code is required only to add functionality or to modify or override specific aspects of the default behavior. Use of the Application Framework thus yields significant savings in programming time and code space.

The Application Framework defines the standard components of an application, including the application's code, an application object that is the control center for the application, a resource file, instance directory, process, and a main window.

Applications have a well-defined life cycle comprising six phases

- creation (create document state in file system)
- activation (create process)
- opening (turn to page)
- closing (turn away from page)
- termination (kill process)
- destruction (delete document state from file system)

In addition to normal applications that run when their page is turned to, PenPoint provides a Service Manager architecture that supports background server applications such as databases and network connections. Applications can interrogate PenPoint as to the presence of services and then establish message-passing connections to these services. For example, a personal-information manager application might provide many views onto one large collection of textual and calendar information. Each view would reside as a page in the Notebook. Actions in one view (your personal calendar) can thus be reflected instantly in another view (your project schedule).

Applications save their internal state in a directory in the file system, but this is invisible to the user, who has no need to save or load the application's state explicitly from one session to the next.

Embedded Document Architecture

The most innovative aspect of PenPoint's Application Framework is its Embedded Document Architecture (EDA), which provides three key user benefits: the document model, live application embedding, and hyperlinks.

The Document Model

In PenPoint, the operating system performs the clerical bookkeeping steps of starting and stopping processes (running applications) and of loading and saving application data. This is called a "document" model because the user never deals with application programs and data files or with the need to associate the two by loading files. Instead, users simply move from page to page and always see their data just as they last left it: scrolled to exactly the same location and with the application apparently still running. Unless the user is transferring information to other computers, there is no need for the user to deal with separate files and programs. Instead, to the user's mind, each document is itself a live, running piece of the user's data.

Live Application Embedding

Live application embedding refers to PenPoint's capability to embed a live instance of one application inside another application. It is PenPoint's most unique technical innovation.

For example, a text document can, with no special programming on the part of its creator, embed any other PenPoint application, such as a spreadsheet or business graphics application, within a text document it creates. Figure 1-2 shows a text document with two embeddees: a live, running drawing program and a live, running signature pad (which is, by the way, a built-in PenPoint object), both with their borders turned off. The result is that all PenPoint applications can provide a true compound document capability in which users are free to mix and match applications seamlessly.

The pen is an inherently multimedia tool; nothing is more natural than quickly switching from writing numbers to writing words to drawing a sketch, all on one piece of paper. PenPoint's live embedding allows every document in the PenPoint Notebook to be a compound or multimedia-ready, paperlike surface.

Other operating systems copy "dead" data from one application to another. This requires the designer of the receiving application to write code to accept a variety of data formats from the Clipboard and dynamic data exchange (DDE) transfer mechanisms. While PenPoint supports this mode of transfer of pure data, the norm is for the receiving application simply to embed an instance of the application that already knows how to edit and display the data.

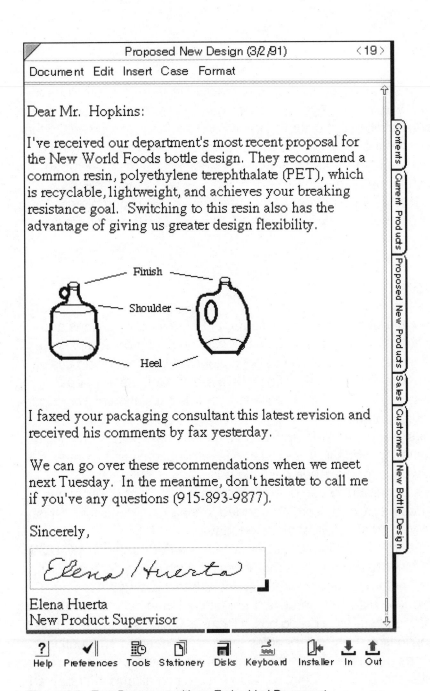

Figure 1-2 Text Document with an Embedded Document

Hyperlinks

Hyperlinks are a standard element of PenPoint's EDA. PenPoint provides a simple gesture with which a new hyperlink button can be created. The resulting button will "jump" (a combination of turning pages and scrolling a document) to the location selected when the button was created. Users can rename buttons and place them anywhere in the Notebook. Since PenPoint supports live embedding, the buttons can be placed inside documents as well as in PenPoint's Bookshelf area. The result is a hyperlinking mechanism that is completely integrated with both the operating system and all applications written for it.

Applications

From what we have said, it should be clear that PenPoint applications and the operating system have a close relationship with one another. The user might form the impression that installed applications and the operating system are simply part of a seamless whole. But the two are, in fact, cleanly separated. This allows easy distribution, installation, and deinstallation of PenPoint applications by third parties.

PenPoint comes with one built-in application, the MiniText editor, which is a pen-aware formatted-text editor. It is available for all applications to reuse, saving them the work of coding their own text editors.

Otherwise, as a general-purpose operating system, PenPoint applications will typically be bought by end users and added to their PenPoint system, just as MS-DOS and Macintosh applications are today.

PenPoint's standard for application distribution is 1.44MB, 3.5-inch MS-DOS disks. Every PenPoint-capable machine has access to such a drive (either built-in, via a base station, or through a desktop system). When the user places an application distribution disk into the drive, PenPoint automatically senses it and displays an application installation dialog box. If the user confirms a desire to install or update the application, PenPoint handles the rest. All needed application code and resources are installed into the PenPoint machine. Application code is also relocated at this time. PenPoint will also ensure that all classes required by the application are installed and are of the correct version.

Mobile Connectivity

PenPoint excels at connectivity to a variety of computers and networks. Mobile connectivity requires an operating system to be different from existing desktop operating systems, which evolved in a world of static connectivity.

> **Desktop Operating System = Static Connectivity**
>
> Desktop operating systems are designed for a world in which a single network connection is present all day. While this makes sense for desktop machines, these limitations are inconvenient for laptop users and unacceptable for mobile, pen-based computers.
>
> Desktop operating systems can typically load only a single network protocol at a time. For instance, with an MS-DOS laptop, no matter how small it is, you have to change start-up and configuration files and reboot your computer to connect to and disconnect from your office network. If you unplug the network wire without rebooting the system, you may lose data or crash the desktop operating system. These are the limitations of a static connectivity design.

PenPoint provides smooth connectivity to other computers and networks through built-in networking APIs that go well beyond the file transfer utilities currently used for laptop computers. PenPoint's networking protocols provide access to file system volumes, printers, and other remote services provided by desktop personal computers and networks.

Mobile, pen-based computers are connected and disconnected many times a day, often to and from different computers and networks. For these reasons, PenPoint supports multiple, "autoconfiguring" network protocol stacks that can be dynamically installed without rebooting the operating system. Network connections can be established and broken at will by the user (in other words, the user simply plugs cables in and removes them or walks into and out of receiving range for wireless communications), and the operating system and applications handle the breaks gracefully, suspending all interruptible operations until the connection is reestablished.

PenPoint's Out Box allows users to initiate file transfers, send electronic mail and facsimiles, and print documents to any destination, regardless of where the user is and regardless of whether the pen-based computer is currently hooked up to a connection that could satisfy the command.

The Out Box is a central, extensible queueing service for all connection-dependent transfer operations. Transfer agent services that extend the Out Box to work with specific destinations such as printers, file transfer, specific electronic-mail protocols (MCI Mail, PROFS, MHS, and so forth), and facsimile can be installed. The user interface for the Out Box is a small floating Note-book that provides a section for each Out Box transfer service.

Outgoing information must, of course, be addressed. PenPoint supplies standard Print and Send commands that allow communication services to be tightly integrated with PenPoint applications. The Send command brings up service-extensible addressing mechanisms that allow the user to send a single document to multiple destinations. PenPoint provides a standard address-book API so that the user's favorite address-book application can be used to store addressing information integrated with the address-book information the user keeps for all other uses.

Few people have the time to read all their electronic mail at their desk when they're plugged into the network. PenPoint's In Box supports quick download-ing of all received mail and facsimiles, so users can disconnect and carry their mail with them for perusal between meetings or at home in the easy chair. The In Box architecture is symmetrical to the Out Box and is similarly extensible by installable transfer services.

PenPoint's file system is designed for compatibility with other existing file systems, particularly MS-DOS, and includes full support for reading and writing MS-DOS-formatted disks.

The PenPoint file system is tied to the MS-DOS file system; all PenPoint-specific information is stored as an MS-DOS file in each MS-DOS directory. This approach is used when mapping to other file systems as well. Additional, installable volume types are also supported.

Compact and Scalable

Desktop operating systems assume large, cheap mass storage and therefore run poorly or not at all in one-tier hardware (RAM only, no mass storage) or require prohibitively expensive amounts of RAM to simulate disk space, or require difficult-to-update ROM memory. Although small applications exist for desktop operating systems, most of the best-selling applications typically require several megabytes of disk space.

In contrast, PenPoint is designed to run as a single, standard operating system on a full range of pen-based hardware, providing the largest possible market for applications. PenPoint runs well on both one-tier and two-tier (RAM with mass storage) memory architectures. As a result, PenPoint users will have a choice between small RAM-only machines and slightly larger machines with or without hard disks.

PenPoint's object-oriented design achieves compactness through a high degree of code sharing. Furthermore, PenPoint keeps only a single copy of code in the computer, because it relocates executable code at application installation time, not at application load time, as is traditionally done. If applications are relocated into memory at load time, there must be an additional copy of unrelocated application code on the disk. This, in effect, doubles total memory requirements. Once PenPoint installs an application, only a single copy of its code (the relocated executable) resides in the PenPoint machine until the user deinstalls that application.

PenPoint applications are small compared with their desktop counterparts. Competitive PenPoint applications often require total storage space of only 100 to 200 KB, rather than the megabytes that existing disk-based applications require.

Because PenPoint hardware will vary in screen size from shirt pocket up to large desktop visual tablets, PenPoint provides full support for all PenPoint user interfaces (including applications) to automatically adjust and scale to a variety of screen sizes. PenPoint's User Interface Toolkit allows applications to specify their user interfaces in the form of a relative constraint language. PenPoint then calculates the actual size and position of all user interface elements during program execution. As a result, applications do not hard-wire screen-size dependencies, as they have in the MS-DOS world.

A Solid Foundation

Combined with its unique support for the pen and mobile computing and its compact implementation, PenPoint is a platform that can provide a large and growing market for applications well into the next century.

All of PenPoint's APIs are 32-bit, and the first commercial version of Pen-Point will run on the Intel 80386 processor in its native, 32-bit, flat-memory mode. In addition, because PenPoint is written in C and is designed for portability, it can be ported to a variety of other processor architectures, including high-performance, low-power RISC (reduced instruction set computing) chips.

PenPoint provides preemptive multitasking similar to OS/2's, enabling smooth user interface interactions, background communications, and smooth background translation of handwriting while the user is writing. Each application runs in its own process. Lightweight child threads are supported.

Reliability is crucial to the mobile, pen-based market. PenPoint therefore takes full advantage of available hardware memory and hardware process protection to provide a reliable and robust environment. If an individual application or process crashes, the rest of the system keeps on running. Even if PenPoint itself crashes, it provides an on-the-fly diskless "warm boot" that preserves all user Notebook data and application code and returns control to the user within one minute. Companies can count on PenPoint for their most critical field applications.

Although we've seen that PenPoint requires little storage space, it can run equally well in high-end configurations with large amounts of memory. PenPoint can directly address up to four gigabytes of physical memory. Furthermore, PenPoint incorporates paged virtual-memory support, allowing it to work efficiently in architectures that include backing store, such as desktop hard disk machines.

Software developers today are forced to write ever larger applications because today's operating systems require every application to be self-sufficient and monolithic. As a result, small developers are increasingly locked out of the commercial application marketplace since large, monolithic applications generally require either large programming teams or long development cycles. PenPoint changes the equation in favor of smaller development teams by providing an object-oriented environment in which applications can build upon each other and share large amounts of functionality.

The event-driven, object-oriented nature of the system minimizes the need to "reinvent the wheel" with each new application. PenPoint's APIs are implemented using object-oriented programming techniques of subclass inheritance and message passing. PenPoint provides more than 250 classes and 1,500 messages for use by the application developer. Programmers can code by exception, reusing existing code while altering or adding only the specific behavior and functionality their own applications require. Because the object-oriented architecture is systemwide, these benefits are not restricted to single applications; in fact, applications can share code with each other just as readily as with the system itself.

Summary

This chapter has introduced the key concepts behind the PenPoint Operating System. As we have seen, this new operating system was created to respond to the unique needs of pen-based computing. Specifically, these needs demand a general-purpose, mobile operating system.

PenPoint responds to these unique needs with such features as:

- Notebook User Interface (NUI) — PenPoint's central organizing concept consisting of pages, tabs and a table of contents. In addition, a new but familiar language of gestures and powerful handwriting recognition completes the NUI.

- Embedded Document Architecture (EDA [TM]) — PenPoint's EDA lets the user embed live, editable documents within other documents and create hyperlink buttons between any two locations in the notebook.

- Mobile Connectivity — Instant-on, detachable networking and deferred I/O permit truly portable computers for mobile workers.

- Compact and Scalable — While expressly designed for small light-weight, portable computers, PenPoint is highly hardware independent and scales to a variety of sizes, from pocket-size to wallboard-size computers.

- Rich OS for the 90s — A true, 32-bit, flat-memory model architecture with pre-emptive multitasking and a powerful, compact imaging model, Imagepoint™.

2

The PenPoint
User Interface

PenPoint is unique in that it is the first operating system designed to be driven primarily by a pen. Because of this, PenPoint includes many new elements not found in traditional GUIs. This chapter will provide you with an understanding of the PenPoint user interface, its design goals, how it relates to traditional GUIs, and the unique ways PenPoint works with the pen. It is neither a complete exposition of the interface nor a user manual.

Ambitious Goals

As discussed in Chapter 1, since mobile, pen-based computers are used in different ways from desktop systems, they have different user interface (UI) requirements than desktop PCs. Briefly stated, users of mobile, pen-based systems require a user interface that is direct and intuitive, yet powerful and flexible.

Early on, GO Corporation established goals that PenPoint's UI would have to

- be based on coherent metaphors—the user's conceptual model is the single most important element in a good UI.
- fully exploit the pen—UIs would have to be rethought from the ground up, if necessary, for the real potential of the pen to be unleashed.

21

- balance visual invitation and visual restraint—visual invitation is important to encourage the user to touch an element on the screen. But it is in tension with visual restraint: Good design is uncluttered, and PenPoint's users would be accustomed to using pens on uncluttered territory (blank sheets of paper).

- strike a balance among simplicity, consistency, and efficiency—that is, "easy at the beginning, powerful at the end." Real head room must exist for users to grow more efficient in their use of PenPoint as they gain experience.

- permit a smooth transition for users of existing GUIs—many PenPoint users would come from a background of using existing GUIs, and they might continue to switch between the two systems. PenPoint would have to be "interoperable." It would therefore build upon and extend GUIs, not gratuitously reinvent every UI technique imaginable.

PenPoint's user interface is the design solution that meets these goals. It is an immediately graspable user interface, even for the rank novice: Use a pen for interaction, and organize your information as you would in a notebook. The simplicity and directness of this user interface are compelling.

PenPoint and Traditional GUIs

If you have used a GUI, you will find many familiar concepts in PenPoint's user interface. User interaction techniques such as pointing to a graphics screen (with a mouse in a traditional GUI, with the pen in PenPoint's), scrolling windows, and pull-down menus are all important foundations of PenPoint. On the inside, application programmers will find that PenPoint has a modern windowing and graphics subsystem that they must use to render their screen display and that their applications must be structured in an event-driven fashion, just as in desktop GUIs.

There is much that is unique about PenPoint's user interface, and this chapter's purpose is to focus on the unique, not the familiar. We will briefly introduce PenPoint's more traditional elements and then discuss those that are unique.

Windows and Their Frames

PenPoint applications run inside of a window and may in fact be sharing the screen with other applications. These windows are called document frames and can be resized and repositioned (except when they are a page in the Notebook, as described later in this chapter). Figure 2-1 shows the standard elements of a PenPoint document frame. As you can see, the standard elements of a window are there.

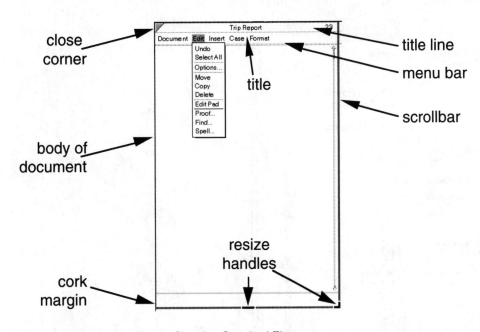

Figure 2-1 Document Frame Showing Standard Elements

Menus and Option Sheets

PenPoint uses Option Sheets in addition to pull-down menus. (See Figure 2-2). Menus are typically used for verblike commands, Option Sheets for setting adjective-like attributes of an object (such as font size). Option Sheets help avoid "menu overload." Furthermore, since attribute settings and commands are different, placing the two in distinct portions of the user interface permits

. . . .

The Power of PenPoint

PenPoint to provide optimum behavior for each. Commands should take effect right away; consequently, menus dismiss (go away) as soon as you choose a command. Options, however, are often set several at a time, and the same settings may be applied to several objects in a row; therefore, Option Sheets allow the user to set as many options as desired. The Apply button applies settings to the selected object. The user may then change the selection and continue using the Option Sheet. The Apply and Close button applies the settings and then dismisses the Option Sheet. The Close button simply closes the sheet without affecting the selected object.

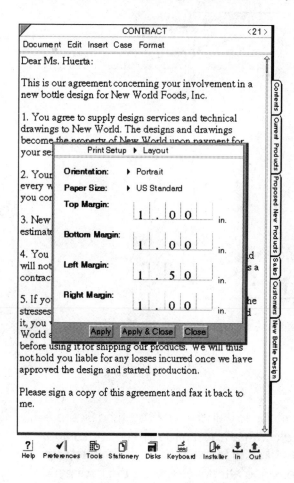

Figure 2-2 Typical Option Sheet

Basic Controls

PenPoint includes a wide variety of the basic GUI controls such as buttons, checklists, and multiple checklists. Of course, to echo the pen-based nature of the system, PenPoint displays choice settings as check marks (as shown in Figure 2-3).

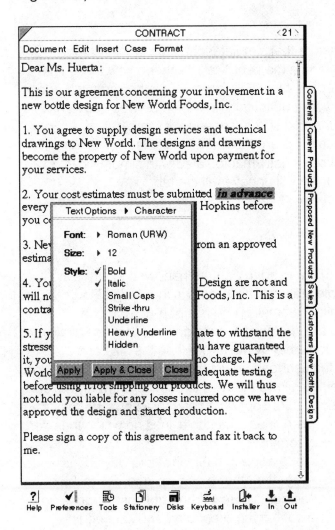

Figure 2-3 Choice Settings Displayed as Check Marks

Some New Items

PenPoint's UI Toolkit includes two items not normally found in other GUIs: notebook tabs and writing pads.

Tabs

Tabs are a user interface feature that simulates the tabs in a three-ring binder (as shown in Figure 2-4). In a moment, we'll describe how these tabs are used in the notebook metaphor itself. But you can use the same tab code to create navigational tools in your application (to switch between screens in a form or sheets in a three-dimensional spreadsheet, for example).

PenPoint's tabs overlap when there are too many to display in a single column. In this case, they can be directly manipulated with simple flicks up and down of the pen tip. A flick left will uncover all the tabs.

Writing Pads

Writing pads (see Figure 2-5) are used to capture handwriting, translate it into ASCII text, and allow simple editing. The larger writing pad in Figure 2-5 is an embedded writing pad, while the smaller one is a pop-up edit pad.

Writing pads provide a natural area for handwriting, since they are similar to lined paper. Because many people handwrite larger than the size of the translated text on the screen, the user can adjust the dimensions of the writing pads. A system preference setting allows the user to choose between boxed and ruled styles of pads. Boxes require separation of characters and may ensure higher recognition rates; ruled lines are simple lines on which the user may write characters more closely together.

The user can cause a writing pad to appear in either of two ways. One command creates an embedded pad, the other a pop-up pad. Embedded pads are typically used for larger amounts of text. The application opens up space around the embedded pad so that the preceding and succeeding context is still visible while the user writes into the pad. Pop-up pads are optimized for small amounts of text. They float at or near the location of the command, and the application does not shift its display. They are great for inserting, editing, or replacing up to a few words.

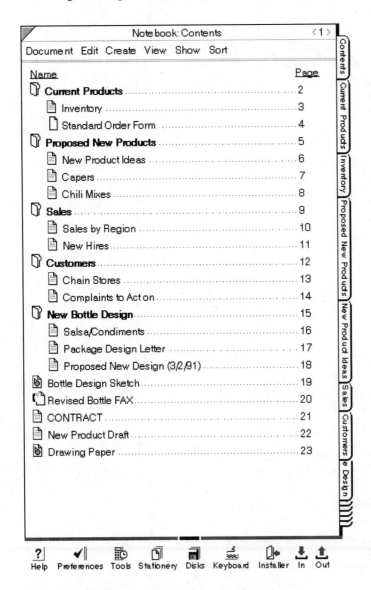

Figure 2-4 Divider Tab Simulation

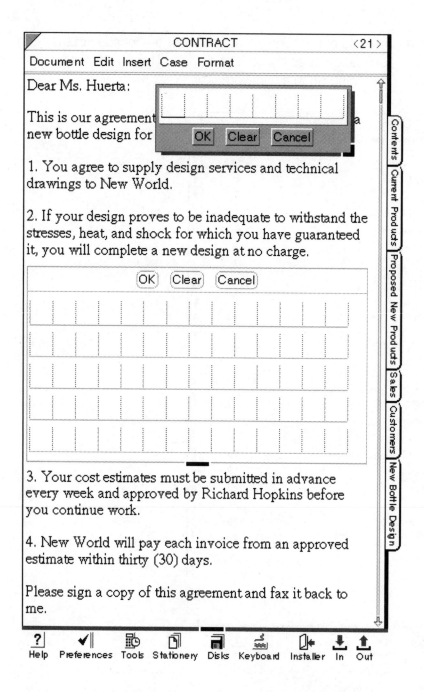

Figure 2-5 Two Types of Writing Pads

All writing pads are essentially the same object appearing with various default sizes in response to user commands. They are resizable. After hand-writing into the pad, the user presses the OK button. This causes the translated text to appear in the boxes. The user can write directly into these boxes to correct any errors. In addition, space can be easily opened up, and characters can be deleted with a simple gesture. The result is a reliable method of entering handwriting and correcting it that is easy to learn and use. When the user presses the OK button again on the translated (and corrected) text, the pad will empty its text into the underlying application.

Applications can use writing-pad objects as an integral part of their user interface. They may, for instance, embed pads into on-screen fields so the user can simply place the pen into the field and begin writing.

Because writing pads provide a rich and comprehensive set of handwriting entry styles, the result is that applications can simply reuse these PenPoint objects for almost all their handwriting input. The user benefits because the user interface for handwriting is consistent across a wide variety of applications.

PenPoint's Notebook Metaphor

PenPoint's notebook metaphor is based on the intuitive organizing principles of pages in a notebook with sections, tabs, and a Table of Contents (see Figure 2-6). All user data exists as pages.

Pages are numbered in the top-right corner. The user can turn pages with a tap or a flick of the pen tip on or near the page number. Page turns include a special graphical effect that looks much like a real page turn.

Notebook tabs appear on the right-hand side of the Notebook and may be attached to any page or section; touching a tab turns immediately to its location in the Notebook. If there are more tabs than will fit on the screen, they overlap and collapse together. Their overlapping can be controlled with flicks of the pen tip.

There are no file load or save commands, nor is there the concept of programs existing distinct from program data files. Instead, each page of the Notebook is called a "document" and is viewed by the user as a live application instance that is always available just as the user last left it.

```
┌─────────────────────────────────────────────┐
│  ╲          Notebook: Contents        ⟨ 1 ⟩  │
│                                               │
│  Document  Edit  Create  View  Show  Sort     │
│ ═════════════════════════════════════════════│
│  Name                                 Page    │
│  📁 Current Products ................... 2    ┌──────┐
│     📄 Inventory ....................... 3    │Contents│
│     📄 Standard Order Form ............. 4    └──────┤
│  📁 Proposed New Products .............. 5    │Current│
│     📄 New Product Ideas ............... 6    │Products│
│     📄 Capers .......................... 7    │       │
│     📄 Chili Mixes ..................... 8    │Proposed│
│  📁 Sales .............................. 9    │New    │
│     📄 Sales by Region ................ 10    │Products│
│     📄 New Hires ...................... 11    │       │
│  📁 Customers ......................... 12    │Sales  │
│     📄 Chain Stores ................... 13    │       │
│     📄 Complaints to Act on ........... 14    │Customers│
│  📁 New Bottle Design ................. 15    │       │
│     📄 Salsa/Condiments ............... 16    │New    │
│     📄 Package Design Letter .......... 17    │Bottle │
│     📄 Proposed New Design (3/2/91) ... 18    │Design │
│  📄 Bottle Design Sketch .............. 19    └──────┘
│  📄 Revised Bottle FAX ................ 20
│  📄 CONTRACT .......................... 21
│  📄 New Product Draft ................. 22
│
│
│
│
│
└─────────────────────────────────────────────┘

  ?⌐      ✓⌐      ▤      🗋      ▥      ≋      🚪⟶    ↓      ↑
 Help  Preferences  Tools  Stationery  Disks  Keyboard  Installer  In  Out
```

Figure 2-6 Notebook Table of Contents

Behind the scenes, the PenPoint Application Framework associates data files with installed application code and operating system processes. To the Pen-Point user, a page of the Notebook and a document are synonymous. To a Pen-Point programmer, documents are also synonymous with "application instance." (In this book, we'll use the latter term since our audience is technical.)

Pages may be grouped into sections. Sections may also contain other sections; arbitrary hierarchies may therefore be created. The first page of the Notebook is a Table of Contents that looks and operates likes its book equivalent. In the Table of Contents, the pages and sections are displayed as an indented outline. Sections may be collapsed and expanded as in an outline processor. Touching a page number in the Table of Contents turns to that page. All contents of the Notebook are always visible from the Table of Contents, and pages may be easily created, moved, copied, deleted, and otherwise manipulated from that point. Entire sections may be transferred in and out of the Notebook just as easily as individual pages.

In Figure 2-7, the user has turned to a text document page. When the page-turning command was given, PenPoint did the following steps:

- cleared the screen and displayed a page-turn effect lasting less than a second
- created a process and application object for the destination page being turned to
- sent a message to the destination application object to restore its saved state from the file system
- sent a message to the destination application object to display itself on the screen

In the background, now that the user is able to view and interact with data on the destination page, PenPoint sends messages to the original page's application to file its data. PenPoint then terminates the process behind the original application.

As you can see from this sequence of steps, it is the PenPoint operating system that performs the clerical bookkeeping steps of starting and stopping processes (running applications) and of loading and saving application data. Users simply move from page to page and always see their data just as they last left it: scrolled to exactly the same location and with the application seeming to be still running. In reality, because PenPoint Notebooks can contain hundreds or thousands of pages, PenPoint automatically starts and stops processes behind the scenes for the user. Otherwise, if PenPoint actually kept these off-page processes running, memory would be consumed quickly.

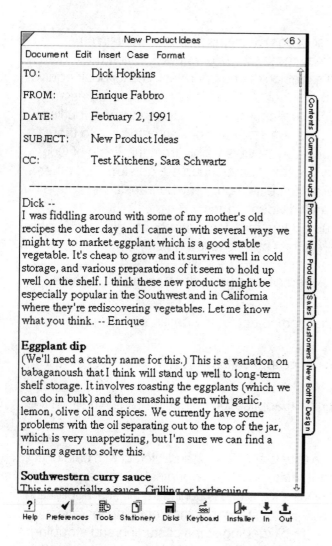

Figure 2-7 Display after User Turns to a Text Document Page

The Notebook metaphor is designed for mobile users who are most often communicating with other users. Mobile users must be able to focus their attention elsewhere than on the computer. The Notebook metaphor supports a quick-reference style of access in which the user must be able to find information with just a few taps of the pen.

Benefits of the Notebook Metaphor

The notebook metaphor stands in stark contrast to the high level of concentration the desktop metaphor requires. This is not surprising: The desktop metaphor was designed for desktop users who are alone with the personal computer and therefore free to concentrate their full attention on the computer. The user of a desktop system is assumed to be doing nothing else while operating the computer. The user of a pen-based, mobile system, on the other hand, may be able to devote only a small portion of conscious attention to the computer.

The notebook metaphor provides these benefits

- It is a physically familiar (like a real notebook) and stable user model (pages and sections remain in the order and state the user last left them in).

- Users need not learn about the unnecessarily technical.distinction between programs and data files, because user data in the Notebook simply exists as live, running documents; there are no file load or save commands to learn.

- Because it is a stable model, users can employ their spatial memory of the unique ordering of their pages and sections to help find and organize their information.

- The Table of Contents provides an instant overview of Notebook contents; all organizational tasks (such as create, delete, move, rename, and so forth) and navigational tasks (page turns) can be performed from the Table of Contents.

- Tabs on any page or section allow the user to maintain a set of documents so that they are instantly accessible with a single tap.

- Sections allow hierarchies to be formed: According to the user's preference and style, the Notebook may either be a simple flat collection of pages with no sections or a rich and deep hierarchical collection of sections within sections.

- The user can move sequentially through the Notebook simply by turning pages.

- The user can move in random order through the Notebook either by turning to a Table of Contents and then turning to any other page or by touching on an attached tab or using Goto buttons for frequently traveled paths. (Note that the terms *Goto buttons* and *hyperlinks* mean the same thing.)

The Bookshelf

At the bottom of the PenPoint screen is a Bookshelf area in which systemwide objects and resources are displayed as icons. You can think of the Bookshelf as the meta-area in which the Notebook is rooted, or resides.

PenPoint's standard Bookshelf includes icons for these objects

- on-line help system
- system preferences
- Tools Palette
- Stationery Notebook
- Disk Manager
- software keyboard
- Installer
- In Box and Out Box
- the selected Notebook

A tap of the pen on any of these objects opens it on the screen, floating over the Notebook.

The power of object-oriented programming is evidenced in PenPoint's use of the notebook metaphor in several of these subsystems: The stationery, reference help, In Box, and Out Box all use floating instances of small, recursive Notebooks for their user interfaces. The user is able to use the familiar concepts of a Table of Contents, pages, and sections to browse through these system services, and PenPoint is able to achieve tremendous code reuse.

The on-line help system provides context-sensitive and reference-style help screens.

System preferences provide the user with configuration options such as the choice between writing in all uppercase or mixed upper- and lowercase, writing-pad styles, system font, portrait or landscape screen orientation, time and date, and whether to enable sound. The user can also see memory usage statistics here.

The Tools Palette provides a pop-up window with icons for a variety of system accessories and tools such as clocks, calculators, and, importantly, PenPoint's handwriting training program.

The Stationery Notebook provides a place for the user (as well as installed applications) to store copies of documents they would like to use as templates. This provides for a standardized form of application templates to be fully integrated with PenPoint's creation user interface.

The Disk Manager allows the user to browse and transfer files to and from external disk volumes. These may be floppy disks, hard disks, desktop PC and Macintosh computers, or volumes on network servers. The Disk Manager user interface is based on the same code as the Notebook's Table of Contents and provides a similar outline view that uses the identical core gestures for all transfer and manipulation of external files.

The software keyboard is a small pop-up image of a keyboard that the user may tap with the pen tip when a physical keyboard is absent and the user would prefer to not handwrite.

The Installer manages all installed applications, listing them and their memory consumption for the user.

The In Box and Out Box queue up incoming and outgoing data transfer operations until a suitable connection is available (see Chapter 16 for more information on these).

The current Notebook fills the screen but is not the root of the PenPoint world. Therefore, an icon representing the current Notebook sits on the Bookshelf alongside the other icons (in the default configuration, it is scrolled out of view).

Because PenPoint ensures that the Notebook contains only user data (and not system objects), advanced users may want to manage multiple Notebooks in a single PenPoint machine. These Notebooks would be created by the user or loaded from disk, and the user would switch between them by choosing their icons on the Bookshelf. There is nothing to prevent a Notebook from residing on disk.

Besides adding Notebooks to the Bookshelf, the user can also place other objects such as documents and hyperlink buttons (described later in this chapter) there. As the Bookshelf fills up, it will automatically wrap the icons to fill into row order. The bottom of the Notebook has a resize handle so the user may draw it up to uncover as many rows of icons as the Bookshelf contains.

Gestures: The Pen Builds on the Mouse

The pen builds upon the heritage of the mouse as a pointing device. As we discussed earlier in this chapter, PenPoint is based on many traditional GUI principles, including the principle that much of the GUI screen is responsive to pointing operations. Pointing is much easier with the pen than with the mouse. With the mouse, you must position the cursor to the correct location and then click the mouse button. These are skills that must be learned. With the pen you simply tap on the screen.

But the pen extends well beyond the mouse's function as a pointing device. Since people can write and draw well with the pen, it can be used for many more classes of operations than can the mouse. In fact, PenPoint uses the pen as its primary input device; it is the only input device the user ever needs to learn or use.

In PenPoint, the pen is used for pointing, data entry, and gesture commands. Of all input devices, it is the only one that can be used for all three. The mouse cannot, because it is too difficult to handwrite with a mouse. The keyboard cannot, because it is difficult to point with cursor keys and you cannot draw gesture commands with a keyboard. Even when voice recognition is sufficiently perfected for unconstrained high-volume data entry and command issuance, it will still be a horrible pointing device. (Imagine controlling your computer through voice commands without a pointing device like the pen in hand: "Delete that word ... no, not that one, two to the left ... OK, now, see that word "abject" four lines up? I want you to move it to just before the ...".)

Because the pen unifies all these input modalities into a single, natural tool, it is the ideal primary input device for a computer. Keyboards (covered later in this chapter) and voice recognition become excellent adjuncts to the pen, to be used in special situations.

Gestures as Commands

The most interesting and useful capability of the pen is not the handwriting you can perform with it, but the gesture commands you can issue with it. Gesture commands specify in a single step both a command and the target of the command. With mouse-based systems, the user must always select the operand object, then select the command verb. With the pen, users simply draw the command directly over the intended operand object.

The pen is so powerful that intensive editing and data entry tasks can be performed entirely with it. In Figure 2-8, the user draws a small caret gesture to request that a "gap" be opened up to write into. In response, the text opens up a gap and fills it with a writing-pad object (one of many standard PenPoint support objects). Figure 2-9 shows the resulting writing pad with some typical hand printing that PenPoint recognizes.

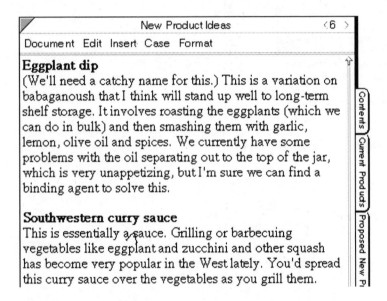

Figure 2-8 Caret Gesture to Request Writing Space

While the user handprints, PenPoint performs the recognition process in the background, so that the resulting text can be displayed nearly instantly after the user closes the writing pad. Upon closing, the resulting ASCII text is passed to the application.

Under PenPoint, the *location* of a gesture controls its intended meaning. For instance, when the letter "O" is drawn in a handwriting area, it is translated into ASCII 79 (a capital "O"), but when it's drawn over application data such as a word, it is translated into the Edit command. When the "O" is drawn into an object-oriented drawing program, it is translated into the command to create a circle object (see figures 2-10 and 2-11). Such location-specific gestures provide an intuitive "do what I mean" style of interface that is free of the confusing modes that arise when a mouse is used where a pen would be more natural.

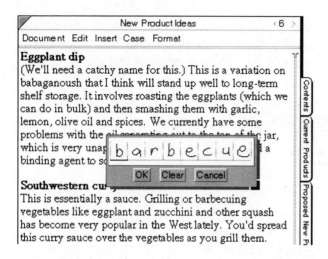

Figure 2-9 Writing Pad Appears in Response to Gesture

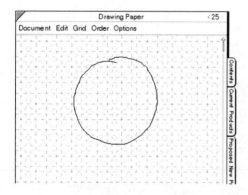

Figure 2-10 User Draws a Circle Gesture

Ideas in Conflict

Even though the pen builds on the heritage of the mouse as a pointing device, it is important to note that the two devices mix together about as well as oil and water. The mouse requires an on-screen cursor; the pen abhors this. The mouse does not trail ink on the screen; the pen requires this.

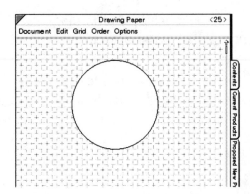

Figure 2-11 Drawing Program Creates Circle Shape in Response to Gesture

As a result of these fundamental conflicts, unchanged mouse-based GUI applications require a mouse cursor. If these applications are running on the same machine as pen-based applications, the user will be confronted with the difficult situation of having a pen with a button on it to switch the pen between mouse mode and pen mode. The user would have to understand the nature of every window on the screen and ensure the pen was in the correct mode before touching it to the screen.

Standard Gesture Language

PenPoint provides a standard, rich gestural language based on intuition about pen editing marks. The heart of the gestural user interface is a set of core gestures shown in Figure 2-12. These gestures work consistently across all applications, providing common commands such as Select, Delete, Move, Copy, Options, and Help. PenPoint provides dozens of additional gestures for application-specific commands (for example, the same letter "B" that applies a style of boldface when drawn in a word processor will toggle document borders on and off if drawn on the title bar of a document).

GO has found that a well-designed gesture is highly mnemonic. The choice of gestures should be driven by two key factors

- They should leverage our society's "collective unconscious" regarding editing marks; for example, scratch-out and pigtail marks are intuitive deletion gestures.
- They must be easy to draw and make; GO's user research has found that many multistroke gestures (those in which the pen tip is typically lifted at least once during drawing) cause users difficulty.

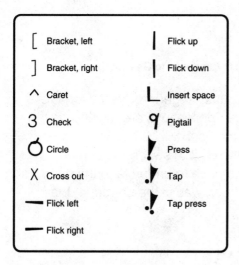

Figure 2-12   Core Gestures in PenPoint

While virtually all commands and operations in PenPoint are available through menus and Option Sheets so that users can easily find them, the most frequently used commands have gesture equivalents. Because these are so direct and efficient, most users will use them rather than other approaches.

Using the Pen for Data Entry

PenPoint includes a powerful handwriting recognition (HWX) subsystem. This system is available to all applications. In addition, it is used by a number of PenPoint objects (such as the writing pads mentioned previously) that are in turn available to all PenPoint applications.

The initial version of PenPoint is shipped with a HWX system developed entirely by GO Corporation that has the following characteristics:

- recognizes neatly printed, mixed upper- and lowercase letters, numerals, and punctuation
- gives the user the option of writing into character boxes or on ruled lines
- tolerates characters that overlap or touch
- recognizes characters independently of stroke and time order
- accommodates several users with or without training.

PenPoint supports these features on an impressive list of naturally shaped characters at very high recognition rates, even when the user is writing random English text. Typical word accuracy rates are 80 percent or better, which is equivalent to character accuracy rates of 90 to 97 percent. For more information on the HWX system see Chapter 13; for more information on evaluating HWX systems see Appendix C.

Under PenPoint, the pen is clearly a respectable data entry device. With time, it will only get better, because PenPoint's HWX is replaceable. HWX APIs exist as standard programming interfaces regardless of what HWX is currently installed. Therefore, PenPoint's algorithms can be continuously improved without disturbing the growing base of applications.

PenPoint's HWX subsystem is replaceable, allowing replacement of GO Corporation's current English-language HWX with engines developed by third parties. This supports placement of PenPoint into foreign markets such as Japan, but it also guarantees that the world's best HWX can be available within PenPoint. Several third-party efforts are already underway to port other HWX technology into PenPoint.

With time, PenPoint will support HWX systems that deliver accuracy rates higher than today's and tolerate messier or cursive handwriting. HWX is a CPU-intensive task, and a better job can typically be done by expending more processor time. GO Corporation's algorithms have been carefully designed to run in real time on current-generation hardware. As faster processors become available, more ambitious HWX goals can be set. Furthermore, as the PenPoint market grows, the market for HWX engines will grow and encourage entrepreneurial development.

Keyboard Support

PenPoint also supports keyboards for high-volume data entry. When users are working at a table or desk and they know how to type and they have a physical keyboard available, nothing beats the keyboard. But it's important to point out that where other operating systems tend to use the keyboard for everything (for example, all commands must be issuable from the keyboard) and the mouse for some things, PenPoint inverts this former primacy of the keyboard; in PenPoint every user action can be done with the pen and the keyboard is supported chiefly for its excellence at high-volume data entry. That is, PenPoint's user interface guidelines do not require the use of Alt key combinations, function keys, or the ESC key.

More Differences

Besides the notebook metaphor and gestures, PenPoint's user interface contains a number of other features not normally found in a traditional GUI. These include

- a non-traditional move/copy model
- the Stationery Notebook
- scroll margins and scrolling with gestures
- cork margin
- Embedded Document Architecture
- hyperlink buttons
- floating pages
- integrated connectivity

Direct Move and Copy

Move and copy operations in traditional GUIs are based on a clipboard model in which the user must first copy or cut data to an invisible clipboard and then issue another command to paste the data into the destination application. In PenPoint, the user employs gestures that immediately initiate a direct manipulation drag and drop move/copy user interface. (See Chapter 8 for a more detailed description of how this portion of the user interface is implemented.) Move and copy work within individual applications, across application boundaries, and across pages in the Notebook.

Stationery Notebook

PenPoint's Stationery Notebook unifies the user interface for creating new blank instances of applications with the user interface for creating copies of application template documents. It is extensible by applications, which can bring templates with them at installation time, and by users, who may add their own templates at any time. All templates (including a blank one for the creation of blank application instances) are stored in the Stationery Notebook. An entry in this Notebook with a check mark next to it will then appear in the Stationery menu, which is a simple menu that appears in the Table of Contents in response to the insertion gesture.

Scrolling

PenPoint contains relatively traditional scroll bars with up and down arrows and a scroll handle that is draggable and indicates your current position in the file. These scroll bars are called scroll margins because they also contain a thin margin into which you can draw flick gestures. These are simple up and down flicks (in a vertical scroll margin) or left and right flicks (in a horizontal scroll margin).

The scroll margins are infrequently used, however, because users may draw the same scroll flicks in the application window itself. The result is direct manipulation at its best: To scroll a line to the top of the window just place the pen tip near it and draw a quick little flick up. Scrolling via flick gestures is much more efficient than scroll bars because the placement of the pen tip can be very imprecise and casual; with scroll bars, the placement of the pen tip (or mouse cursor) must be precise.

Cork Margin

The cork margin is a unique standard part of every PenPoint document frame (although it is turned off by default). It is a simple little border area at the bottom of the document frame (see Figure 2-13) that can contain any PenPoint object. It is called the cork margin because you "stick" things there in a fashion similar to a small cork bulletin board. In fact, the cork margin's capabilities as a general-purpose repository are similar to the Bookshelf, which we previously described. Both cork margins and the Bookshelf can contain hyperlink buttons, closed documents (appearing as icons), and other PenPoint objects.

Because the cork margin is attached to a document frame, it goes wherever the document goes. You might put several hyperlink buttons in the cork margin that point to various locations in the document that you want to mark. Because the Bookshelf is always at the bottom of the screen, it is global. In essence, the cork margin serves as a local buffer for objects, and the Bookshelf as a global buffer.

Embedded Document Architecture

One of PenPoint's most impressive technical capabilities is its Embedded Document Architecture, in which live applications may be placed inside each other to produce true compound documents. (This book devotes Chapter 8 to this topic.) While complex software technology is required to implement this capability, to the user the embedding user interface is straightforward.

```
┌─────────────────────────────────────────┐
│ ◤        Inventory           〈3 〉        │
├─────────────────────────────────────────┤
│ Document Edit Insert Case Format          │
├─────────────────────────────────────────┤
│        CUSTOMER STATUS REPORT          ┬  │
│                                        │  │
│        AS OF OCTOBER 30, 1990          │  │
│                                        ┌──┤
│                    PREV  CURR    %     │C │
│  CUST    PRODUCT LINE  YTD   YTD  CHANGE│o │
│                                        │n │
│  WHOLE FOODS                           │t │
│  10 Marinara      1,240  1,800  30% +  │e │
│  20 Garlic Bomb   670    640    7% -   │n │
│  25 SW Curry      8,009  5,340  40% +  │t │
│  30 Loco Coconut  400    590    20% +  │s │
│  40 Fish's Friend 130    106    25% -  ├──┤
│  50 Outstanding   44     78     90% +  │C │
│  60 Mellow Yellow 120    120    0% -   │u │
│                                        │r │
│      TOTAL        12,008  12,987  8% + │r │
│                                        │e │
│  UNCLE BOB'S GROCERY                   │n │
│  20 Garlic Bomb   130    108    25% -  │t │
│  40 Fish's Friend 44     79     95% +  ├──┤
│  50 Outstanding   118    118    0%     │P │
│                                        │r │
│      TOTAL        2,400   2,600   8% + │o │
│                                        │d │
│  RED LABEL STORES                      │u │
│  25 SW Curry      105    100    5% +   │c │
│  30 Loco Coconut  40     75     95% +  │t │
│                                        │s │
│      TOTAL        150    175    20% +  ├──┤
│                                        │S │
│  PRESCOTT'S                            │a │
│  10 Marinara      1,240  1,800  30% ±  │l │
│  20 Garlic Bomb   670    640    7% -   │e │
│  25 SW Curry      8,009  5,340  40% +  │s │
│  30 Loco Coconut  400    590    20% + ↓├──┤
├─────────────────────────────────────────┤
│ (REAL FOODS) (SUPER G ROCERY) ▯ ToDo  2:00 P.M. │
│ (WHOLE FOODS) (UNCLE BOB'S) (RED LABEL)(PRESCOTTS) │
└─────────────────────────────────────────┘

  ?│   ✓│    ▤    ◫     ▦     ↗    ▯◀   ⬇    ⬆
  Help Preferences Tools Stationery Disks Keyboard Installer In Out
```

Figure 2-13 Cork Margin at Bottom of Page

To create a document inside of another, the user simply opens the Stationery menu inside of the host document and chooses the new document type, just as he or she normally would. Embedded documents may be closed to a small icon (in which case the application is no longer running) or they may be open. When the document is open, the user has full control through standard document Option Sheet settings over whether the document menu bar, scroll bar, and borders are on or off.

Hyperlink Buttons

PenPoint includes hyperlink buttons as a first-class, integral part of the operating system. The user creates these links by selecting the target for navigation and drawing a simple gesture at the location where the hyperlink button should be placed. PenPoint creates a button that points directly to the selected destination. Hyperlink buttons can point to any page in the Notebook or to locations within pages. When a hyperlink button is pressed, PenPoint creates an automatic page turn to the destination page. The location within the destination page is selected and scrolled into view. Hyperlink buttons are correctly preserved across all filing and other data transfer operations.

Floating Pages

Pages in the Notebook may be floated by the user double-tapping on the page number in the Table of Contents (or on a tab or hyperlink button pointing to the page). A single tap on any of these goes to the page while a double tap floats the page. You can think of floating pages as being temporarily "torn out" of the Notebook, while remembering their original location, to which they return when the floater is closed.

Floating gives PenPoint a general overlapping window model for those users and situations in which this is appropriate. In other GUIs, overlapping windows are the only organizational style, so users simply must learn to use it. In Pen-Point, this style is treated as an advanced approach; users can confine their systems to the more intuitive page-turning model.

Integrated Connectivity

PenPoint includes an extensive set of user interfaces for connectivity. Because data transfer is so integral to mobile, pen-based computers, PenPoint allows documents being transferred to queue up in the In Box and Out Box. These services fill and empty when the appropriate communications connections (for instance, a connection to a desktop PC or network) are available (see Chapter

16 for more information). Both the In Box and Out Box use small floating Notebooks as their user interfaces, allowing the user to employ the familiar organizational power of pages, sections, and the Table of Contents.

The Send command in PenPoint is available from within every application to send a copy of that document as electronic mail or facsimile (if the appropriate transfer services are installed). The Send command brings up a standard addressing user interface that works with a systemwide Send List (a form of address book for addresses and phone numbers), and the pending transfer operation is then entered into the Out Box.

User Interface Consistency

PenPoint encourages application user interfaces to be consistent with one another in several areas. In our previous discussion of gestures, we pointed out the concept of a core set of approximately one dozen gestures that all applications implement in a consistent fashion. In addition, there is a set of Standard Application Menus (SAMs), commands, and Option Sheets that all applications must implement. (As you may have guessed, the Application Framework provides default implementations of these features that are sufficient for most applications.)

SAMS specifies two required menus: a Document menu and an Edit menu. The Document menu contains (at least) Checkpoint, Revert, Print, Print Setup, Send, and About commands. The Edit menu contains (at least) Undo, Select All, Options, Move, Copy, Delete, Find, and Spell. In addition, SAMS provides standard document Option Sheets that provide option cards to describe document title and information, access controls, and application information.

To ensure appropriate application UI consistency, the PenPoint Software Developer's Kit includes UI Guidelines that specify the full set of consistency requirements.

Summary

This chapter has looked at the PenPoint user interface primarily from the user's perspective. While this interface shares many features with existing graphical user interfaces (GUIs), PenPoint incorporates some new ideas, including notebook tabs for navigation among documents and writing pads for insertion of handwritten text.

As we have seen, PenPoint is organized around the concept of a notebook, including sections, tabs, and a Table of Contents. PenPoint also includes a Book-shelf area along the bottom of the notebook where system-wide objects can be stored for easy access regardless of where in the notebook the user is working.

We have looked at the core gestures and handwriting recognition tech-niques that make up one of PenPoint's most unique and visible user interface elements. We have noted that the pen is not intended for high-volume data entry and that PenPoint therefore also supports keyboard data input.

3
Developing Applications for PenPoint

· ·

PenPoint is radically new in many ways. Yet, in other ways, it builds on ideas that have preceded it, some of which may be familiar to you. As with any new technology, PenPoint offers some intriguing challenges to programmers who want to develop applications to take advantage of its new features and capabilities.

Mindful of this challenge, GO Corporation provides a significant amount of support for your programming efforts. From training to a Software Developer's Kit (SDK) that contains all of the class libraries, source code, development tools, and sample applications you'll need to build PenPoint applications, PenPoint's developers offer you a range of help and encouragement as you embark on your programming effort.

Why Develop for PenPoint?

At the outset, you may still be unconvinced that you should spend your valuable time and resources developing applications for the PenPoint platform. There are at least four reasons you should seriously consider doing just that.

First, many, if not most, of the major computer hardware vendors will be producing systems that run PenPoint. GO Corporation's strategy is to license the PenPoint operating system and support software to as broad a range of hardware manufacturers as possible. To that end, GO has made a conscious decision not to become a hardware company itself. When it formally announced PenPoint, significant industry support was also announced. For you, that means that there will be many sales representatives, retailers, OEMs, and others selling PenPoint-based computer systems, resulting in widespread knowledge and acceptance of the operating system as an emerging standard.

Second, the market for pen-based computers will grow very rapidly over the next few years. By the end of the 1990s, the pen-based market will be just as large as the desktop PC market was at the end of the 1980s. This large market will use pen-based computers for new tasks for which it will require new software; existing desktop PC-based applications will, for the most part, not simply be ported to PenPoint. As you will see throughout this book, a pen-based system creates a new set of expectations and affords a host of opportunities for rethinking application design. New software companies will be founded; new software companies will flourish.

Third, the fact that you are reading this book means you have a chance to get into this emerging and potentially huge market early. There are no established, dominant players in this arena. You can enter the software market with a product that has as good a chance as any of becoming a success.

Finally, the fundamental paradigm shift from desktop to pen-based notebook computing opens many new opportunities for creative products and designs. The old rules are no longer valid. This will be an exciting platform for which to develop software simply because it will give you an opportunity to stretch your creativity and your mind to envision and implement new kinds of software that were heretofore either unheard of or not feasible because of the limitations of desktop computing.

The Learning Process

Obviously, all of this potential requires you to invest some time and effort in learning the new paradigm and in mastering some new tools.

Before you begin your approach to PenPoint, you should already be a C programmer. In its first release, PenPoint supports ANSI (American National Standards Institute) C. (Chapter 4 describes the C support in PenPoint in more detail.) You should also have some familiarity with object-oriented programming (OOP) since PenPoint is strongly oriented toward OOP development with class libraries, messages, and inheritance. Note that it is not necessary that you learn a new OOP language. PenPoint uses only standard ANSI C, not C++. The object-oriented aspects of PenPoint are concentrated largely in the Class Manager (see Chapter 5), which you will need to learn. Thus the learning curve for this aspect of PenPoint development is less steep than for undertaking a transition to a fully object-oriented language like C++.

Once your background includes C and OOP programming, you should learn the PenPoint Application Framework (see Chapter 6). This is the most important and often-used portion of the PenPoint class library. A working understanding of this aspect of PenPoint is essential to success in developing PenPoint applications.

Next, you'll want to learn some additional material about PenPoint's class library and development support. Of particular importance are portions of the windowing system (see Chapter 7), the graphics interface (see Chapter 9), the file and resource systems (see chapters 11 and 12), and the User Interface Toolkit (see Chapter 10). This book furnishes an overview of how those activities are organized and implemented, providing you some background that will prove valuable when you tackle the SDK documentation, which covers these subjects in greater detail.

Don't Be Intimidated

As you look over the topics in this book and the size of the class library and corresponding SDK documentation, you may feel overwhelmed at the size of the learning curve in PenPoint. Don't let the bulk of the product deceive you, though. Because PenPoint is an object-oriented operating system, it makes more application programming interfaces (APIs) available than you are used to in other operating systems. But, as with those environments, just because these APIs are available does not mean you must use all of them all the time. In fact, one purpose of this book is to cull through PenPoint and focus on those APIs that are most important for you to learn.

After you have a reading knowledge of the main classes and functions in PenPoint, you should study and modify the sample problems that come with the SDK. These applications are well-commented and are explained in SDK documentation so that you can grasp how and why they work. By making judicious modifications in them, you will begin to get a feel not only for how PenPoint programs work, but also how programming for PenPoint feels.

With this background, you're ready to design and build your application.

The Development Process

Object-oriented design and development require different approaches from those you may have used with procedural languages and designs. One key difference to keep in mind is that rapid prototyping is so easy in PenPoint that you can afford to spend some time building multiple prototypes before you write much code.

Even before you prototype, though, you should think seriously about your application design in the context of the pen-based computing paradigm.

Thinking about Your Application

You should think of your application as a specialized building block dealing with a single data type. It may, in fact, turn out to be a collection of such components, but if you begin thinking of it in terms of this key idea, you'll find that it is easier to design, prototype, build, test, and sell.

With PenPoint's capability to embed applications inside other applications dynamically (a subject covered in detail in Chapter 8), you can often create sophisticated applications by relying on other applications' capabilities. For example, you may be able to create an application that integrates an existing text editor and an existing spreadsheet program into a problem-solving tool such as a business plan generator.

> **Entirely New Application Category**
> Because of the embedding capabilities of PenPoint, a whole new category
> of applications may emerge. Programs whose sole purpose is orchestrat-
> ing other programs and organizing them for the user may become an
> important new concept in software design. For example, you might create
> a bulletin board (not an electronic bulletin-board system but a simulation of
> the cork-based bulletin board of your youth) with which a user can orga-
> nize overlapping windows representing opened and closed applications.
> This would provide a user with a "desktop on a page" approach to applica-
> tion usage, which is useful when users have sets of documents they always
> use together and that they need to juxtapose together on the screen.

Prototyping Your Application

The PenPoint SDK comes equipped with prototyping tools that enable you to
craft an empty shell of a program and demonstrate how it would work on the
PenPoint system without having to write any C code. This makes it possible for
you to prototype your application with several different interfaces or approaches
and then get feedback from potential users about its design.

Market testing of this kind is important, but it is often difficult in traditional
development environments because the only way to show how a program will
work is to build it. By the time that's done, the cost and time involved in chang-
ing it may be prohibitive. With PenPoint's object-oriented approach and its
prototyping tools, however, you can take advantage of early market feedback
to modify a design so that it will sell better after you have invested all of the
time and energy you put into coding it.

Even if you are building a PenPoint application for a captive market, such as
an in-house department or work team, this kind of market testing and user
feedback is important to its success. You can let users participate in the
design process; in fact, some of the PenPoint prototyping tools are easy
enough to use that you can even teach your potential users how to create the
interface the way they want to see it. Then you can help them fine-tune it
before you begin coding. The benefit of this early user buy-in and ownership
lies in the degree to which users will not only accept but embrace the finished
product and make extensive use of it.

Designing Your Application

Object-oriented design is an important subject that is beyond the scope of this book. One piece of advice that you'll find most useful in this regard, however, is that you should decompose your design into objects defined by their behaviors. In other words, you should examine your design for bits of behavior that can be used as the basis for constructing individual objects. One way to approach this problem, suggested by software designer and consultant David A. Wilson, is to write a narrative description of your program. The nouns in the description become candidates for objects and the verbs become candidates for messages those objects need to understand.

As you design an application for PenPoint, try to keep in mind the need to be as thoroughly pen-oriented as possible. This requires you to think about the appropriate uses of ink, gestures, and data entry techniques.

As with any object-oriented environment, the real efficiency and power of PenPoint derives from maximum reuse of PenPoint components. Don't reinvent the wheel where you don't have to do so. You will find that it will almost always pay off to spend more time looking through the PenPoint class library for an object that matches or nearly matches the behavior you need than starting from scratch writing a new object.

Taking the idea of reusing code a step farther, you should design code so that it creates reusable components. This will result, over time, in a library of reusable objects dealing with behaviors you often need. Over time, you should find that the amount of new code you have to write for each new application is reduced. You might even come up with such interesting reusable components that you'll find you can market them as well.

Exploit the Application Framework (see Chapter 6), the view-data model (see Chapter 8) and the observer model (see Chapter 5) in PenPoint to make your application behavior efficient and predictable. Using the view-data and observer models permits you to create multiple views of the same data element and benefit from automatic updating of the view when the value of the data changes. This can be a powerful technique.

Consider using the Service Architecture (see Chapter 15) to create some or all of the parts of your application. Any element of your program that does not require a user interface might be a candidate for implementation via the

Service architecture. For example, if you have a database engine in your application, you can create it using the Service architecture, make it a separate component, and gain not only efficiency but, potentially, another marketable product.

Rethinking User Interfaces for the Pen

As you rethink your application's user interface to make it as pen-oriented as possible, you should keep a number of things in mind. Think about

- ink as a data type — not all ink needs to be translated into text or geometric shape or gestures; some can be simply stored in image form (for example, signature pads). You should think about attaching data structures describing pen movement and drawing to your application in strategic ways. For example, you can include note-taking data fields in which the user's entries need not be translated into text at all.
- gesture recognition — gestures are efficient. You should exploit their use in your application as much as possible.
- ink as a markup medium — you can use ink as a way of marking up a document without altering its contents. This opens the way to such applications as a groupware word processor that displays proposed edits in multiple markup layers.
- context specification — look for places in your application where you can define or delimit the "type" of data a handwriting field can contain so that you can pass to the handwriting translators more detailed information, thus leading to improved accuracy and speed in translation.
- ink as "labels" — when ink is captured in PenPoint, you can store it and use internal pointers to reference it. You could use these pointers as labels so that the user uses the pen to indicate document contents and what to do with them.
- alternate data entry means — rather than having the user handwrite a list of entries as you might expect in a keyboard-based system where the user could type those responses, consider using prompted branching and predefined lists from which the user can select options.

PenPoint supports memory-mapped files, which allow you to address data in a file as if it were in main memory. You should consider using this approach to data access in your application because of its efficiency.

In designing your PenPoint application, be sure to provide data connectivity to desktop PCs and Macintoshes, particularly to the most popular file formats with which you wish your application to be data-compatible. The PenPoint remote file system (see Chapter 16) and Import/Export support (see Chapter 11) make it easy to provide this support.

Make your user interface scalable so that its size and aspect ratio can be adjusted to the hardware environment in which it is run. The automatic layout feature in PenPoint's User Interface Toolkit provides excellent support for this; use it. Particularly in view of the number of hardware manufacturers who will build PenPoint-based systems, it is important that you not lock your application into a particular assumption about screen size and orientation.

Mapping to the PenPoint Class Library

You will want to map all of your objects to the PenPoint class library to the maximum possible extent. Before you can do this, you need to learn enough about the class library that each new search for an object need not start from scratch. This book is designed to introduce you to and summarize the operations of the important classes and groups of classes in PenPoint.

When you've studied and become somewhat familiar with the class library, then you can search for objects that have some or all of the behavior you've defined for your application's objects. By understanding what the PenPoint classes do, you can quickly narrow your search. The SDK documentation then enables you to focus quickly on the likely candidate objects.

Having identified an object to work with as the basic behavior definition for your application object, you will then either subclass that class, customizing your newly created object class, or create an instance of the original object if its behavior exactly matches that required by your object. Resist the temptation to create new objects at the root level of the object hierarchy; more often than not, you'll find that this means some reinventing of the wheel.

The SDK

We strongly encourage you to take the Application Developer's Course (ADC) from GO Corporation as part of your training in PenPoint. This class is offered frequently and includes a great deal of hands-on laboratory experience building applications. If you take this program, an SDK is included as part of the course materials. Otherwise, you can purchase the SDK documentation separately.

Contents of the SDK

The SDK contains the software and documentation you need to build PenPoint applications. The main elements of the SDK are

- a set of application developer's guides that focus on broad issues and the use of development tools
- a comprehensive architectural reference that describes in detail all classes and messages in the PenPoint class library
- an API reference that reproduces all header files, formal message and parameter definitions, and data structures
- all necessary header and include files
- an object-aware, source-code debugger
- a database-driven class browser
- prototyping tools
- a special version of PenPoint that runs on PCs

Language and Software Support

PenPoint development requires an ANSI C compiler. The PenPoint Class Manager provides all the object functionality developers have come to expect from environments such as Smalltalk and Object Pascal. Because the Class Manager is a subsystem of PenPoint rather than a language extension, its capabilities are available via standard C syntax. In addition, these same capabilities can be made available to other languages such as Pascal and C++.

Virtually all PenPoint APIs are based on Class Manager messages and objects. This means you can reuse and modify system code at many levels in the system.

A comprehensive set of debugging capabilities is an inherent part of the SDK. Not only can you set and monitor debug flags in a separate debugging window in the PC-based development environment, you can also use a source-level symbolic debugger. It allows the programmer to examine clsMgr objects and messages, set break points in the source code, manage multiple threads, and execute sophisticated debugging scripts.

Runtime Function Support

PenPoint supports most standard C runtime functions. Because of differences between pen-based and other kinds of user interfaces and due to the special needs of an object-oriented operating system, some of these functions are modified and a few are not relevant.

Chapter 4 describes C runtime function support in more detail..

General Usage

The general development process for a PenPoint application involves creating the original source code files on an MS-DOS-based machine, preferably one with an 80386 CPU. You can undertake some testing and debugging in the PC environment, though it is obviously difficult to test fully the pen-based aspects of your user interface without a pen.

Ultimately, you download your application to a PenPoint-based computer. You might do this either by physically creating and reading a disk with the application or via a fast communications link between the PC and the PenPoint-based computer. The GO debugger will function in a remote debugging mode in this case, with the debugger user interface and symbol table on the PC while it debugs your application in the target hardware.

As you undoubtedly know, the development process then becomes iterative until you have a debugged application working as you want it to work. At that point, you create the distributable product. We recommend you distribute your product on a 1.4MB disk with an MS-DOS format and that you follow certain directory structure requirements discussed in Chapter 11 to ensure maximum compatibility with the PenPoint-based hardware system on which the user will install your program.

Hardware Requirements

To develop PenPoint applications, you need a development platform and a run-and-test platform. The development platform must be an MS-DOS-compatible computer system. The run-and-test platform can be either a 80386-based PC with an EGA or VGA display and a mouse or digitizing tablet to simulate pen activity or a PenPoint-based system if you want to run PenPoint on the target hardware. We recommend the latter, but it is not required.

GO Corporation maintains a list of supported computer systems; you can obtain the latest list from the company.

With either a mouse or a digitizing tablet, you can simulate at least portions of the pen-based user interface in your application. However, you cannot get the true feeling of using a pen on the display any other way than with actual PenPoint target hardware; we recommend every development team have access to at least one.

If you want to connect your desktop development platform directly to a PenPoint-based system, you can do so through one of the high-speed point-to-point network interfaces supported by GO Corporation. Chapter 16 provides more details on this point.

User Interface Design Guidelines

GO Corporation puts a great deal of emphasis on the consistency of the user interface in PenPoint applications. Experience has shown that this is important to the adoption and efficient use of any graphical user interface.

60

. . . .

The Power of PenPoint

Users come to expect certain kinds of behavior from applications running in a particular environment. Applications that meet these expectations are almost always more successful than those that do not.

To facilitate your program's user interface design, GO Corporation publishes the *PenPoint User Interface Style Guide*. The SDK contains a copy of this document.

We strongly encourage you to obtain and study these interface guidelines and to comply with them. You should deviate from the guidelines only when there is an overwhelmingly compelling reason to do so.

Summary

This chapter has briefly examined some global issues surrounding the development of applications for PenPoint-based computer systems. There are at least four good reasons to develop such applications.

As we have seen, there is a learning curve for programmers interested in developing applications for this new operating system, but the object-oriented nature of the system makes it possible to learn development techniques efficiently. This object orientation also requires that you think differently about your application and its design from traditional procedural approaches.

Finally, we have examined the contents of the SDK with which you will work as a PenPoint developer.

4

The PenPoint Kernel

....

A robust, multitasking kernel is the foundation of any modern operating system. PenPoint is built on just such a foundation: a 32-bit, preemptive multitasking kernel with functionality similar to both OS/2 and UNIX. PenPoint's kernel is responsible for the orderly operation of the hardware on which Pen-Point is running. You will rarely need to access the kernel directly except for memory allocation and deallocation, but understanding how the kernel works will assist you in dealing with the rest of the system with which you have more-frequent programming contact and also satisfies your natural curiosity about what's "under the hood."

The basic role of the kernel layer is the adjudication of resource ownership and allocation. The resources the kernel arbitrates are of two primary types: time and space. Time refers to execution time on the CPU; space encompasses not only memory but also such space-constrained entities as I/O ports. The kernel uses the two basic concepts of privileges (for space access) and priorities (for CPU allocation) to manage these resources.

Because the kernel is the foundation of the system, it is the least object-oriented element in the PenPoint operating system. A specialized adjunct to the kernel is PenPoint's Class Manager, which we discuss in detail in Chapter 5. Taken together, the kernel and Class Manager include a well-defined API (application programming interface), but the kernel's interface consists exclusively of functions rather than messages. The Class Manager provides the object and class technology that the rest of PenPoint uses to behave in an object-oriented manner.

61

Even though most of your interaction with the kernel involves memory allocation and deallocation, we will look first at time management because you need to understand how the kernel handles tasks and processes before you can understand how that management process affects memory allocation and utilization.

Task Management

A task in PenPoint is defined as any executing thread of control. It is the basic executing entity in the system. You can think of tasks as consisting of hardware tasks and software tasks. The latter can be further subdivided into processes and subtasks. These processes and subtasks are scheduled and run by a software scheduler based on a priority scheme that determines which task should run at any given time. The only kind of hardware tasks available in PenPoint are interrupts.

A process is the first task that runs when an application is instantiated. A new process requests local memory. Processes own all the resources used by the application instance, including memory, subtasks, and the semaphores that are used in locking and interrupt management schemes. When a process is terminated, all resources owned by it are returned to the system.

You can envision a process as a single address space unit. Everything inside any process is accessible to the rest of the process. In other words, inside a process, everything is shared as in a family. In fact, we will refer to a process and all of its subtasks together as a task family. Other processes, however, cannot access any of the resources owned by a process without specific permission and knowledge.

A subtask is a thread of execution started by either a process or a subtask. Subtasks created by other subtasks are called sibling subtasks. The process that creates a subtask owns that subtask in a parent-child relationship. A subtask has the following characteristics:

- It shares local memory with its parent process as well as any sibling processes.

- It owns no resources.

- It has its own registers and stack.
- It can lock semaphores as well as send and receive messages.

The PenPoint software task scheduler handles the initiation and execution of processes and subtasks. To start a process, the kernel creates a new execution context consisting of local memory, a local instance pointer to the executable code, and a new stack; it then initializes data values.

A process can be started by another process or by a subtask, but there is no hierarchical relationship between processes. In other words, a process that creates another process does not therefore own the created process. This also means that there is no special impact on a created process by its creator. The created process will not terminate when the creator does (or even be notified of its termination unless specific instructions exist to do so), and the created process can decide to associate itself with other processes any time and in any way.

Memory Management

Since PenPoint-based computer systems are by nature strongly focused on memory as a storage medium and less reliant on alternative media such as disk drives than are traditional operating systems, memory residence and memory allocation have somewhat different meanings than you may be accustomed to. All components of the operating system, all applications, and all application data are kept in RAM.

The PenPoint kernel uses privilege settings to determine which of the various tasks and processes (see next section) running in the system has access to which memory and other space-related resources.

Memory can be private to a process, although there is also global memory. We will look at how processes deal with their private memory in the next section. Global memory is shared by all processes, and any task can allocate memory in the global area of RAM. The memory manager keeps track of global memory usage through identifiers and counters that track how many instances of which application processes are sharing a given piece of global data. It will not free the data area, even though a specific instance may attempt to do so, until all of the processes have finished using it.

PenPoint memory management uses a flat-memory model in which you can create heaps and allocate memory within those heaps.

> **NOTE**
> The initial developer's release of PenPoint supported only the 80286 segment-heap memory model, but the final commercial release, an 80386-based environment, supports the flat-memory model described.

Multitasking Support Functions

There are, as you may know, two major approaches to multitasking: preemptive and yield-based. In a preemptive multitasking environment, the operating system is able to preempt an executing task and regain control of the processor. In a yield-based approach, applications must follow a rigorous set of rules that define a "well-behaved" program. These rules typically require the application to "call back" into the operating system periodically so that the system can regain CPU control if needed.

PenPoint uses a preemptive approach to multitasking.

Why Preemptive Multitasking Is Preferable to Yield-Based

Preemptive multitasking is completely transparent to the application. The kernel in PenPoint can efficiently switch CPU time among many processes while remaining able to regain control of the CPU even if an application crashes (for example, by the application entering into an infinite loop).

Microsoft Windows 3.0 and the Apple Macintosh operating system both use yield-based multitasking. As we saw previously, this approach requires the additional coding effort of programs following the rules. It also has the disadvantage that the multitasking is "jumpy" because applications will often not yield soon enough to make transitions smooth. If an application crashes in one of these environments by entering into an infinite loop, the operating system and all other executing applications will also crash because the operating system will never regain control.

In brief, then, preemptive multitasking is easier to program, offers smoother responsiveness, and provides a greater level of reliability than yield-based multitasking.

How PenPoint Handles Multitasking

Relating this approach to multitasking to the discussion earlier in this chapter about tasks and processes, you can see how PenPoint deals with multitasking.

A process is the first task run when an application is instantiated. Therefore, all processes are owned by their application instances. This gives processes a kind of schizophrenic perspective. Seen from the kernel level, a process is exactly the same as an application instance. In other words, the kernel sees only the process. Seen from the top level of the system, including from the viewpoint of your application, an application instance has other items besides the process associated with it. These other items include memory and resources.

Processes generate subtasks, which are then managed by the software task scheduler as previously described.

The scheduler uses priority levels to determine which subtask to execute. All software tasks have a priority associated with them. Those with higher priority values execute before those with lower priority values. These values are defined at two levels. They have a priority class (high, medium high, medium low, and low) and, within each class, a priority rating of 1 to 50. One rule of prioritization in PenPoint is that all on-screen applications always have a higher priority than off-screen pages and applications. Tasks of the same priority share (time-slice) the processor.

Multitasking within an Application

Most applications are a single process. They do not contain separate subtasks. Therefore, they will not typically use the kernel's task management or its other task-related functionality. This is in part because PenPoint single-threads all of your application's interactions with the operating system, the input system, and other executing applications.

A Preferable Limit

It is clearly true that this approach of single-threading your application's task limits true concurrency between two applications. In a multitasking environment, you might justifiably wonder why PenPoint is designed this way.

Simply put, this approach makes your job as a programmer much simpler than it would be if we took another approach.

Some applications, however, may want to create separate subtasks. For example, a spreadsheet might create a subtask to handle calculation in the background, asynchronously with the user interface's view of the data. Any application that wants to create its own subtasks must use the kernel's task management as well as the kernel's intertask communication routines. If you do create an application that consists of multiple subtasks, you must be extremely careful to avoid deadlock. PenPoint supplies a semaphore architecture to support this requirement, but since it is rarely necessary for you to delve into this area, we do not discuss this process here.

> **New to Multitasking?**
> If you have never programmed in a multitasking environment and if the concept of deadlocking is unfamiliar to you, then we strongly suggest that you obtain a good book about operating system design and study it thoroughly before building an application that uses subtasks internally.

Reliability

The kernel of PenPoint is essential to the operation of the entire system. Therefore, it is important that it be designed to be as reliable and crash-proof as possible. Reliability in PenPoint involves three key issues

- a protection model for the kernel's contents
- enabling the operating system to survive an application crash
- enabling the operating system to recover quickly from a crash in the operating system itself

> **Against What Is PenPoint Protecting Itself?**
> You may wonder what kinds of behavior or events PenPoint is designed to protect itself against. The emphasis in the PenPoint protection scheme is on inadvertent misbehavior, rather than on malevolent software such as viruses. Thus, if your application accidentally creates a pointer to a wrong location or attempts to modify a protected object in the class hierarchy, the protection scheme will intervene to prevent that from happening.

Protection of the Kernel

The kernel's protection model must protect the system in ways that are far different from those of object-oriented systems that do not attempt to perform operating system functions. In an object-oriented environment (as you'll see shortly), programmers spend most of their time subclassing existing classes in the hierarchy to give them slightly different behavior.

In an environment such as Smalltalk, it is virtually impossible to separate your application code from the system code. You are frequently called on to examine system source code, understand what it does, and then either use it or subclass it to achieve some specific behavior omitted by the system designers.

The problem with allowing such rampant object access in PenPoint, of course, is that here the class library is in large part also the operating system that holds things together in the environment. It could be disastrous to permit any programmer to make a modification that could in turn alter how any other application runs.

PenPoint uses hardware-level protection schemes to protect its core objects from accidental alteration.

Survival of Application Crashes

As we have pointed out, PenPoint uses a preemptive multitasking model. As a result, the system will always retake control even from an application that crashes. It will regain this control within a few milliseconds of the occurrence of the application crash.

Once the operating system has regained control, it can follow an orderly application shutdown procedure to keep the rest of the system intact. This means that if one of several executing applications enters an infinite loop, the problem will not propagate to the other executing processes in the system. Instead, within a short time of the occurrence of the crash, PenPoint will be operational again.

Recovery from Operating System Crashes

If the PenPoint operating system itself crashes, the user warm-boots to recover.

Warm booting involves scrapping all running processes, including those running at the kernel level. All applications and installed code resources, as well as data files, are carefully preserved, and dynamic memory is cleared.

The system then shuts down all of the processes that were running when the crash occurred and clears their resources, including dynamic memory. Each process is started from a clean slate. With the probable exception of the page to which the user was turned when the crash occurred, everything in the system should be restored to its precrash condition. Depending on exactly what was happening and on its stage of development when the crash occurred, even the active page may be preserved.

PenPoint is designed to handle this entire crash recovery process in less than a minute. It is, in essence, an on-the-fly diskless reboot process.

The Loader

Traditional operating systems always have two copies of the code for the system and for any executing applications. One of these copies exists in its unrelocated form on disk and one in its relocated form in the system's memory. In PenPoint, of course, this executable code can exist only in the system's memory since it has no guarantee that an external storage medium will be available.

PenPoint loads a single, relocated copy of binary code into memory. This single copy is shared by all instances of an application and is preserved even across operating system crashes. This obviates the need for the unrelocated form of the code to be anywhere but on application distribution disks. If you write a word processing application and your user has thirty-five documents stored on his or her computer system, each of which uses your application, there is still only one copy of your executable code. Each of these documents is an instance of your application and owns a pointer to the executable code

70

. . . .

The Power of PenPoint

as well as some data that helps it keep track of where in the execution process it last stopped.

This is clearly a major gain over traditional operating systems in terms of memory utilization as well as overall efficiency.

Date and Time Services

The kernel, since it lives closest to the hardware, is of necessity closest to the clock chip in the system on which PenPoint is running. As a result, Pen-Point places some useful date and time services in the kernel.

The most interesting of these services is the alarm subsystem. It keeps track of a queue of alarm dates and times. As each alarm time arrives, even if the machine is turned off, action dictated by the alarm when it was set will be taken. PenPoint systems need this capability because to conserve batteries they need to be powered down when not in use. With the clock on a separate chip and this alarm system, we can permit application designers to build such applications as calendar-based alarms. It is possible, for example, to build an application that will wake up the system and carry out a telecommunications task when rates are favorable or traffic is low.

More-traditional timer interrupts as well as setting and getting the date and time are also supported by PenPoint.

Machine Interface Library

Part of the kernel layer of PenPoint is known as the Machine Interface Library (MIL). This library supports the efficient porting of PenPoint to new hardware environments and is of interest only to developers with that assignment.

The MIL is an extensible part of the PenPoint Adaptation Kit (PAK), about which you should contact GO Corporation if you want to deploy PenPoint in an environment in which it is not now implemented.

Other Kernel Services

Floating-point math is supported through a library of C routines. These routines are relatively standard and include functions to handle

- addition and subtraction
- multiplication and division
- trigonometric functions
- logarithmic functions
- conversion between floating-point and fixed numbers

The PenPoint C runtime library provides as much of the functionality of leading C libraries as is reasonable in view of hardware and operating system requirements and differences. Functions specific to the MS-DOS or IBM BIOS environments are not implemented. Functions that make calls to those omitted functions have been modified accordingly.

All functions are reentrant, including some that were not designed to be so in the Microsoft library. Some time-related functions were completely replaced with newly named functions to avoid problems involving differences in parameter list sizes.

For the most part, however, you will find that PenPoint's C runtime library closely resembles the Microsoft library.

An ANSI (American National Standards Institute) C compatible stream I/O library is also part of the PenPoint kernel layer. This library is a robust and flexible architecture for file and serial I/O support.

Summary

This chapter has examined the kernel layer of the PenPoint operating system, the layer that is closest to the hardware on which PenPoint is implemented. The kernel handles task and process management, memory management, and multitasking support.

As we have seen, the kernel is designed to ensure reliability of the operating system from alteration by programming or by system or program crashes.

The kernel also includes other functions such as a loader, date and time services, and a Machine Interface Library.

5

The Class Manager

PenPoint is an extensible, object-oriented operating system. It uses a Class Manager to support object-oriented programming (OOP) concepts. The Class Manager provides all the object functionality that developers have come to expect from environments such as Smalltalk and Object Pascal. Developers can use calls to the Class Manager to create classes and class hierarchies, to create and destroy objects or class instances, to inherit functionality from other objects, and to define and send messages between objects.

Virtually all PenPoint application programming interfaces (APIs) are based on Class Manager messages and objects. This means you can reuse and modify system code at many levels. As a result, applications are smaller and provide a more consistent user interface (see Chapter 2) because they share standard functionality provided by PenPoint subsystems. Traditional operating systems, of course, are not object-oriented at all. These facts lead to some observations about the differences between PenPoint and earlier operating systems.

One of the most intriguing of these relates to the intimacy between applications and the operating system. In a traditional operating system, most applications interact with the operating system relatively infrequently, for specific reasons and at widely spaced intervals. These interactions are generally calls from the application to the operating system requesting access to facilities managed by the system. The application can only call the surface (public) APIs, not the operating system's internal building blocks. Applications must "take it or leave it" in regard to the way the operating system carries out its core tasks. This situation is depicted in Figure 5-1.

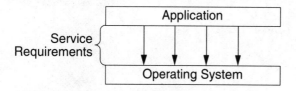

Figure 5-1 Typical OS/Application Interaction Model

In PenPoint, on the other hand, there is a close working relationship between the operating system and applications. As we will see in great detail throughout the rest of this book, the development process can be viewed as extending the operating system to encompass your application. Many of the functional elements of your application may in fact turn out to be instances of facilities furnished by PenPoint, perhaps with a bit of customization. Because all of PenPoint above the kernel layer (see Chapter 4) is object-oriented, your application can "reach" into PenPoint's class hierarchy and call ancestor classes as well as surface classes (leaf nodes). The result is a system that provides many more entry points than a traditional operating system and therefore supports a much greater degree of code sharing. (For example, PenPoint has more than 1,500 messages compared with about 600 function calls in Microsoft Windows 3.0.) This situation is depicted by Figure 5-2.

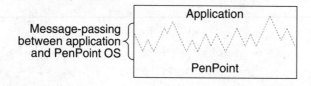

Figure 5-2 PenPoint OS/Application Interaction Model

Features Supported

To function as an object-oriented operating system, PenPoint has a number of fundamental capabilities that traditional operating systems do not provide. Among these are

- user-controlled installation/deinstallation of classes, including sharing of classes between applications and message sending across process boundaries
- versioning support so that new releases of application and system code can work correctly with objects created by earlier versions
- support for objects that are global to the system and therefore shareable between the system and applications
- means for protecting the operating system from being damaged as a result of the subclassing that is an inherent part of object-oriented programming
- support for prohibited or controlled access to objects that are either private or protected (for example, operating system file objects that must be protected)
- unique IDs for all objects in the environment so that message passing can be handled efficiently and correctly, even when data objects are transferred from one PenPoint machine to another (which means that PenPoint objects are persistent)

We will examine many of these facilities in this chapter, though many will be dealt with in greater detail later in the book.

By providing these capabilities, PenPoint brings object-oriented technology right to the foundation level of the operating system, enabling everything that happens in a PenPoint-based system to have all the intuitiveness, efficiency, ease of learning, and other characteristics of good object-oriented systems.

Why Not Use an OOP Language?

PenPoint does not use an object-oriented language because none of the available object-oriented languages offers the ability to handle the requirements previously outlined without extensive and non-standard modifications. They are typically designed to support a single application on a traditional disk-based, procedural operating system, rather than for all applications and the operating system to be an object-oriented multitasking environment with classes and applications dynamically installing and deinstalling during the life of the system.

In addition, it was important to make PenPoint application design accessible to as broad a range of programmers as possible. You will have to learn some object-oriented concepts to build PenPoint applications, but you can write all of your code in ANSI (American National Standards Institute) C. That means your code is highly portable between C compilers, so you have one less thing to learn to be up and running in PenPoint.

PenPoint's solution is to provide a subsystem called Class Manager. You will interact a great deal with this subsystem and its important messages as you create PenPoint applications. The Class Manager is an integral part of the PenPoint kernel (see Chapter 4 for other elements that share the PenPoint kernel with the Class Manager). Because the Class Manager is part of the kernel, all the rest of PenPoint can use the Class Manager; this permits those other elements of the system to package their functionality as classes. Whenever you build a PenPoint application, two of your main tasks will be to define new classes and create new objects. This process involves the Class Manager interaction.

In PenPoint, classes are used to package all public APIs. You can think of this as a way to describe and encapsulate highly flexible code modules. However, these code modules typically use traditional C code with function calls and pointers to implement their public APIs. The result is a system that combines the efficiency of C in its internal implementation with the power of object-oriented programming in its external programmatic interface.

Programming Efficiencies

Message handling does not require any special language constructs. A message is constructed with standard C function calls, except that message arguments must be stored in data structures before making the C function calls. The resulting C code looks a little unusual but this implementation style is efficient and implementable in ANSI C.

Object creation in PenPoint is also straightforward. Typically, you send the message msgNew to a class you wish to instantiate. For example, to create a new list object, you would send msgNew to clsList. You must always precede msgNew with msgNewDefaults to initialize a data structure to default values before you override some or all of those default values and then send msgNew. In either case, the process is simple and standard.

Unique Identifiers

PenPoint uses 32-bit unique identifiers (UIDs) to help the system keep track of all classes and objects. A UID encodes information indicating whether the object it references is global or local, and well-known (that is, permanently defined at compile time) or dynamic (that is, created by the Class Manager at runtime). Global well-known UIDs are assigned and administered by GO Corporation to avoid conflicts. Because applications can embed other applications (see Chapter 8), it is important that any well-known UID you plan to use in your program be assigned by GO Corporation and therefore guaranteed to be unique among assigned UIDs.

PenPoint also supports the use of UIDs within filed data. These UIDs must be persistent (that is, unique across all time and space). PenPoint accomplishes this with Universal UIDs (UUIDs), which are 64-bit quantities that include a unique machine ID from the hardware on which PenPoint is running. UUIDs can be used to point to PenPoint objects even when they've been filed to external media and then loaded back into PenPoint, regardless of which machine they are loaded into.

Why UIDs Are Important

One of the fundamental acts of program code is to reference some entity. References to memory locations (using pointers), files (using names), and other elements of a system are either dynamic or static. Dynamic references are passed into your code from other code or as the result of an act of creation on your part. They are generally numbers or pointers (memory addresses).

Static references pose more difficulties because they are placed into your code at compile time. If a static reference is a memory address or interrupt number, your code will not be very portable. Classically, static references are given some measure of independence by expressing them as strings (for example, the name of a library reference). But strings are clumsy to process, difficult to guarantee uniqueness of, and inefficient to pass as an argument.

PenPoint unifies both dynamic and static references into a single "naming" facility called UIDs. Combined with GO's administration service to guarantee uniqueness when needed, UIDs are efficient, expressive, and convenient. In PenPoint, everything from a small temporary object you just created through a static reference of another application is referenced by a UID.

PenPoint has two root classes in its class hierarchy. All objects descend from clsObject, but classes additionally descend from clsClass. Note that clsClass is a meta-class, so that for each class in the system there is a corresponding object that stores information about the class as a whole (including the code that implements its methods) and implements class-level operations. In an idealized sense, objects encapsulate data and behavior (with behavior, of course, expressed as code). But you obviously would not want to duplicate the code with every object instance. To avoid this, clsClass supports classes as a special kind of object that provides the shared behavior (code) and information for a type, or class, of objects.

Major Programming Tasks

As you create PenPoint applications, you are likely to find yourself involved with the following activities that fall within the province of the Class Manager:

- setting up message arguments
- sending messages
- creating new instances
- controlling object access and capabilities
- creating new classes
- setting up observer objects

We will take a look at each of these functions so that you can get some of the flavor of programming with PenPoint's Class Manager.

Setting Up Message Arguments

For all practical purposes, you can think of all processing in PenPoint taking place as a result of one object sending another object a message. Conversely, all objects in PenPoint respond to messages. So whenever you build an application, you will find yourself spending a good deal of time designing and creating messages and their arguments for your objects to respond to so they can perform their function in the application.

Each message takes a single 32-bit parameter when it is sent. If you need to pass more information than fits in 32 bits, you can use this parameter to pass a pointer to a structure containing argument data.

Objects can respond to messages in one of two ways: by returning a status token indicating success or failure of the operation requested in the message or by returning data in the argument structure supplied by the message sender.

Sending Messages

You send messages to objects to elicit from them behavior that they know how to carry out. This behavior is either part of their class's definition or contained in a parent class. You need not know the details; all you have to know is that a particular object is able to respond to a specific message you send to it.

Message passing in most object-oriented systems is purely local and synchronous. Objects can only send messages to objects that reside in the same application instance. When an object sends a message to another object, all processing halts until the receiving object responds. In PenPoint, message passing can be synchronous or asynchronous. This feature is obviously essential to a multitasking operating system.

Table 5-1 lists the four functions provided by PenPoint's Class Manager for the sending of messages. In choosing which Class Manager function to call, you must understand whether the destination object resides in a separate task. You must also determine if you want synchronous (application code execution is blocked) or asynchronous (application code continues executing concurrently with the called code) tasking semantics.

Table 5-1   Message-Sending Functions in the Class Manager

Function	Usable across task boundaries?	Usable asynchronously?
ObjCall	No	No
ObjSend	Yes	No
ObjPostAsync	Yes	Yes

Use ObjCall for objects local to (that is, owned by) your task. To send messages to objects in other tasks, you must use ObjSend or ObjPostAsync. This is because processes have separate memory address spaces, which means that argument data structures must be copied by the Class Manager from the caller's task space into the address space of the called task.

ObjSend is synchronous. Most application developers will use ObjCall and ObjSend.

If your application requires true concurrent multitasking between its tasks, use ObjPostAsync. The caller and the responder will then execute concurrently. This is a valuable technique for applications such as a spreadsheet that wants to perform recalculations in the background while allowing the user to continue to interact with the program's user interface.

Because most PenPoint programs test the returned status codes after sending a message (just as they would if they were calling a C function), the Class Manager defines a number of macros to assist you in message-passing tasks.

An Example

Figure 5-3 is a stylized example of sending a message in PenPoint. Three pieces of information are essential

- the message to be sent
- the object to which the message is to be sent
- the argument values required by the message

```
position.x = 1;
position.y = 2;
ObjCall (msg, object, position);
```

Figure 5-3 Stylized Message-Sending Example

As we said earlier, the argument value is 32 bits; to pass more data, you use some or all of the 32-bit argument to pass a pointer to a data structure whose values you first initialize (in this example, the structure is called "position").

As you can see, ObjCall is a normal C function that takes these three parameters; it then uses the Class Manager's internal method table machinery to pass the argument and object to the appropriate method (C code) where the message is implemented. ObjSend and ObjPostAsync work identically, except that they may copy their arguments.

Creating New Instances

Because msgNew takes many detailed arguments that many programmers will not need to initialize, all PenPoint classes respond to msgNewDefaults by supplying default values in the P_ARGS block for msgNew. You should therefore always precede a msgNew with a msgNewDefaults.

To create an instance of an existing class, you will generally follow this process

1. Send the class you wish to instantiate msgNewDefaults, passing a pointer to an appropriate argument structure.
2. The class initializes the new argument structure appropriate for this class.
3. Change fields you want to override.
4. Send msgNew to the class. This is where the actual instantiation occurs.

Controlling Object Access and Capabilities

One of the main issues in an object-oriented operating system, as we have indicated several times, is the need to protect objects from unintentional modification. Not all objects, of course, require such protection. But, clearly, any object that the system depends on must be able to be protected from alteration.

PenPoint implements this capability by using keys and locks. All objects can have a key associated with them. This key limits access to certain kinds of operations to applications that have the key. Several messages that request basic object operations like freeing (removing) the object require the use of a key unless the object has set certain of its capability flags to allow the operation without a key. You can also require keys for messages you define.

Capability flags include those that permit a sending object to change the class of an object, free it, use an object as an ancestor for a new class, make an object observable, and control the messages that this object honors. Each of these flags is a binary value that has different default settings depending on whether the object is an instance or a class. Capability flags can be changed dynamically by code with the appropriate key.

Keys and locks, along with the Kernel's usage of hardware-protected memory and process protection, are good examples of PenPoint's defensive efforts to protect against misbehaved or buggy applications. These features also support rapid application development because many bugs are caught immediately by the PenPoint Kernel and the Class Manager. A highly reliable operating system and applications are the result.

Creating New Classes

There are two stages to creating a class. First, you write code that defines the new behavior the class will exhibit. The only reason you ever design and create a new class in PenPoint is because your application requires some behavior that is not defined in an existing PenPoint class, so behavior definition is the key design step. Once you've coded this behavior, you compile the new class and install it into a running PenPoint-based system.

The second stage takes place at runtime in PenPoint. There, the new class is created by PenPoint sending msgNew to clsClass. The message arguments are passed to clsClass in a structure called CLASS_NEW, which contains, among other things, the name of the parent class, the name of a compiled method table (see following section) to associate with the class, and the amount of memory required for instance data.

Method Tables

How does a message to an object actually "look up" and call the appropriate C function? PenPoint's Class Manager maintains a method table for each class in which message UIDs index into the table that contains the memory addresses of the associated C routine. During development, the programmer creates a table that associates each message's UID with a C function call, then compiles this table using the special Method Table Compiler that comes with the PenPoint SDK. This results in an object file. At runtime, when you create your new class by sending a msgNew to clsClass, you pass it a compile-time symbolic reference to the method table and the Class Manager binds the class to its method table.

Setting Up Observer Objects

A unique capability of clsObject (and therefore of all PenPoint objects) is its observer capability. Any object may register itself as an "observer" of any other object that is capable of being observed. Objects may have multiple observers. Subsequently, the observer will be notified whenever there is a change in the state of the observed object. This allows an efficient, data-driven style of programming, rather than forcing objects to continuously poll or invent ad hoc protocols just to coordinate among themselves.

The benefits of the observer architecture are significant. It is used as the foundation of a variety of automatic notifications and updates in PenPoint, ranging from applications being notified that a new service has been installed to PenPoint's Application Framework views observing their data objects.

Why Observer Notification Is Important

There are two ways of finding out when an event has occurred in a system: polling and notification.

In a polling architecture, you must periodically inquire whether the event has occurred yet. This is something like using a microwave oven whose alarm bell has been broken. To find out if your food is cooked, you have to watch it continuously or look at it periodically. This is not very convenient.

Fix the microwave's alarm and you have a notification process. You can go off and do other things, confident that when the food is cooked, you'll be informed.

The user interface and APIs to many traditional operating systems require the user and programmer to poll for events like inserted disks and electronic mail arrival at the terminal. The user has to look for the event in some way.

PenPoint urges all software and user interfaces to be based on the friendlier notification concept. To make this convenient for applications, PenPoint incorporates an efficient notification mechanism at the heart of its object system.

To be able to notify observers of state changes, an object must have its appropriate capability flag set, contain a list of objects to be notified (though the list is maintained by the Class Manager in response to messages), and an argument structure pointer if data is to be passed with the notification.

Once an object is set up so that it is observable, any notifications it posts will automatically notify any dependent or interested objects of a state change; you need do nothing to make this happen.

Summary

This chapter has examined the Class Manager in PenPoint, the repository of the object-oriented behavior in the system. As we have seen, the Class Manager supports such features as

- user-controlled installation and deinstallation
- versioning
- global, sharable objects
- operating system protection
- controlled access to critical objects
- unique IDs for all objects

We have seen that application development through the Class Manager involves setting up and dealing with messages and objects as well as creating new classes of objects.

We have also seen that observer objects are essential to the nature of PenPoint.

6

The Application
Framework

· ·

As you can tell, applications written for the PenPoint Operating System interact far more intimately with the system than do applications written for more traditional operating systems. In older-style applications, the user had to be aware of details of the system, including such issues as which application to open to work with a specific document, the name and location of the data file, and a host of other details. These users must explicitly save their data or run the risk of losing it when the machine on which the operating system is running is turned off. This is in stark contrast to a PenPoint application where the user simply turns to a page in a notebook and the system locates the appropriate document, identifies the application to run, and sets things up for the user. When the user turns away from a page, the system saves the closed document without user intervention.

This level of intimacy between the operating system and the application would be an all but impossible feat if the operating system didn't provide significant tool support for the designer. The Application Framework is the home of the tools that enable you to handle this close-knit interaction between what you build and the environment in which the user will work.

In windowing environments on other operating systems, you generally have the choice of using the support framework supplied by the operating system designer or going your own way. This is not the case with PenPoint applications: Using the Application Framework as the basis for your application is not an option, it is the only way you can get your application to install in and run on a computer system using PenPoint.

Every PenPoint application, no matter how trivial or complex, must respond to certain messages sent by the Application Framework. As we'll see in this chapter, these messages are provided so that the user can install your application neatly into PenPoint, create new instances of your application (by creating an associated document as a new page in the Notebook), and intermingle your application and its documents with other documents on the same machine.

> **NOTE**
> We will often treat the Application Framework as if it were a single entity, but you should keep in mind that it is a collection of classes, messages, and protocols. Thus, when we say the Application Framework sends messages to your application, we are over-simplifying a bit to avoid cluttering the discussion with references to specific classes in the Application Framework.

The Application Framework also makes it easy for you to build your application so that it follows the life cycle pattern of all PenPoint applications. As we'll see later in this chapter, all PenPoint applications have life cycles. Most of the programming necessary to support this paradigm is included in the Application Framework.

> **Why an Application "Life Cycle"?**
> A well-defined life cycle allows PenPoint to manage the creation and destruction of processes and running programs. In other operating systems, the *user* must determine when to run them and when to shut them down. Thus the notion of an application life cycle allows PenPoint to make overall system usage more transparent to the user.

Purpose of Layer

Essentially, the Application Framework layer of PenPoint serves two purposes. First, it is a collection of classes that define the protocols that make up a PenPoint application. Second, it is a complete implementation in its own right of a generic PenPoint application.

Common Functions Handled by Application Framework

Architecturally, the Application Framework is a set of classes that define protocols to implement common application behavior. These behaviors include

- installation via the Installer
- creation of application instances
- activation of an instance of your application (typically by turning to a page in the Notebook)
- saving and restoration of application data
- deactivation and deletion of application instances
- deinstallation of applications

The Application Framework layer also provides the class and message support needed to facilitate the use of the standard elements present in all PenPoint applications.

Advantages of Application Framework

As we have said, you must use the Application Framework layer in building a PenPoint application. But this is neither an arbitrary requirement nor an onerous burden. In fact, you'll find that a number of advantages arise from your full use of this layer's functionality.

First, like all of the other classes in PenPoint, the Application Framework layer's classes make extensive use of inheritance to save code. By grouping common behaviors and support for standard elements in a single collection of tightly integrated classes, PenPoint makes it possible for you to focus on your application's objectives rather than on its presentation to the user.

Second, because the Application Framework structures all applications in a well-defined, standard way, they all can be manipulated by common software. For example, the operating system can install, deinstall, and perform other operations for all applications rather than each application being required to reinvent this wheel.

Third, applications can even manipulate one another in a standard way. The concept of applications interacting closely with other applications is probably foreign to you. In most traditional operating systems, interaction between applications is an arm's-length situation. You may be able to share data with other applications or perhaps even launch them. But in PenPoint, the user can create arbitrarily complex documents that embed multiple applications in a single page of the Notebook. For example, for users to place an illustration in the text of a word processing document, they create an instance of a drawing program. PenPoint provides full support for all actions on the outer document (in our example, the text document) to be applied to contained documents (such as the illustration) as well. Furthermore, the PenPoint concept of application development will almost certainly lead to a plethora of small, independent programs that serve highly specialized purposes. These applications may be accessible to all other programs running in the Notebook, and thus be subject to control by those programs. This complexity would be a nightmare if the operating system didn't provide strong support for it. Fortunately, as you'll see in this chapter, PenPoint does.

Fourth, you can implement a family of related applications extremely efficiently. Since the Application Framework, like the rest of PenPoint, is class-based, it can be extended. For example, you might write a family of related applications so that they share a common subclass of the Application Framework. This would link them together more intimately than possible with other operating systems, and it would do so efficiently.

In short, the idea of the Application Framework is one you'll come to appreciate as you develop PenPoint programs.

Architectural Overview

Figure 6-1 is a class hierarchy diagram of the Application Framework layer's principal classes. Viewed in its entirety, the Application Framework layer makes use of approximately sixteen classes. Of these, you will find yourself most often using eight

- clsClass
- clsAppMgr
- clsApp
- clsAppDir
- clsEmbeddedWin
- clsView
- clsAppWin
- clsAppMonitor

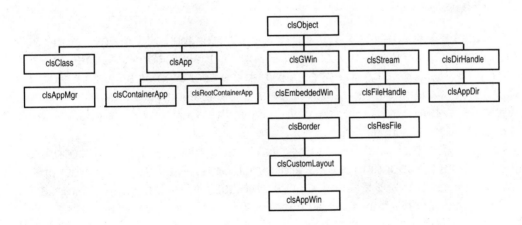

Figure 6-1   Application Framework Class Hierarchy

In Appendix A, we take a closer look at each of these classes, including the messages defined by each that you will need to know and use most often. For now, we are interested in taking a bird's eye view of the layer's architecture, so we'll save the details until later.

As you saw in Chapter 1, all named classes in PenPoint are instances of clsClass. They are also descendants of clsObject. We briefly touched on this dual-inheritance structure in Chapter 1; now it is time to take a closer look at it in the context of your application.

All applications are instances of clsAppMgr and descendants of clsClass. This means that a user-created instance of an application, while obviously an instance of the application's class itself, is a descendant of clsApp. This rather complex interrelationship of classes is shown in Figure 6-2.

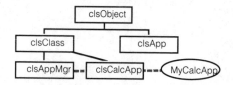

Figure 6-2 Typical Application Class Hierarchy

In Figure 6-2, the dashed lines indicate instances the solid line descendancy. Your application would, of course, occupy the position in the diagram where the class clsCalcApp appears. When the user creates an instance of your application, that instance occupies the final leaf in the tree diagram in Figure 6-2, labeled myCalcApp. As you know, the user can create multiple instances of any application.

To make sense of what seem to be parallel structures, you should recognize that PenPoint is supporting two parallel dimensions here: The obvious dimension is instantiating application instance objects; the less obvious is instantiating clsAppMgr itself (that is, application installation). For application classes to be installable and efficient in memory use, PenPoint extracts all code resources and behavior that are common across all application instances and places this in clsAppMgr. In other object-oriented systems, class hierarchies tend to be static; they do not support the grafting of new classes into the hierarchical tree structure. PenPoint's class hierarchy, by contrast, is dynamic. In PenPoint, not only is it possible to graft new classes onto the tree, it is even possible to do this under user installation and deinstallation control.

This capability requires architectural and user interface support for gracefully handling the application's dependency tree. If an operating system is truly designed to encourage code sharing, it must handle the case in which some of an application's dependencies are not present. This is what the "meta level" of clsAppMgr is about.

The messages defined by clsAppMgr deal with maintaining common instance data about an application as well as with creating, activating, and deleting instances of applications. On the other hand, the messages defined by clsApp deal with application instances while they are activated. (We'll have much more to say about these and other phases of a PenPoint application's life cycle shortly.)

The class hierarchy is not the only way to look architecturally at PenPoint applications and their interaction with the Application Framework. Any application that is running (typically those that are currently visible on the display) can be viewed from any of four separate but closely related aspects: its display, its file directory, its process, and its object.

Figure 6-3 shows the screen of a computer system running PenPoint with five applications open: the Bookshelf, the Notebook, the Notebook Contents, a text-editing application called New Product Ideas, and a charting application called Charting Paper.

You can see how this display of five applications relates to the file system's handling of these applications and their elements by examining Figure 6-4.

As you can see, the Notebook that serves as the fundamental metaphor for PenPoint applications uses the file system to organize its documents so that they parallel the structure of the Notebook Table of Contents. Each document and section has its own directory in the file system. If a document is contained in a section, its file entry is a subdirectory of the section's directory. Similarly, if a document has an embedded document, the embedded document's directory is a subdirectory of its enclosing document's directory. The Bookshelf acts much like a section, providing a "home" for all of the other top-level subdirectories and documents in the Notebook.

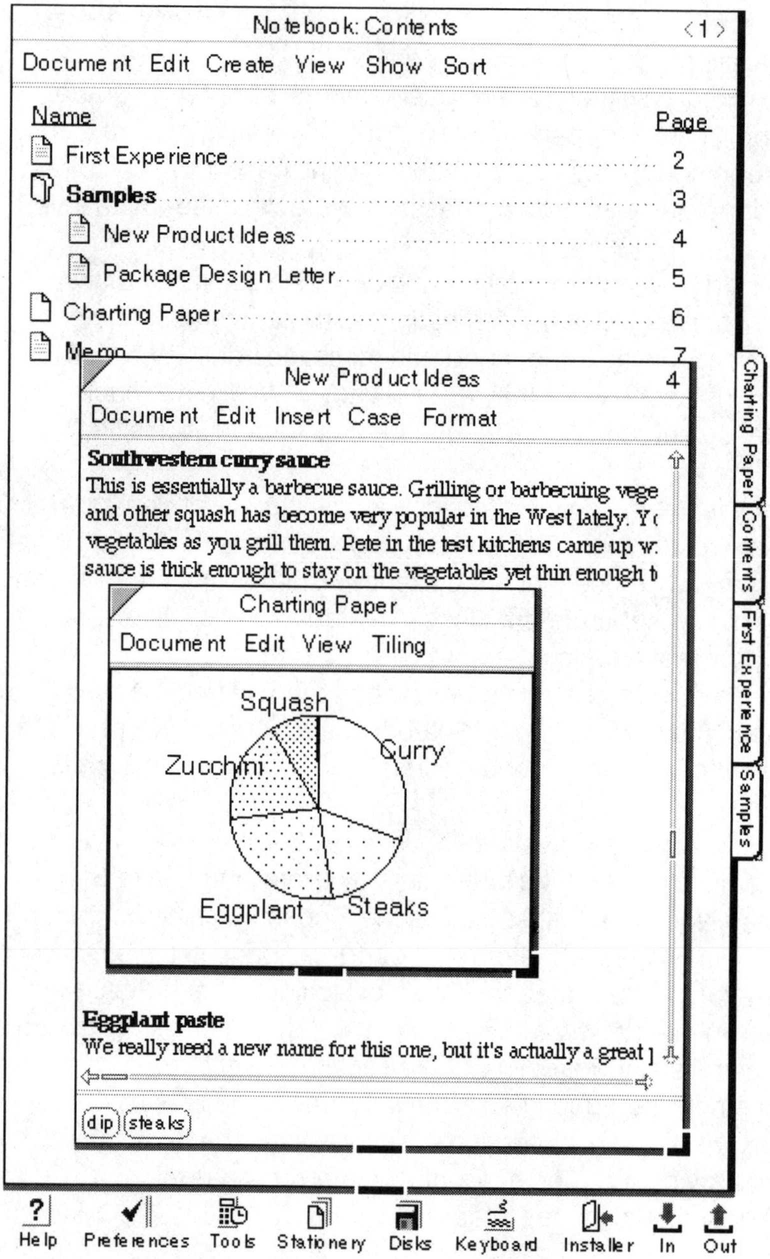

Notebook: Contents ⟨1⟩

Document Edit Create View Show Sort

Name	Page
First Experience	2
Samples	3
New Product Ideas	4
Package Design Letter	5
Charting Paper	6
Memo	7

New Product Ideas 4

Document Edit Insert Case Format

Southwestern curry sauce
This is essentially a barbecue sauce. Grilling or barbecuing vege
and other squash has become very popular in the West lately. Y (
vegetables as you grill them. Pete in the test kitchens came up w.
sauce is thick enough to stay on the vegetables yet thin enough t

Charting Paper

Document Edit View Tiling

Squash

Zucchini   Curry

Eggplant   Steaks

Eggplant paste
We really need a new name for this one, but it's actually a great]

dip steaks

Help Preferences Tools Stationery Disks Keyboard Installer In Out

Charting Paper Contents First Experience Samples

Figure 6-3 Screen Display of Five Typical Applications

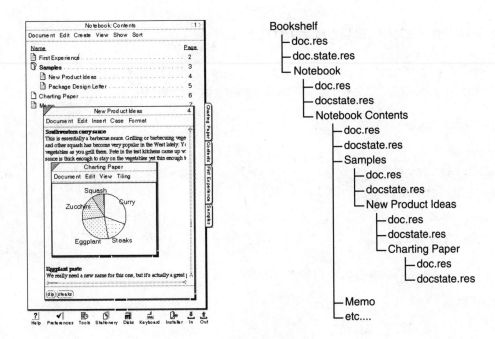

Figure 6-4 File System Entries for Five Typical Applications

A process is associated with each running application in PenPoint. Much of the work performed by the Application Framework involves the management of this process in accordance with the application life cycle. The Application Framework creates the process and sets up its application object to receive messages. When the user turns away from the application, the Application Framework destroys the process and saves its data (although you can design your application to run in "hot mode" so that this behavior is not applied to instances of it).

As we saw earlier in this chapter, an open document is an instance of an application class, which is always a descendant of clsApp. Therefore, an open document is an object capable of receiving and responding to messages defined in its own class and in clsApp.

Standard Application Elements

All PenPoint applications consist of a number of standard elements. The six most important from the viewpoint of the software designer are

- application code
- document directory
- document process
- application object
- resource files
- main window

Let's take a brief look at each of these standard elements in turn.

Application Code

The most obvious standard application element from the designer's viewpoint is the executable code for the program you write to create your application. You generally will write this code in a high-level language (probably C) using the PenPoint Software Developer's Kit. You will then use special linking tools to create a PenPoint application from that source code. The resulting executable file is the application code element of the application.

In addition to the executable code itself, any Dynamic Link Libraries (DLLs) that your application needs to run are also part of the application code element of a PenPoint program. DLLs generally are collections of classes or external service routines that are frequently shared across applications and that perform common tasks such as database access or special calculations.

Application code does not share memory with the PenPoint file system where instances of applications and their related data are stored. Instead, applications and the PenPoint operating system share a special area of RAM that is protected against accidental erasure and is carefully managed by PenPoint. Application instance data is forever linked to its code by a global, well-known unique identifier (UID). Since this UID includes built-in version numbers, all application instance data is globally marked with a unique identifier defining which version of which code generated it.

One Copy of Code

Traditional, disk-based operating systems require memory storage for two copies of code: an unrelocated executable file on disk, and, at execution time, a relocated copy in memory.

PenPoint significantly reduces the weight and cost of pen-based hardware by requiring only one copy of application code. Applications are distributed as executable files on floppy disk, but when PenPoint installs the application, the code is relocated into memory and then permanently retained, obviating the need for a disk-based copy. PenPoint even preserves the application code in memory across operating system restarts. All application code is fully reentrant, so a single-copy of code supports an unlimited number of application instances.

Document Directory

By now, it probably has become second nature for you to think of all documents as instances of the applications that created them. As you have seen, every document has a corresponding directory, and when the user turns to a document that requires a particular application, PenPoint determines from the directory which application created the document, then creates and activates an instance of that application.

The mechanism by which this automatic launching of the right application takes place involves the class ID of the application in the file system, specifically in the instance directory for the document in question. This attribute connects the document to its application.

98

. . . .

The Power of PenPoint

Why a Directory for Each Document?

You might wonder why PenPoint uses an entire directory for each application instance rather than just a file. This design enables applications to gain the freedom of using multiple files to store portions of their instance data and permits subdirectories to be used for embedded children. A file could not contain a child subdirectory because files do not inherently handle storage of such objects, but a directory can deal with this need quite nicely.

Each instance directory entry in the file system, when opened in an application process, is an instance of clsAppDir, which in turn is a descendant of clsDirHandle.

Document Process

The Application Framework, as you have seen, creates and manages a separate process for each active application in a PenPoint environment. This process is the vehicle by which the active application is managed by PenPoint as long as it remains active.

An application process has several attributes, including

- a message queue where messages sent by various parts of the system to the application instance are stored until they can be forwarded to the appropriate object within the process

- an entry point that defines the means by which process startup takes place

- an AppMain routine, which is the event loop within which the program starts the application life cycle and waits for a user event to which it should respond

- a method table that maps message names to method handlers; in other words, where the names of messages to which the application responds locally are related to the names of the procedures that contain the responses

Application Object

The application object is the core of the application. It processes information and responds to messages sent to the object via the process associated with it. As with all PenPoint objects, an application object has a unique identifier that makes it possible for the object to receive messages from external events or other objects, including the Application Framework.

In addition to dealing with messages that are part of its specific functions, an application object creates other objects for the application and assigns responsibilities to these objects. In general, all of the activity that makes up the application's functionality can be found in the application object's structure and processing.

Because all application instances are objects and because of their inheritance (as described previously), all instances will receive and must process messages from the Application Framework. This is the basic means by which almost everything in the PenPoint environment happens. An Application Framework class sends a message to an instance of an application, and that instance either handles the message or passes it up the inheritance hierarchy for one of its ancestors to handle.

Resource Files

Resource files in PenPoint are general-purpose storage mechanisms whose format and contents are application dependent. They are administered by PenPoint's Resource Manager (see Chapter 12). All application instances have at least one resource file associated with them. This file is the repository for all objects created by the application.

The Resource Manager provides your application with a persistent object store in which you need only read and write. The Resource Manager deals with locating objects on request and with space allocation and compaction.

Your application can use multiple files in the document directory, including multiple resource files. To the degree your application structures its instance data as objects and you use resource files for this data, you will find that filing requires very little code under PenPoint. You need only ensure that each object can read and write its own instance data.

The most important feature of a resource file is that it remains in the system's memory after the user turns away from the application. In fact, when the user closes your application instance by turning away from it, the resource files and other files in its document directory, the directory itself, the application code, and any associated DLLs and processes are all that remain of the application.

Main Window

All visible PenPoint applications must have at least one window. (PenPoint supports "invisible," or background applications as well. A database server is an example of such an application.) This window is referred to as the main window.

This window belongs exclusively to your application. You can do whatever you like in this window. This includes, for example, bypassing PenPoint's built-in drawing routines (see Chapter 9) and using direct, low-level graphic primitives if you need to do so.

The primary purpose of your main window, of course, is to display data relevant to your application. In addition, it gives the user a place to respond to that data by giving your program instructions. PenPoint includes a great deal of class support for the display of data by an application. (See Chapter 9 for details.) But, as with drawing routines, you can always choose to bypass this support completely and handle your own data management and display.

In general, you will have more than a single window. You will almost certainly create child windows as part of any reasonably robust application. In particular, if you are displaying many pieces of information, you will probably want to build a special child window, called a view, for each data object.

Application Framework Standard Behavior and Inheritance

Like all good windowing environments, PenPoint's primary purpose is to make life simpler for users. Users come to expect consistency from systems like Pen-Point. As they move from one application to another, they expect to be familiar with the interface. This standardized behavior is a key part of the PenPoint system and a major reason for the existence of the Application Framework.

As you might imagine, given PenPoint's highly object-oriented approach to the world, most of this standard behavior comes by inheritance. This makes it easy for you to provide consistent applications to your users, and difficult to avoid doing so.

While there are literally dozens of things that PenPoint applications tend to have in common, we will focus in this section on a baker's dozen

- installation behavior
- creation of new application instances
- on-line help
- document properties
- move/copy
- gesture recognition
- Goto buttons (also called Hyperlink buttons)
- standard application menu support
- file import and export
- printing support
- spell checking
- search and replace
- application stationery

We will look at each of these in turn; a few of them will be covered in detail elsewhere in this book.

Installation Behavior

Issues concerning installation are often ignored by developers until a product is almost ready to ship, or even until a later version. As a consequence, installation is often a confusing and error-prone experience for the user.

To remedy this and to speed application coding, PenPoint provides a comprehensive and subclassable set of installation-related behavior for PenPoint applications. As a result, installation is straightforward for the user and consistent across all applications. For example, when an application distribution disk is placed into a PenPoint floppy drive, PenPoint recognizes it as an installable application and automatically brings up a simple user interface by which the user can confirm a desire to install. PenPoint handles the rest for the user, and for the application.

Classes such as clsInstallMgr and clsAppInstallMgr together provide for

- application installation and deinstallation
- deactivation (temporary deinstallation) of an application to its "home" on an external volume

Deactivation is useful for the user who wants to free up room on the Notebook by temporarily removing an infrequently used application. The application will be automatically reinstalled when the user turns to an instance of that application, assuming the PenPoint system is connected to a device where the Home volume can be found.

In addition, clsAppMonitor provides a single object and single execution thread (known as "instance 0" of an application) that represents the installed application. This class is therefore where you can place code concerned with your application's unique configuration and installation needs.

Creation of New Application Instances

We have already said a good deal about how and when PenPoint creates new instances of your application. The mechanics, however, may be of some interest to you.

103

. . . .

The Application Framework

When the user issues a Create command, the PenPoint system creates a new instance of your application. The Application Framework sends your program's application class a message to create an instance of itself. Your application class, by inheritance from clsAppMgr, then creates a subdirectory entry at the appropriate place in the file system (depending on whether the instance is contained in a section, embedded in another document, or is a new stand-alone instance) and fills in key attributes to help it keep track of what is going on.

If this new instance is created in the Notebook Table of Contents, then it is not automatically run immediately after it is created. On the other hand, if this new instance is created within another document so that its expected behavior is to run immediately, it will do so.

On-Line Help

There are two ways your application can supply on-line help for the user. PenPoint makes it quite simple for you to furnish such help. The basic ways of providing help are

- Quick Help on an individual object (roughly corresponding to context-sensitive help in other systems)
- support of the PenPoint built-in Help Notebook with supplemental information about your application (roughly corresponding to reference help in other systems)

Each method of help is implemented differently.

To provide Quick Help, you will define a special resource for each type of object for which you want to offer assistance. For example, each visual element of your program (such as menu commands or control regions) should be able to respond with an appropriate Quick Help text. Protocols in clsGWin will then automatically interpret the user's help gesture correctly, decode the object for which the user has requested help, and display the correct resource.

The most convenient way of providing help is by adding your own application's content to the built-in PenPoint Help Notebook. You can add your help to this Notebook in the form of text files that are managed by the system or in the form of one or more help applications that you embed in the Help Notebook. If you prefer to use the first approach, simply define a text file for each type of help you want to supply, put the files into an appropriate subdirectory structure, and let the installation process take care of the rest. (These text files can use rich text formatting, or RTF. They need not be "plain" text files.) The system then uses its default help application, clsHelpApp, as the means of displaying and handling user interaction with your help files. To use the second approach, you create separate Help applications and place them (rather than text files) into the appropriate subdirectory of your distribution medium. You might use this approach, for example, to use an on-line, interactive tutorial as a help process that you want integrated into the Help Notebook.

Mechanically, you place the appropriate type of help data in a predefined subdirectory of your distribution medium; the installation manager detects its presence, finds it, and installs it correctly. That's all there is to it.

Document Properties

All documents in PenPoint have associated properties. Properties can include characteristics such as author, comments, font used, page size, access control, and additional descriptive information.

Users see these properties as personality traits they can examine and change by asking for an Option Sheet describing the current document. This sheet (see Figure 6-5 for a typical example) usually consists of a collection of traits and values for those traits. The user taps on a trait to add or remove it from the list or to change an attribute that can have only one value.

You define Option Sheets for your application using messages in clsOption, which is part of the PenPoint User Interface Toolkit (see Chapter 10).

Move/Copy

The ability to move and copy information between documents is an important feature of the PenPoint system. As you undoubtedly can appreciate, implementing such a protocol takes on some new dimensions when you must account for multiple instances of a single application and for applications embedded within other applications.

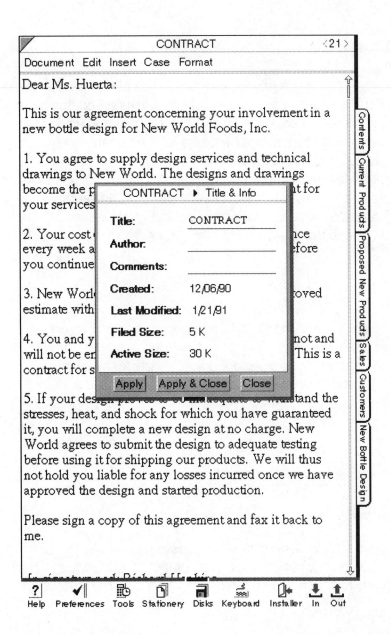

Figure 6-5 Typical Document Property Sheet

PenPoint provides a robust set of messages to support move and copy operations for all applications. This protocol is discussed in Chapter 8.

Gesture Recognition

As you saw in Chapter 2, one of the unique characteristics of computer systems built around PenPoint is their recognition of pen gestures, combinations of strokes that may resemble an alphabetic character, proofreading mark, or other symbol whose presence, position, size, and orientation may have meaning for the system and the application.

Unless you plan to provide custom gesture recognition for your application, you will have to do very little to provide users with this gesture-interpretation support. All the necessary messages are provided as part of the input portion of the PenPoint system. These matters are discussed more fully in Chapter 13.

Goto Buttons

Users of your application may define Goto buttons within documents created by your program. These buttons (see Figure 6-6 for an example) permit the user to create cross-references to other documents and other portions of the same document. They act as links in the system.

Figure 6-6 Typical Goto Button

The creation, management, and use of these buttons is handled in clsEmbeddedWin and some of its subclasses. The subject of embedded windows and their management, including Goto buttons, is covered in detail in Chapter 8.

Standard Application Menu Support

PenPoint provides default implementation for a number of standard menus, menu commands, and Option Sheets. These are collectively referred to as PenPoint's Standard Application Menus (SAMS). Chapter 2 contains a complete list of SAMS-related commands. PenPoint's User Interface Design Guidelines require all applications to provide these commands. The Application Framework makes it easy to comply with the guidelines by implementing SAMS for you.

When your application receives msgAppOpen, it must create its user interface, including the menu bar. At this point you can either create the menu bar without SAMS and then pass the msgAppOpen message to your ancestor class, clsApp, or you can allow clsApp to create the menu bar and then merge your unique menus or menu commands yourself later. In the first case, clsApp will merge SAMS menus with those you've created; in the latter case, you do the merging. The end result is the same.

In general, clsApp has default responses for all SAMS commands. For instance, in the Document menu, the Print, Print Setup, and About commands are fully implemented to display standard dialog and Option Sheets with no coding on your part. You must write new code if you want to modify or extend these standard behaviors (as you might for fancy printer settings, for example). Menu options that are not available or appropriate are automatically grayed out by clsApp. For example, the Move, Copy, and Delete commands from the Edit menu only work if you have a selection. If there is no selection, clsApp makes sure these menu items are grayed for you.

File Import and Export

On most computers, users generally can ignore the formats of data files with which they work. They typically open an application, and once they are running that program, all of the files they work with are in a format the program understands. Except for the occasional need to create a text-only (ASCII) version of a formatted word processing file for telecommunications or other purposes, most users remain blissfully ignorant of details of file format. On the other hand, the relatively more frequent operation of launching the right application for a particular document is more cumbersome on those systems, requiring the user to have some knowledge of the connection between programs and data files.

Computers built around PenPoint precisely reverse this process. A PenPoint user, as you repeatedly have seen, opens an application by the simple expedient of turning to a Notebook page containing a document created by that application or understood by it. This means that moving files into and out of PenPoint requires an application to be selected by the user.

When importing data files from a traditional operating system into PenPoint, the user must identify the application that will deal with that data. When users attempt to move such files into PenPoint, they are asked to choose an installed PenPoint application to manage or present the data. Then PenPoint's built-in file import mechanism creates an instance of that application and sends to it a message instructing it to translate the incoming data to its own format.

Similarly, when exporting data from PenPoint to other operating systems, the user must choose an export file format that can be understood by the application on the receiving system.

As a developer of PenPoint applications, your responsibility is simply to define the file formats used with or created by your programs. You provide this information in data structures called IMPORT_DOC and EXPORT_LIST. Once you've coded this information into your application, you can simply respond to the five messages PenPoint sends to indicate a need to import or export data

- msgImportQuery
- msgImport
- msgExportGetFormats
- msgExport
- msgExportName

Printing Support

Printing a document created using a PenPoint application is straightforward. In fact, it requires no programming support. Printing is nothing more than drawing a document's image on a device that produces hard-copy output rather than a screen display. PenPoint's device imaging technology is very PostScript-like in this sense.

Support for specific printers is furnished at the system level rather than at the application level. Your application need not understand anything about the device to which it is sending the image of the document and its data.

We cover the subject of printing as part of Chapter 9 when we talk about graphic device images.

Spell Checking

Your application automatically supports spell checking unless you disable this capability (as you might, for example, in a paint program where it would not make sense). Spell checking is part of PenPoint's standard application menu support (SAMS), described in detail in Chapter 10.

You may provide your user with custom dictionaries that are specific to your application or to your class of users (for example, attorneys or doctors). PenPoint is equipped with a built-in 77,000-word dictionary. The user also can define new dictionaries.

The spell checking technology is part of the handwriting and input component of PenPoint (see Chapter 13).

Search and Replace

You will not have to undertake much, if any, programming to support robust search and replace in your PenPoint applications. Through clsSR and the Search and Replace Library, the operating system has powerful built-in support for this common operation in text-based documents.

The process of searching and replacing text in a PenPoint document is complicated by the possibility that it may be necessary to deal with embedded documents. When ordering a search-and-replace operation, users can specify whether to include embedded documents. If they choose to do so, the search-and-replace mechanism must be intelligent enough to deal with different document types and oftentimes with different formats.

Because of this complexity, search-and-replace operations technically are part of a broader issue called application traversal. PenPoint defines numerous messages and procedures for dealing with this need. We will examine them more closely in Chapter 8.

Application Stationery

All PenPoint applications automatically support the notion of stationery. You need not provide specific programming support for this capability. The stationery unifies creation of blank application instances along with default templates. Stationery therefore acts as a sort of template with which users can create new instances to give them a head start on creating a document.

For example, a text-editing program might include templates for the usual forms for memorandums, business letters, even legal documents in the appropriate directory of your distribution disk. So when users want to create a document that follows the template's format, they simply choose the proper stationery. PenPoint then creates an instance of the application. Users can also define new stationery by creating templates they frequently use and saving them as stationery documents.

If you wish to provide one or more stationery documents as part of your application, you simply furnish them on your distribution medium in an appropriately defined subdirectory. The PenPoint installation process takes care of the rest of the work, placing instances of all template documents in an area where the system can find them when requested.

PenPoint Application Life Cycle

Figure 6-7 depicts the life cycle of a PenPoint application as a state diagram. All PenPoint applications go through this life cycle process each time the user creates an instance of them. Your application manages the transitions between the various states in response to Application Framework messages it receives. The Application Framework messages usually are caused by user actions, such as page turns, but could be programmatically generated as well.

In the following discussion, we will outline each application instance state in terms of how it is generally entered and what messages your application must respond to as it manages itself through the process. A more detailed discussion of the messages themselves appears in Appendix A.

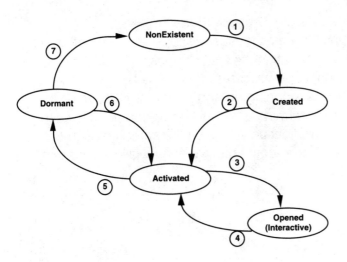

Figure 6-7 Application Instance State Diagram

Instance Creation

Most often, the user creates a new instance of your application by tapping on the Create menu and selecting your application or by copying a blank piece of application stationery owned by your application into the Notebook Contents. There are, of course, other ways an instance can be created (for example, by the user importing a file and selecting yours as the application to manage and display its data).

When PenPoint needs a new instance of your application, it will send the message msgAppMgrCreate, which is defined in clsAppMgr, to your application class.

Why Separate These Actions?

You will notice that PenPoint separates the tasks of opening and activating an application in addition to separating the tasks of closing and terminating an application. In traditional operating systems, these tasks are typically connected, in other words, opening an application also activates it, closing an application normally terminates it. This approach permits us to draw a distinction among an application visible on the screen, one that is active but invisible, one that is quiescent (inactive and invisible), and one that is deleted.

Activation

When the user turns to a page containing an instance of your application, PenPoint recognizes that the user wants to activate that instance, previously dormant. Two steps take place when the user turns to a Notebook page that requires activation of an instance of your application. PenPoint activates the instance, then the system opens the document.

PenPoint sends msgAppMgrActivate to your application class, followed by msgInit to your application object when it receives a request to activate a dormant instance of your application.

Opening

As we indicated in the preceding section, opening an application (from the user's perspective, a document) is a logical continuation of the process started with the activation of your application's instance. During this step, the contents of the document become visible to the user.

You must respond to msgAppOpen to handle the processing involved in opening your application instance.

Closing

When the user turns away from a page containing an instance of your application, PenPoint sees this as a request by the user to close that instance. Notice that this is true even if the user is moving to another page in the Notebook that is an instance of the same application.

PenPoint sends msgAppClose; you respond to that message to handle any processing you wish.

Terminating

PenPoint may terminate your application instance when it closes it. In other words, termination is a logical continuation of closing in much the same way that opening is a logical continuation of activation. There are times, however, when your application must remain active. For example, if it is handling a background task such as a long file transfer, the user may turn away from it but not want to terminate its operation. Applications can avoid being terminated by being in hot mode (in other words, being defined as a process that is always running). Only user deletion ends a hot-mode application. Closing and terminating messages require application compliance and are asynchronous with page turns. This allows you to finish ongoing computations off-screen before terminating the application, even after the user has turned the page away from your instance.

You must respond to msgFree and msgSave to handle the processing involved in terminating an instance of your application.

Destruction

When the user deletes a document, usually via the Notebook Table of Contents, PenPoint removes the application instance associated with that document. You don't need to do anything extra to handle this step; PenPoint deals with it automatically.

Summary

This chapter has described the Application Framework, where the tools reside that permit you to handle a close-knit interaction between the applications you build and the operating system. As we have seen, this aspect of PenPoint supports important common application behaviors such as

- installation
- creation of application instances (new documents)
- activation of instances
- saving and restoring application data
- deactivation and deletion of application instances
- deinstallation

The Application Framework consists of some 15 classes, eight of which will be of most interest to you as a developer. This framework also provides support for a set of standard elements of which all PenPoint applications consist, including application code, installation behavior, document directories, processes, application objects, resource files, and main windows.

This chapter has examined a number of standard application behaviors and seen how they are largely implemented in your applications by inheritance from built-in PenPoint classes and their behaviors. In addition, it looked in depth at the PenPoint application life cycle.

7

The PenPoint Windowing System

. . . .

Windows are the most visible part of the PenPoint user interface. Windows are everywhere in PenPoint; even some design elements you don't intuitively think of as windows, such as menus and buttons, are windows.

It should be clear, then, that the windows we talk about in this chapter are not what the user often thinks of as windows. To the PenPoint programmer, a window is a rectangular region of the screen with the capability for customized display and input behaviors. Furthermore, every window has a well-defined relationship with all other windows: position, overlap order, opaqueness or transparency, and so forth. PenPoint windows themselves are invisible to the user; only their displayed contents are visible. What the PenPoint user calls a window we will call a document frame. This term refers to the rectangular border, document title, scrollbars, and menu surrounding a document. The document frame is a complex assemblage of parts, each of which uses one or more windows.

You can, of course, write PenPoint applications without creating your own windows. If your program doesn't need to interact with the user (as a device driver may not, for example), then you won't need to create windows. But it is safe to say that if your application has a user interface, it is likely to use windows.

All drawing, including text display, takes place within a window. Most windows have an associated drawing context (discussed in Chapter 9), which handles the drawing of images on the screen in response to user and program control. Thus if your application displays any information on the screen or expects the user to provide any pen input, it will use one or more windows.

115

Windows execute four types of operations

- input and hit detection (see Chapter 13)
- painting and repainting (placing images in a window and refreshing the images when needed) (see Chapter 9)
- obscuring (overlapping windows)
- clipping (preventing windows from drawing outside their confines)

The last two of these are closely related automatic behaviors.

As with most of PenPoint application development, the basic behavior of windows is built into the extensive class library. PenPoint windows feature multiple coordinate systems, clipping, and protection. They are integrated with PenPoint's input system (see Chapter 13) so that pen input events are automatically directed to the proper window. The windowing system also supports a separate screen display plane, called the acetate plane, where the system displays a representation of pen ink as the user moves the pen across the display surface. To produce this behavior and use the windowing system features described in this chapter, all you generally have to do is subclass existing PenPoint window classes and provide your application-specific behavior. As usual in PenPoint, you describe this additional behavior by overriding messages and supplying information in special data structures.

NOTE

You will actually use the User Interface Toolkit, described in Chapter 10, to create windows. The point here is simply that you can also create windows directly using this subclassing technique.

As you might expect, the fact that windows can contain embedded windows that may belong to other applications (see Chapter 8) complicates the kind of support needed for windowing in PenPoint. PenPoint structures windows into a tree hierarchy. This relationship is described as a parent-child window relationship, beginning with a root window that corresponds to the physical screen. By designing windows this way, PenPoint gives you and the system maximum flexibility regarding the placement, use, and management of windows. We will have much more to say about this as the chapter develops.

Why a Hierarchy of Windows?

PenPoint's hierarchical windowing structure permits the division of the screen real estate into potentially hundreds of ownership units. Since applications can be embedded inside other applications, a PenPoint screen display is often a complex assemblage of dozens, even hundreds, of windows. By using a tree hierarchy with a parent-child relationship in which the child is always clipped to the parent and never visible unless the parent is visible, PenPoint makes this complexity manageable. This approach supports efficient searching of the window hierarchy. For example, when the pen touches the screen, PenPoint's window system must instantly search to find which of potentially hundreds of windows is the unique owner of that pixel. This can be handled quite simply as a classic branch traversal operation. Starting at the parent window as a root, the window system walks down the branch of the tree that contains the region being searched.

This chapter discusses windows in a logical progression, beginning with basic concepts behind windows and then moving to the programming considerations involved in creating, showing, laying out, managing, and filing windows.

Note that in this chapter we do not discuss the process of placing contents into the windows. Drawing in a window is part of the graphics component discussed in Chapter 9. Windowing and graphics are so closely related that the PenPoint developer documentation discusses them as a single topic, referring to them together as the windowing and graphics subsystem.

Basic Concepts

The PenPoint document frame has many constituent parts, each of which is at least one window. Figure 7-1 shows the various components of such a document frame. This is the type of document frame the user understands by the term "window." Of course, as we have already indicated, there are many other windows in a PenPoint application that the user would not be as likely to recognize as a window.

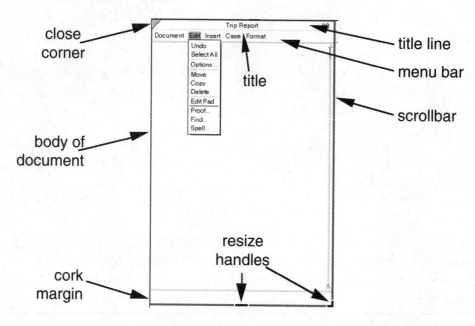

Figure 7-1   Typical Window and Its Parts

You can choose not to use some of these parts, depending on your window's functions. Within an application, you may have several windows, each of which uses different elements of a typical window. You make decisions regarding which parts to use; it's a matter of choosing the right class to subclass or instantiate.

Figure 7-2 shows the windowing portion of PenPoint's class hierarchy. As you can see, it is quite complex. On closer examination, however, you can see that typical parent windows (those that contain other windows shown in Figure 7-2) are derived from the top level of the hierarchy. The class clsGWin is a gesture-interpreting window class; clsEmbeddedWin supports embedded windows.

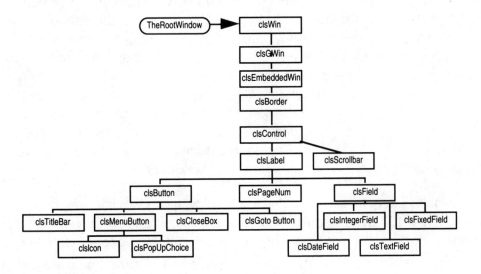

Figure 7-2 Windows Class Hierarchy

Notice that there is a special instance of clsWin called theRootWin in Figure 7-2. This window is always present in the PenPoint windows hierarchy because it is part of the way the system organizes itself. You can think of theRootWin as the display of your system.

While windows are normally thought of in relation to a computer display, PenPoint window trees can be rooted to any image device. As a result, window trees can be used to create virtual, in-memory displays. An important consequence of this design is that window trees can be rooted on printing devices. The printed image is constructed in memory as a window tree with graphics in each window, and the entire page image is then sent to the printer.

120

. . . .

The Power of PenPoint

Because PenPoint allows the same window and graphics systems to be used for printers and displays, applications get printing behavior at virtually no cost.

It is generally not terribly useful to create instances of clsWin because this class does not know how to process input or repaint itself. You will probably find yourself most often creating a subclass of clsView or clsEmbeddedWin when you create your application's main window.

As we indicated earlier, windows do not know how to draw on the screen directly. You can view them as canvases, which can display themselves, and assuming you give them the appropriate behavior by subclassing or overriding, repaint themselves on demand. But they do not know anything about how to display images on the screen.

Drawing is handled via something called a drawing context. You create a drawing context and bind it to a window, then send drawing messages to the context, which translates those messages into ink on the display within the window to which it is connected. There are a number of significant advantages to this approach, three of which are worth mentioning here

- It minimizes memory consumption. PenPoint windows are lightweight (occupying about 100 bytes each), which means you can afford many of them. Drawing contexts, on the other hand, take a minimum of about 500 bytes.

- It allows you to carry drawing state from window to window. You simply bind an existing drawing context to a different window.

- It sets the stage for image-model independence. If for some reason you wanted to draw with an imaging model other than the PenPoint default drawing context (for example, a custom model of your own) you can do so. This provides a measure of flexibility not usually offered by other windowing systems.

The PenPoint windowing system involves the use of five different coordinate systems, four of which will be of some concern to you as a designer. Figure 7-3 shows the five coordinate systems with a sample application running.

There are five coordinate systems because different levels of software have different needs and it is most efficient for code to deal with a coordinate system that accurately maps into its needs. Otherwise, expensive mathematical conversions would have to be performed too frequently. To understand each coordinate system, you must know both its user and its unit of measurement.

LUC (Logical Unit Coordinates) Coordinate system of drawing context. Use whatever units, origin, and rotation that are most convenient for your drawing.

LWC (Logical Window Coordinates) Coordinates in device units relative to your window: (0,0) is its lower left corner.

PWC (Parent Window Coordinates) Coordinates in device units relative to parent window.

LDC (Logical Device Coordinates) Device units transformed so that origin is in lower left corner). Takes into account rotation of the Lombard (Landscape mode).

DU4 (Device Units 4th Quadrant) The coordinate system used by the imaging primitives and the display hardware.

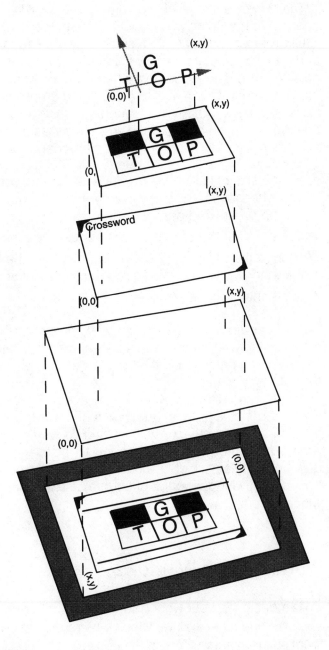

Figure 7-3 Window System Coordinates

The two lowest-level coordinate systems (DU4 and LDC) are really only of concern to PenPoint; we will not deal with them here.

Of greatest interest to you, since they're used for most drawing, rendering, and general measurements within your own window, are Logical Unit Coordinates (LUCs). This is the coordinate system that the drawing context uses. It can measure in much higher resolution than pixels, which permits it to perform transformations with minimal rounding errors and allows it to render accurately on high-resolution output devices such as laser printers.

Furthermore, LUCs are very flexible because you can

- set the size of LUC units to whatever is most convenient and efficient for you, choosing from such measurements as points, metric, mils, twips, screen pixels, and pen-tracking pixels
- scale LUC units (so that one unit equals one inch, for example)
- change the origin (0,0) to a point other than the default lower left corner of the window (a process referred to as translation of the origin)
- rotate the coordinate system

All of this flexibility is well beyond what is necessary to describe the positions of windows, which cannot be translated, rotated, or scaled, and which do not need fine precision in their placement. As a result, windows use pixels for their measurements.

Window coordinates come in two flavors: logical and parent. Logical Window Coordinates (LWCs) are local to the window in question; they describe the position of an object (typically a child window) inside the window. If you want to measure where your window is relative to its parent, use Parent Window Coordinates, which are nothing more than your parent window's LWCs. Your parent window would, of course, use its parent LWCs, and so on up the window hierarchy.

Working with Windows

As a designer, your work with windows in PenPoint involves creating them and inserting them into the window hierarchy, showing and hiding them, laying them out, managing them in the context of your application, and filing them.

Creating a Window

As we have indicated previously, you generally will start the window-creation process by creating a subclass of clsWin or by using an existing subclass. You may also subclass or create a subclass of clsGWin, particularly if your application needs to respond to gestures the user makes with the pen.

Once you have decided which class to work with, you create a new window by sending that class the message msgNew. The class returns a window (or WIN) object. When you send msgNew, you must supply a WIN_METRICS structure as an argument. Although we discuss this data structure later in the chapter in detail, it is useful for you to know the kind of information it requires you to furnish. At a minimum you must tell PenPoint the following information about your new window:

- its parent or device
- its size and location (bounds) relative to its parent
- flag settings that determine such things as how layout, clipping, and repainting are to be handled, and what kind of input it may receive

Now that you have created this new window, it is only an object. You must insert it into the window hierarchy. You do this by sending message msgWinInsert, supplying a WIN_METRICS structure for the window as an argument. This inserts your window as a child window; if you wish it to be a sibling window (in other words, at the same level as another window in the hierarchy), then you can send msgWinInsertSibling. Generally, when you are inserting a subtree of a window tree, you should create the window that will be the root of the subtree first, without inserting it. Next, create its children and insert them into it. Only when the entire subtree has been created should you insert its root window. When the parent window is inserted then its child windows appear on the display. This has the effect of allowing you to create all your windows off-screen and to then display them simultaneously.

Showing Windows

Just because you've created a window and inserted it into the hierarchy, its graphic contents are not automatically visible. You must ensure that the wsVisible flag in the WIN_METRICS structure described later in the chapter is set to True if you want the window to appear on the display.

Furthermore, child windows are only visible if their parent window is visible. Therefore, you must make sure that the parent window is visible first, even when the child window's wsVisible flag has been set. This is due in part to two basic rules about parent and child windows

- Children are always on top of the parent.
- Drawing in a child window is always clipped by the parent. (We'll have more to say on this later.)

By the way, this chain of windows into which all windows are inserted goes all the way back up the hierarchy to theRootWin, which we mentioned earlier.

With your windows properly inserted into this hierarchy, PenPoint can now give you a great deal of help in managing your windows, as we'll see later. For example, it keeps track at all times of which windows are "dirty" (that is, those that need repainting) because they have been moved or resized or obscured or revealed after being obscured or had other events happen to them.

PenPoint includes a flag in WIN_METRICS that is particularly interesting as we discuss the tree hierarchy of windows. If you insert a window into the hierarchy and later remove it (when the user closes it, for example), it may uncover a window that had been beneath the newly removed window. This now unobscured window must be repainted. This process can take time, but you can save time by setting the wsSaveUnder flag in WIN_METRICS to True. When this is set, the window creates a copy of the physical screen region underneath the screen area where newly inserted window will be displayed. This means that when it is time to repaint the screen area under the newly inserted window, PenPoint doesn't need to send a message to the formerly obscured window or wait for it to process such a message. It simply copies the bit image stored when it was inserted. You can see this process in operation when you retract a PenPoint menu; the screen beneath the menu window is instantly redrawn. It is better to use this flag for windows that you expect to be on the screen for a brief time and only when you are sure the contents of the windows under yours will not change while your window is displayed.

Laying Out a Window

> ### What's Behind the Idea of Window Layout?
>
> Other windowing systems leave it to the application to calculate the actual position of each child window inside a window. PenPoint allows this approach but encourages the use of layout. This concept in PenPoint means that the application specifies the contents of a window and the design goals for the appearance of the window, and PenPoint handles the calculations of the positions of all child windows. One consequence of this design approach is that PenPoint is a more device-independent, scalable user interface than the interfaces generated by other windowing systems. It is scalable and adaptable in terms of language, screen size and orientation, fonts, and user preferences.

Because the layout of child windows is controlled by the parent, the overriding issue in window layout is the relative positioning of children within a parent. Like any good parent-child relationship, this process involves negotiation. There are three attitudes a parent window can be designed to take toward how child windows lay themselves out within its borders

- Permissive. Using this model, the parent window is set up so that child windows can display themselves anywhere, even to the point of completely covering the parent window.

- Strict. With this approach, the parent makes all the decisions. The parent window is given an opportunity to intercept and veto all messages to its child windows that could affect layout.

- Flexible. If you program this attitude into your parent window, it will attempt to meet child windows' layout requests but can override them if those messages result in layout conflicts that the parent window has been designed to prevent.

Window layout is far more complex than meets the eye. Much of the work in this area of your PenPoint design is handled through the User Interface Toolkit, particularly its clsLayout (see Chapter 10), so we will not attempt to deal with the issue in depth here.

Managing Windows

Because of the object-oriented way PenPoint deals with window layout, you'll find that handling such things as the resizing of your windows is straightforward. As far as the system is concerned, such activities require laying out the window anew. So the process of repainting the screen after a window is resized is for all practical purposes, identical to the original process of laying out the window.

Sometimes you will want to adjust or modify some or all of the child windows in your parent window. You can use the process of enumeration to obtain a list of all immediate child windows or all windows (recursively, including grand-children, great-grandchildren, and so forth) contained in your parent window. Depending on how you ask for this information, you can also obtain basic information about these windows (such as their UIDs and the style flags).

There are times when you want to arrange child windows in a predetermined sequence. In that case, PenPoint supplies a message, msgWinSort, that permits you to do so. You tell PenPoint how you want the sort handled by providing a callback routine that compares two windows. PenPoint then will rearrange the child windows according to the instructions in that routine.

Filing Windows

When the user turns away from a page in the Notebook or closes a floating window, a parent window may need to file its state and contents. When you file a window in PenPoint, you usually file its child windows as well. This means that you often may find yourself filing many more windows than you thought you were filing.

Why File Windows?

The notion of filing windows is new with PenPoint and may at first seem peculiar. But it will seem quite logical if you remember that at any given time, an application's display state reflects the results of recent user commands and actions. PenPoint supports shutdown and restart of an application at any time (via page turns). When users turn a page and then turn back to the application, they expect things to be in exactly the state they were when they left it. This includes even the possibility that an Option Sheet was open at the time, for example. As a result of these behaviors and expectations, a PenPoint application must, in response to close and terminate actions, save all of its display state. To make this process easy, PenPoint allows the application's current window hierarchy to be filed and retrieved. Other operating systems don't address this because they require the user to launch a blank application and load a file that is not guaranteed to be in the exact state it was when it was last exited.

Some child windows may set a style flag that prevents their being filed. This is done, for example, with temporary windows that are going to be re-created the next time they are needed. The important thing to remember is that all windows are given the opportunity to file when your application is told to save its state.

PenPoint keeps track of the window environment (such as the orientation of the device, pixel size, default system font and size, and other data) for you. When your application must open a window it previously saved, it has access to this environmental information so that recalculating position and orientation is simple if you even need to use it. If nothing has changed since the window was saved, you do not need to do anything.

Summary

This chapter has examined the windowing system in PenPoint, focusing on the most common behaviors of this most visible element of the user interface. It has examined the basic components of windows and the various coordinate systems used to identify the locations of objects within the system.

As a designer, your involvement with windows includes their creation, insertion into a window hierarchy, showing and hiding them, laying them out, managing them, and filing them.

8
Recursive Live Embedding of Applications

. . . .

The concept of embeddable applications is one of PenPoint's most important and useful distinguishing characteristics. PenPoint users can embed, or nest, documents inside one another without having to know anything about the application responsible for creating and managing the document. This power is unique to PenPoint.

Supporting a function so complex obviously requires extensive programmatic support, all of which is built into the Application Framework. As you'll see, you don't have to do anything to make your programs embeddable and it takes very little work to permit them to accept other embedded applications. However, you do need to have knowledge of actions that must take embedded documents into account.

PenPoint provides you with a carefully designed set of classes to deal with these issues. We will discuss those classes, their metrics, and their messages, later in this chapter. But first, we must take a close look at this unfamiliar new concept.

What It Is

PenPoint's ability to support embedded applications and their documents begins with the fundamental notion built deeply into the operating system that there is an essential correspondence between applications and their documents.

130

. . . .

The Power of PenPoint

Every document has an identifier that tells PenPoint which application to run when the user turns to a page containing that document. Without this intimate connection between documents and applications, embedding programs inside one another would be difficult at best.

PenPoint's embedding capability is recursive: The user can embed an application inside an application that has already been embedded inside another application. Theoretically (that is, within memory limits), this recursive embedding can be made arbitrarily deep. To simplify discussions of embedding, this chapter refers to the application hosting the embedded application as either the embedder or the parent and to the hosted application as the child or embeddee.

As you will also notice from the title of this chapter, embedding is "live." What do we mean by that? In this context, the word "live" has two important connotations

- It means that the embedding takes place dynamically, "on the fly," while the application in which another application is about to be embedded continues to run. This makes the embedding process transparent to the user.

- It also means that the applications actually execute inside one another. This is not a process of copying documents or compound document support via established clipboard/scrapbook metaphors. When the user embeds a document inside another, the embedded document's application is running just as the host document's application is running.

Traditional operating systems that support the notion of multiple applications running at the same time (such as Microsoft Windows 3.0 and the Apple Macintosh system) require that every application be in immediate contact with the operating system. Stated another way, only the operating system can act as the host to an application. Figure 8-1 shows this situation. The word processor and drawing program are both running, but the user must choose between them by selecting one to be active. Generally, the user does this by activating a window belonging to the desired application.

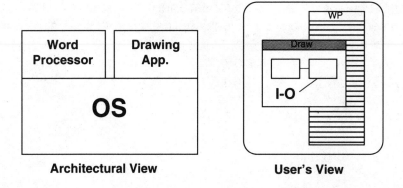

Architectural View   **User's View**

Figure 8-1 Traditional Operating System with Two Applications Running

In PenPoint, any application can host another application. In fact, as you will see in detail later in this chapter, every application actually is embedded in the PenPoint Notebook application. Figure 8-2 depicts this. The word processor document, which is embedded in the Notebook, is running when the user decides to incorporate a drawing into the document. By creating an instance of the drawing application, the user embeds the drawing program and its document directly inside the word processor. There is no need to choose an application — or even to be aware that there is more than one application running. To draw, the user draws in the drawing document. To edit text, the use draws gestures in the word processing document.

Why It's Important

As computer power on the desktop has increased in the past few years, users have come to demand more and more robustness and to expect the ability to solve more complex problems. At the same time, the emergence of graphical user interfaces has led users to demand more simplicity of operation. Designing programs that are more powerful and easier to use than last generation's is a major challenge, one that the software industry has seen as its Gordian Knot. PenPoint's architecture suggests that the right way to approach this problem is not by building larger, more integrated, more robust applications but by providing an environment in which building-block applications with specialized capabilities can coexist transparently.

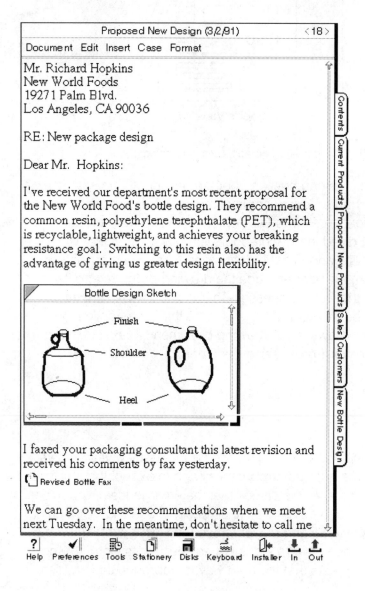

Figure 8-2 PenPoint With Two Applications Running

Compound documents are becoming commonplace. What was only a dream a few years ago — being able to prepare published reports combining text, database reports, spreadsheet data, and graphics — is now an everyday expectation in many business offices around the world.

Creating compound documents, however, is not as transparent as users would like. Traditional operating systems, even in more modern garb, force users to launch an application, typically with a blank document, then choose the document with which they want to work. They can also select the document they want to work with from their system's file directory and, if the document knows which application was used to create it, they can launch the right program that way. But notice that in each case, the user must have some knowledge of the system. The process is not transparent.

The problem is worsened when the user wants to move information from one document to another in an effort to create a compound document. Most operating systems handle this interaction by means of automated clipboard integration. As a result, data gets converted to its lowest common denominator, losing some or all of its richness and formatting in the process of being moved. In addition, this architecture builds on the notion of a separate file for each portion of a compound document. This, again, requires that the user be more aware of operational details of the system.

Users want to create documents, not run programs. They don't want to know about programs, files, directories and subdirectories, and the other myriad details that make up a minimal level of knowledge needed to run even the most user-friendly systems on today's microcomputers. PenPoint permits the user to operate the environment and to see everything in terms of documents and solutions.

What the User Sees

To the user, the process of embedding applications has a natural feel to it. Users can choose to combine documents from two or more programs in either of two ways:

- by creating the documents on separate Notebook pages and then copying or moving them to a destination document, with no loss of content or formatting
- by embedding applications on the fly, creating new documents within existing documents as needed to build the compound result

Either way, the embedded applications appear in embedded windows that are instances of clsEmbeddedWin. We took a brief look at this class in Chapter 7, but we'll spend more time examining it in detail later in this chapter. Users, of course, are unaware of the existence of this class; what they see are embedded windows they can control (by choosing to show or hide borders, for example).

Embedded windows can be in-line, overlapping, or even take up the entire application frame. We will examine some of the programming issues involved in these placement decisions later in the chapter.

The purpose of embedding applications should be clear. The user need not be aware on any level of doing anything other than creating documents to meet needs and solve problems. PenPoint will determine which program to run based on the document type chosen by the user, and will take care of the filing details.

How It's Done

The major obstacle to the implementation of an architecture such as PenPoint's is how to deal with embedded documents when the user requests an action that should cross traditional application borders. Commands issued to an embedder should transparently apply to all embeddees. In a classic operating system, if the user has two kinds of documents open, performing operations like printing, proofreading, and filing data requires separate actions and files for each application. If PenPoint required the same kind of user involvement and awareness, it would lose most of the value of embeddable applications.

Solving this problem requires PenPoint to incorporate a number of features and capabilities, outlined in this section.

135

· ·

Recursive Live Embedding of Applications

The Problem of Data Storage

A classic problem with compound documents involves the question of filing their contents. Do you reduce contents to a least common denominator so you can file all of a document in one place? Or do you create separate files for each type of document and then leave it to the user to try to reassemble them when needed? Traditional operating systems create a separate file for each type of document. PenPoint, as you know, stores each embedded document as a separate directory. Embeddee contents are therefore placed into a subdirectory of the parent document's file system subdirectory.

With this approach, PenPoint is able to treat every embedded application (recall that this includes all applications, since even top-level documents are embedded in the Notebook application) as a cohesive whole containing all of its embedded windows regardless of the application responsible for the contents of those windows.

Basic Concepts

To understand how embedding works we must clearly distinguish among three separate, but parallel dimensions. What the user sees as a single document hierarchy is implemented at runtime by a dynamic combination of entities in each of these three dimensions. The three parallel dimensions are the file system, process space, and window hierarchy.

The file-system dimension is a hierarchy of document directories with one document directory for every embedded application, regardless of whether it is currently running or opened. Because the file system even has entries that correspond to closed and terminated applications (that is, off-screen documents), it is the only dimension of the three that fully captures the entire hierarchy of embedding at all times.

The process-space dimension consists of processes that correspond to running application instances. The set of running processes is driven by the embedding hierarchy in which every activated (running) embedded child application has its own process. Terminated (not running) applications do not have a process associated with them. Furthermore, since PenPoint processes do not have hierarchical relationships with other processes, the process dimension is a "flat space" in which processes are created in response to traversals of the hierarchy in the file system, but the processes themselves do not have a direct parent-child relationship.

The window hierarchy dimension consists of windows that subclass clsEmbeddedWin. This window hierarchy captures the hierarchical visual relationship of the embedder and embeddee applications.

Of the three dimensions the windowing relationships may seem most straightforward, but windows build upon the file system and process dimensions. We will therefore discuss those two dimensions first, and then discuss how embedded windows "front end" this complex assemblage of behavior.

File System Hierarchy

The simple hierarchy in Figure 8-3 shows the file system's representation of application C embedded inside application A. As we mentioned earlier, the file system contains a document directory for every embedded application. Each document directory contains files that belong directly to that application instance (data files, resource files). In addition, each document directory contains attributes that record the class of application associated with the directory, the Unique Identifier (UID) of the application (if it's running), the current state of the application (active or open), and the Universal Unique Identifier (UUID) of the document itself (so that other objects can point uniquely to this document).

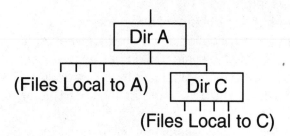

Figure 8-3 File System's View of Embedding

Process Space

Figure 8-4 shows that applications A and C have their own processes, and that these processes are not directly related to each other. Within each process are the windows that are owned by that process: windows A and B (B will be explained shortly) are owned by process A; window C is owned by process C.

Every running application must have a process, but PenPoint cannot have every off-screen page be running simultaneously, since hundreds of processes use too much memory and processor time and since users will want notebooks with hundreds or thousands of pages. PenPoint therefore shuts down off-screen processes. As a result, only processes for on-screen applications run (with the exception of server applications, special system processes, "hot-mode" applications, and the application that currently holds the selection).

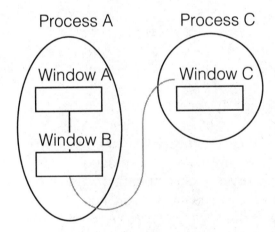

Figure 8-4 Process Space View of Embedding

Embedded Windows

The on-screen relationship of the hierarchy of windows for applications A and C is depicted in Figure 8-5. As you can see, C is nested inside A. But surprisingly, there is an intermediate window B inside A that encloses C. Both B and C are embedded windows: B is embedded inside A, and C inside B.

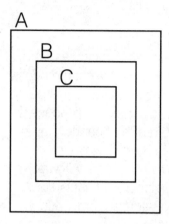

Figure 8-5 Window Hierarchy in Embedding

Why does PenPoint include this extra level in the window hierarchy when it is not present in the user's model or in the file system? To explain, it is first important to mention that PenPoint's user interface allows the user to close an embedded application into a small icon. When this has been done, the embedded application is no longer running.

Close examination of Figure 8-4 explains why the extra level of window B is necessary. Notice that window B belongs to (in other words, is in address space of) process A, while window C belongs to process C. Embedder applications always need an embedded window, even when the embedded application is shut down. The extra window B serves as an embedded window that wraps the embedded application and hides its changes in state from the host embedder application. Because window B belongs to process A, B will always be available to A, even when process C has been shut down (and window C therefore destroyed) after the embedded application C has been shut down to an icon by the user.

That explains everything except why the host embedder applications always need an embedded window. To answer this, we must discuss the typical relationship between embedder windows and embedded windows. Remember that windows are essentially objects that support the cooperative partitioning (sharing) of screen display space. Indeed, this is the major purpose of the embedding window relationships: the host embedder and the embeddee must frequently communicate about the embeddee's exact location and current size. They do this chiefly through four important messages: msgWinInsertOk, msgWinFreeOk, msgWinExtractOk, and msgWinDeltaOK. The embedder window can (and often does) choose to intercept these messages before they take effect; it can then approve, modify, or refuse their intended operations.

To make this clearer, consider Figures 8-6 and 8-7, which depict a drawing program embedded inside of PenPoint's MiniText application. In Figure 8-6, the drawing program is closed; therefore it is represented by a small icon. Unbeknownst to the user, this icon is actually wrapped by an embedded window (B in our example) that represents it to MiniText's main view window (which is itself an embedded window).

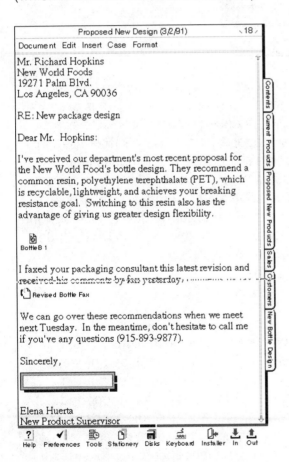

Figure 8-6 Embedded Drawing Program Closed

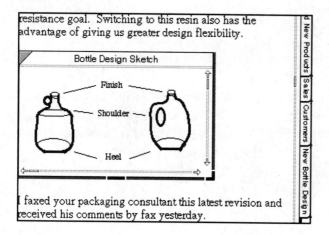

Figure 8-7 Embedded Drawing Program Open

When the user taps on the icon and PenPoint opens the drawing program, its window obviously must get much larger, as shown in Figure 8-7. It is exactly this kind of change in size and state of an embedded window that must be carefully worked out between embedder and embeddee. In this case, MiniText intercepts the messages that change the size of the embeddee wrapping the icon and learns that this embedded window is about to get much larger. MiniText approves, but, because it was warned of the change before it occurred, MiniText can cooperate and make room on the screen for the larger window (notice how the text paragraphs are further apart in Figure 8-7 than they were in Figure 8-6).

clsApp

The window dimension in embedding is, as we have seen, handled by clsEmbeddedWin. This leaves the process and file system dimensions, which are both handled by clsApp. This class defines all file system and process behavior your application needs to be either an embeddee or embedder.

clsApp handles the startup and shutdown of processes for embedded applications. Its default behavior is to run all embedded applications whenever the embedder is running. That is, when the user turns to a page, not only is the document on that page run (opened), but corresponding processes for all embedded documents within it are also opened.

Lightweight Embedding with Components

Now that we've demonstrated how embedded applications work, we must point out the drawbacks of this approach so we can explain the concept of components in PenPoint. From the preceding discussion it should be clear to you that embedded applications are somewhat costly in memory and processor cycles: each embedded application requires its own process and a separate document directory. (These are not costs without merit: because the embedded applications run in their own processes, even if they crash, the embedder can continue running.) While these are perfectly reasonable for normal embedded applications (for example, embedding a drawing or table inside a word processor), they are too costly for embedded data types entailing a small amount of application instance data.

PenPoint components, on the other hand, are a lighter-weight alternative to embedded applications. Because components execute within their host application's process and file their data in the host application's data file, they don't need a process or document directory of their own. Components are instances of subclasses of clsEmbeddedWin and are therefore embedded windows themselves. PenPoint includes three predefined components: clsAppWin (the class used for the wrapper window B in our example), Goto buttons, and Signature Pads. Applications may define their own additional components.

What Your Application Must Do

Don't be too concerned if all this seems like a lot of work: it would be if not for PenPoint's strong object orientation. But clsApp and clsEmbeddedWin handle virtually all of the work for you with appropriate default behavior. You don't need to do any work whatsoever to be an embeddee. To embed, the typical embedder needs to respond only to the four clsEmbeddedWin messages mentioned earlier.

Embedder applications only rarely need to modify the default clsApp behavior for starting and stopping processes. One exception is an embedder that hosts dozens or hundreds of embeddees. Such an embedder would probably want to manage the startup and shutdown processes of its embeddees. Otherwise, it would find all embeddees running all the time. This is just what clsSectApp (the Notebook's Table of Contents) does: it modifies startup behavior to be the opposite of the running process for every embeddee. In this way the only embeddee with a process is the current page (and any floating pages).

Embedded Window Marks

PenPoint keeps track of embedded documents using embedded window marks. A mark is a special data structure containing

- the UUID of the document containing the mark
- the UUID of the component within the document
- a component-specific token that specifies a location within the component
- a label for the mark

Both Goto buttons and the traversal engine use these marks to point to embedded windows.

The Problem of Traversal

Many document operations must include and take into account the contents of child embedded windows. The three most common such operations are search (and its relative, search and replace), print, and spell check, but there could conceivably be many others. In each case, the parent application must know something about the contents of the windows created by other applications and embedded within the parent. At the very least the parent application must be able to find out if the child application defines behavior for the task at hand. For example, it is unlikely (although not impossible) that a painting program would include the notion of spelling checks, because its contents normally are not viewed as text. Such an application might simply tell a proof-reading process to skip over it. But its contents determine this.

This need poses some obvious problems with windows containing documents of different types. Content-dependent behavior is simple in a simple document, but it becomes increasingly complex when we deal with compound documents. PenPoint's answer to the problem is the notion of traversal. Traversal works with both the window and file system hierarchies to visit all user data in the correct order regardless of the complexity of the embedding.

Traversal is actually implemented in PenPoint using a driver-slave model (see Figure 8-8).

The process shown in Figure 8-8 is a typical one, but is not necessarily indicative of the way all traversals are handled. For example, some traversals might not require the slave to locate any data. In that case, the steps associated with that processing are of course eliminated from the steps shown in the figure. Regardless of the details, the driver (the object requesting traversal, generally an application or the PenPoint traversal engine which we'll discuss later) and the slave (either a document or a component) interact to visit all embedded documents and scan all data within a specified range.

In many cases, the user determines the scope or method of traversal by choices or commands. The user is not aware of the traversal issue, but by selecting operations to be performed and defining their scope, the user can play a role in determining the behavior of the process.

As you can see from Figure 8-8, the driver-slave model keeps the traversal process in synchronization through a mechanism called a traversal context. This context is a protocol between the driver and all the slaves it encounters as it carries out its processing on a parent document and its child embedded windows. You can think of this context as a structure that contains the scope of the traversal and its direction as well as the current position within the scope. As traversal processing takes place, the current position is updated to keep the driver and slave in synch.

The traversal process, like most PenPoint processing, uses a message-sending model. The driver sends messages to each slave it encounters. Slaves respond to these messages, depending on the traverse style defined in the traversal context. The four types of behavior an application can define for its instances are

- Don't enter any embedded windows.
- Enter all open embedded windows.
- Enter all embedded windows.
- Invoke a call-back routine.

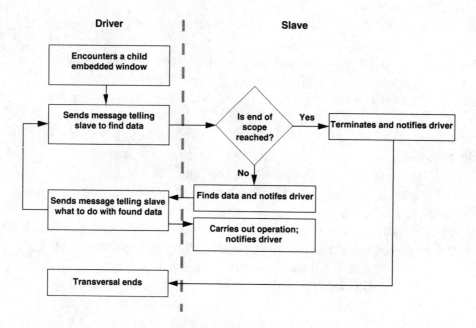

Figure 8-8 Driver-Slave Traversal Model

The Notebook as an Example

Understanding the concept of embedding applications will be much easier after we have looked carefully at an example. The best example to use is the Notebook application, which is integral to PenPoint's organization and behavior.

Each element of the Notebook is a document of some type. Even some items that don't appear to be documents (such as sections) really are documents. They just have a slightly different purpose from what we usually think of as a document's purpose, serving an organizational rather than data-related role.

PenPoint's Notebook is written using the Application Framework (see Chapter 6) and is a child embedded application of the Bookshelf, which is the top-level organizer of the PenPoint system. The Notebook's primary role is to act as an organizing vehicle for all other applications running on the system. Like all PenPoint applications, therefore, the Notebook can be looked at from several perspectives. We focus on the two that are most important for an understanding of recursive live embedding.

Figure 8-9 shows the visual representation of the Notebook as a document. Actually, there are five applications visible on the screen in Figure 8-9: the Bookshelf (across the bottom of the screen), the Notebook, the Notebook Contents, a text-based application called New Product Ideas, and a graphics application called Charting Paper. As you can see from the Table of Contents, New Product Ideas is a document in the Samples subdirectory.

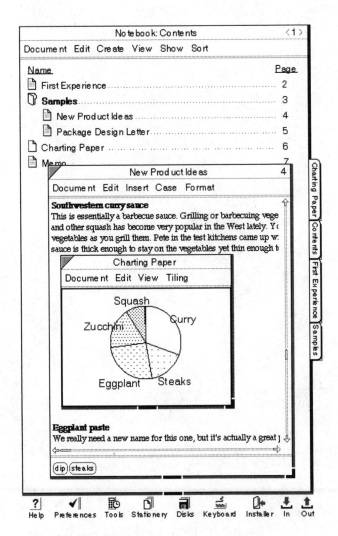

Figure 8-9 The Notebook: A Visual Representation

We can also look at the compound document of Figure 8-9 from the perspective of the File System. This viewpoint is depicted in Figure 8-10. As you can see, the root directory is called Bookshelf. The Notebook application is a subdirectory of the Bookshelf. Notebook Contents is in turn a subdirectory of Notebook. You can see by examining Figure 8-10 that this hierarchical approach is followed through to the most deeply embedded child document, Charting Paper. Each document has at least two files associated with it. One of these files holds the document's contents and the other holds its display state.

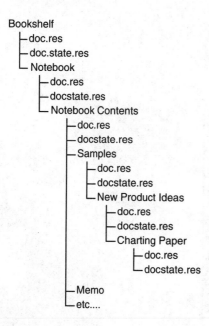

```
Bookshelf
  ├ doc.res
  ├ doc.state.res
  └ Notebook
      ├ doc.res
      ├ docstate.res
      └ Notebook Contents
          ├ doc.res
          ├ docstate.res
          ├ Samples
          │   ├ doc.res
          │   ├ docstate.res
          │   └ New Product Ideas
          │       ├ doc.res
          │       ├ docstate.res
          │       └ Charting Paper
          │           ├ doc.res
          │           └ docstate.res
          ├ Memo
          └ etc....
```

Figure 8-10 The Notebook: A File Representation

How You Program for Application Embedding

On one level, you don't have to do much to support recursive live embedding. Your application automatically supports this behavior because it's a PenPoint application. But to strengthen your application's support, you need to think about three issues

- placement of embeddee windows
- moving and copying information between applications
- traversal support specific to your application

Where to Place Embedded Windows

When the user creates an instance of an application inside your application, you must consider the placement of the embedded window that contains the document. There are two ways to place such a window: unconstrained and constrained.

Unconstrained placement of the window is the easiest way to handle embedding. Using this method, the new window acts like a floating window atop your main document window, which is its parent. Since every window already keeps track of its position relative to its parent, this placement style takes no work on the parent's part. This is the default behavior for clsEmbeddedWin.

Constrained window placement requires more parental control. To some degree, this approach means you must determine where to place the child embedded window based on the kind of display item it represents. For example, a drawing document embedded in a text document could be treated as a large single character appearing immediately adjacent to the character in the document after which it is inserted, or it might be handled as an item that should only appear on a line by itself. In any event, your application, as the parent, will choose where to position the child window when the user embeds it.

Move/Copy Protocol

You must implement a move/copy protocol for your application object. If the system default move/copy behavior is acceptable, you can, of course, simply use the inherited approach. Otherwise, you should plan to write your own protocol.

Users can begin a move or copy process between embedded windows by selecting the information to be moved or copied and then issuing the move or copy command via menu or gesture. Once movement or copying is initiated, the system generates a move/copy icon (an animated border around the object or a symbol for the object being moved or copied). The user then indicates a position to which the object should be moved or copied; the system handles the rest of the processing transparently to the user.

Once the user has indicated what is to be moved or copied and its destination, there are two locations for this object: the source (where it starts) and the destination (where it ends up). Obviously, if the user is copying rather than moving, then the source and destination will both have copies of the object when the process is complete. If the user is copying or moving data within a single instance of a document, then the source and destination object are identical, and many of the messages we refer to later in the chapter will be sent to the special symbol, self. The source sends a message to the destination object instructing it to move or copy the selection data.

The destination determines the type of data that the source has selected and, if it is a data type it understands, tells the source to send the data. The source now knows what type of object the destination is and it can determine whether it wishes to move its data into an instance of that type of application or not. For example, a graphics program may reject the idea of sending its data to a text program.

Assuming both parties agree to the data move or copy, the source determines the location of the destination in the PenPoint file system. With this setup processing complete, the source moves or copies the data. The destination then determines precisely where to put the data, which may or may not be identical to the user's requested location.

Viewed at the message-protocol level, Figure 8-11 shows the processing involved.

Traversal Protocol

Although it is not mandatory that your application support traversal, we strongly recommend that it do so. Another major benefit of implementing traversal is that PenPoint's built-in support for printing, spell checking, and search and replace are available to your application with little additional programming. If you choose not to implement traversal, you should have a very good reason for not doing so. Some specialized applications, such as device drivers, may choose not to support traversal, but if your program has a user interface, it probably should support traversal.

You can support traversal as a driver application, as a slave application, or as both. Appendix A defines the messages involved in each case.

Creating a Traversal Driver

If your application defines some behavior that will require it to traverse embedded child documents, you will have to create a class to handle the traversal. Most of the time, you will use clsStdTE, the standard traversal engine class. There are two other possible classes: clsTraverse and clsTE, a generalized traversal driver that implements the protocols described by clsTraverse. You will normally use clsStdTE because it automatically creates a traversal context as well as an instance of clsTE.

If you write a traversal driver, your driver will send messages defined in clsTraverse.

You will also have to create an initial traversal context. There are five ways you can accomplish this

- for a specific document
- using the current selection
- in response to a gesture
- in response to a gesture over a word
- containing a specific embeddee

Each of these approaches corresponds to a message in the traversal protocol described in detail in Appendix A.

Traversal drivers merely send these messages and receive responsive messages and data from the slave processes.

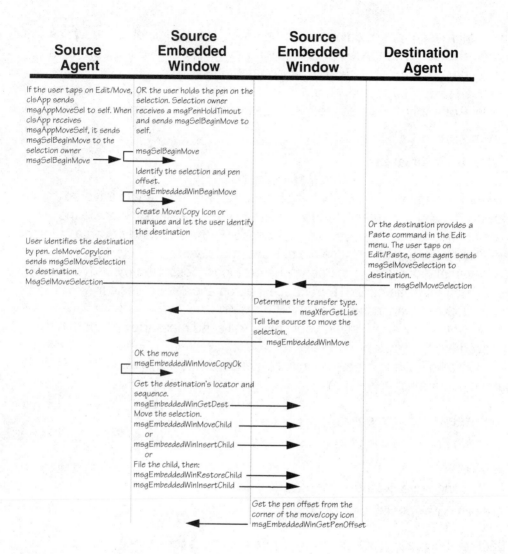

Figure 8-11 Move/Copy Protocol Messages

Supporting Traversal as a Slave

If your application is to support traversal as recommended by GO Corporation, then you should define methods in your class to respond to clsTraverse messages. Alternatively, you can subclass an existing class that already handles clsTraverse messages. Fortunately, clsEmbeddedWin includes such support, so making your application's view class a subclass of clsEmbeddedWin accomplishes traversal processing support automatically.

Summary

This chapter has examined one of the most important new ideas in PenPoint: recursive live embedding of applications and documents. After examining what this concept means and why it is important, we looked at embedding from the user's perspective.

As we saw, embedding applications involves subclassing and using instances of clsEmbeddedWin as well as some aspects of clsApp. Embedded applications create compound documents that can be viewed from the perspectives of file system, process, or window relationships. You must be aware of the need for traversal operations, which require a particular operation such as spellchecking to operate across embedded documents created using different applications.

To clarify the meaning and use of embedding, we examined the PenPoint Notebook as an example of its implementation.

9

ImagePoint: Graphics and Imaging System

....

PenPoint is based on a graphical user interface. Everything that appears on the display of a computer running the PenPoint operating system is created using graphics techniques. PenPoint uses these techniques to implement a powerful graphical user interface tuned to the needs of the pen.

Because of the way graphics have been implemented in PenPoint, however, graphically produced elements are more powerful and flexible than you may be accustomed to seeing in older operating systems, even those with a strong graphic orientation. For example, text is fully unified with all other graphics in PenPoint, and all images can be scaled, rotated, translated, and used for both screen display and printing. PenPoint graphics are most like PostScript, but with a message-based API rather than a language-based API.

NOTE
We won't be discussing in this chapter the pen strokes and ink-related aspects of graphics. These issues are more accurately part of the input system and are discussed fully in Chapter 13.

As you probably know, the basic common building block of all graphical computer displays is the pixel. A pixel can be thought of as a single definable location on the display, a dot of the smallest possible size that the system hardware is capable of controlling. The word comes from the term "picture element," which has long since fallen into disuse.

In this chapter, we look at PenPoint graphics first in overview, then from the perspective of drawing contexts (a concept introduced in Chapter 7). With that background, we can examine, in turn, the following graphics topics:

- the clipping and repainting of windows
- graphics primitives
- color
- dealing with prestored images
- fonts
- drawing text
- printing

Overview of Graphics in PenPoint

As we indicated in Chapter 7, all drawing in PenPoint takes place in a window. However, in PenPoint, you don't send drawing messages directly to a window. Instead, you send drawing messages to a special object called a drawing context, as in Microsoft Windows. Drawing contexts render your drawing messages in the window to which they are connected. The concept of drawing contexts is crucial to PenPoint graphics and is discussed fully in the next section.

To ensure that your drawing affects only that portion of the screen that is under your control and within the borders of the target window, the system enforces clipping.

PenPoint Drawing Primitives

PenPoint defines a number of messages for drawing specific kinds of shapes. Each of the shapes and its associated message is described later in this chapter, but a summary will help you understand the scope of PenPoint's support for graphics.

Shapes in PenPoint come in two varieties: closed and open.

A closed shape is any shape that starts and ends at the same point, completely enclosing an area. PenPoint supplies messages for drawing the following closed shapes:

- rectangles (including those with rounded corners)
- ellipses and circles
- polygons with an arbitrary number of sides
- sectors
- chords

An open shape is essentially a line. But PenPoint's definition of a line is quite sophisticated, including messages to draw the following open (line) shapes:

- multiple-segment lines (polylines)
- Bezier curves
- arcs

PenPoint also allows you to fill the enclosed areas of closed shapes with a pattern or solid color.

Painting and Repainting Windows

Drawing becomes visible to the user when your program paints in a window in response to msgWinRepaint. To an application there is no distinction between painting and repainting a window; the application cannot determine if this is the first time it's being asked to repaint itself.

Depending on your application, you may find yourself continually repainting all or a portion of a window(s) or only repainting when some relatively infrequent and unpredictable event makes it necessary. In the first case, you may, for example, be building an application in which the user is drawing, writing, or typing information into a window. As each new stroke or character is received, you will have to repaint at least that portion of the window in which the drawing event occurred, or the user will not see the result of his or her actions.

Two events—user input and windowing activity—can result in some or all of the pixels in your window becoming "dirty." When this happens, your program must repaint the window.

PenPoint does not automatically remember the contents of your windows; it is your responsibility to keep track of what your window is displaying and to redraw to the window when necessary.

Role and Use of System Drawing Contexts

The real meat of graphics on a PenPoint system is the system drawing context (more commonly called the SysDC, or the DC). From your perspective as a designer of PenPoint applications, all drawing takes place by sending messages to a DC. Figure 9-1 depicts this.

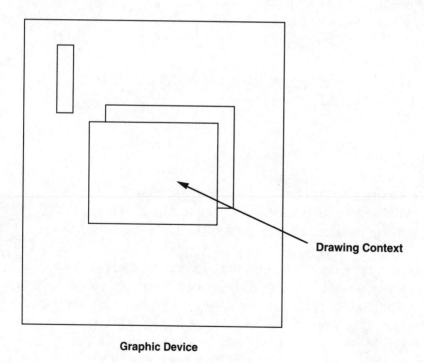

Drawing Context

Graphic Device

Figure 9-1 Bird's-Eye View of Graphics Architecture

A DC is always bound to one window at a time. You can change the window to which a DC is connected so that you can draw similar pictures in multiple windows, but at any one time only a single window is bound to a DC. It should be obvious to you, however, that if you bind a DC to a window, do some drawing in it, then bind that DC to another window, the drawing you did in the first window doesn't disappear. It simply won't be updated if you address any new messages to the DC, because the drawing context is now drawing in a different window.

As you undoubtedly have gathered by now, you send all drawing messages to a DC. As we saw in Chapter 7, the reasons for this extra layer of message processing in PenPoint have to do with memory efficiency and flexibility. A DC entails a relatively large amount of overhead. In fact, it occupies about five times as much memory as a window. Since PenPoint DCs allow windows to be relatively lightweight, applications can use dozens or even hundreds of windows to construct and control their user interfaces without consuming too much memory.

Creating a Drawing Context

Drawing contexts are instances of clsSysDrawCtx. You create a new DC the same way you create any other object in PenPoint, that is, by sending msgNewDefaults and then msgNew to the class.

A drawing context can be viewed from a programming perspective as a set of values that describe the state of the environment in the window to which the DC is attached. As you may imagine, this results in a fairly complex data structure. PenPoint defines defaults for all these states. When you create a new DC, it starts with these default values. Table 9-1 summarizes the elements of a DC you may often want to modify. It also indicates the default value assigned to these elements when you create a new DC.

Table 9-1 Important DC Elements and Their Defaults

Element	Default Value and Meaning
Units	Unit = point (1/72 of an inch)
Drawing mode	Keep narrow lines visible
Plane mask	Don't draw into the acetate layer where pen ink is "dribbled"
Line cap	Square off ends of lines
Line join	Use miters for line joins
Line thickness	One point
Foreground color	Black ink
Background color	White ink
Fill pattern	White
Line pattern	Black
Font scale	One unit
Default font	Unknown (no default)

While the listed default values for a DC are probably adequate for most cases, you should expect to change one or more of these values fairly regularly. As we will see in Appendix A, PenPoint defines messages that enable you to examine and change each of these important values individually.

Binding a DC to a Window

To bind a drawing context to a particular window, you send the DC the message msgDcSetWindow and pass it the ID of the window to which you want to bind it. PenPoint returns the ID of the window, if any, with which the DC was formerly associated.

You can also find out the ID of a window to which a DC is bound by sending it msgDcGetWindow.

A DC must be bound to a window before most of its messages will have any meaning, and a DC may be bound to only one window at a time. However, a single window may be bound to multiple DCs, which you might use to create a particularly complex picture.

Drawing with a DC

The process of drawing in a window with PenPoint is relatively simple. It requires only two steps

1. Ensure that the graphics state is correct (that is, that the DC has all the right values for the drawing you are about to do).
2. Send the DC one or more drawing messages to create shapes or text.

When the window to which the DC is bound is repainted, the drawing created by the messages you send will become visible to the user. If you need to do so, you can make the window repaint by sending it the message msgWinRepaint.

Storing DC Drawings

It is important to realize that when windows are filed, they don't store the screen image displayed within their borders. They store just the information necessary to re-create the window. There are three ways to store actual window display contexts

- capture a bitmap of the window (a memory-intensive and device-dependent approach)
- store application data structures from which you can regenerate the display (usually the best way)
- store your image as a sequence of DC drawing instructions

Sequences of DC drawing messages can be stored in a compact, efficient, and manageable way so that you can retrieve them later and even modify them dynamically. To support this use of graphics, PenPoint defines a special type of object called a picture segment, or PicSeg.

You can think of a PicSeg facility as a recording device that you insert between your drawing commands and the DC. You create and bind a PicSeg the same way you set up a DC. In fact, a PicSeg is a subclass of a DC. The

PicSeg remembers all drawing commands you issue. It stores each of these commands in a special compressed format called a *grafic*. Each grafic in a PicSeg contains information to reproduce a single drawing action. Grafics can be individually manipulated so that the PicSeg's operations can be reordered or modified without it actually drawing anything.

The PicSeg is an efficient way to store graphic information in the PenPoint system. PicSegs also can serve as a convenient data structure for your use if you are creating a drawing program.

In some ways, PicSegs correspond to the meta-files used in other graphics systems.

Clipping and Repainting Windows

While Chapter 7 covers PenPoint windows in detail, some aspects of window behavior are directly related to the drawing context with which they are associated. These two types of behavior are clipping and repainting.

Clipping the Drawing Area

If you send a DC one or more drawing messages that result in the creation of an image that extends beyond the boundaries of the selected window, the DC draws only the part of the image that is inside the window. This is the most obvious and common example of the process of clipping, and it happens automatically.

As a rule, windows cannot draw within one another's boundaries. Such behavior would be startling to the user, as well as difficult to manage. Since the user is to a great extent in charge of what happens on the screen, the ordering of windows is only partially under your control. The drawing context ensures that drawing will remain confined to the window to which it is bound.

Figure 9-2 depicts two situations in which clipping becomes an issue. In the first, the target window has no embedded windows, but the user draws outside its borders. The dashed line portion of the drawing is not displayed. Nevertheless, all drawings will be captured by PicSegs, even those that are clipped. The right side of Figure 9-2 shows an "intruder" window overlapping the window in which drawing is taking place. Note that here, clipping ensures that the drawing of a continuous line does not disrupt the contents of the overlapped (and perhaps embedded) windows.

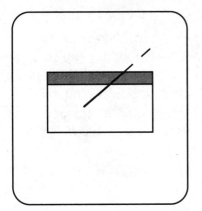 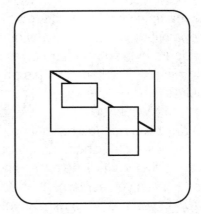

Figure 9-2 Clipping in Two Situations

We saw in Chapter 7 that you can override this normally polite behavior of windows within the relationships of a family of windows (parent and children) so that they share some common drawing area. If you do this and then draw into a window whose visible area overlaps into a parent or sibling window, the DC will behave accordingly, drawing in these other windows' boundaries.

There is another way you can alter the clipping region within which drawing takes place. You can define a subset of your window's total area as the area for drawing. If you do this, then all draw messages sent to the DC will be clipped within that defined area.

Ultimately, however, all drawing takes place through a DC and appears within a clip region that can be an entire window (the common situation), a larger area (in the case of a family of windows that cooperate to permit such behavior), or a portion of an entire window.

Repainting a Window

When part of your window gets dirty, it probably will need repainting. For example, if another window overlaps your window and is moved by the user, this dirties the previously overlapped portion of your window. Fortunately, you need not keep careful track of the status of your window in this regard; Pen-Point will notify your window if it requires repainting.

When you receive a message (msgWinRepaint) indicating your window needs repainting, you send your window msgBeginRepaint. Thereafter, all drawing operations you perform on the window affect only the dirty region until you send msgWinEndRepaint. This process of confining repainting to the area that requires it makes the use of a multiple, overlapped window system more efficient than it would be if every window completely repainted all its contents any time any pixel needed repainting. It also reduces to an absolute minimum any screen flicker or flash the user would see.

You can further control the repainting operation by sending an argument to the window when you send msgWinBeginRepaint. This is sometimes important if the drawing you are performing involves a significant amount of computation, because it can accelerate the update process. Normally, however, you simply don't worry about what portion of your window requires repainting; you let PenPoint handle it.

It probably appears that repainting your entire window is never necessary or appropriate unless all of its contents have been made dirty and require updating. While that is generally true, it is not always the case. You can repaint your window any time you need to without waiting for an instruction from the system. For instance, you would do this every time the data values or content of your window changed and needed updating. There may be times when you want to handle the repainting this way; PenPoint does not get in the way of your desire to do so. You would simply send msgWinDirtyRect to the window, followed by msgWinUpdate, msgWinBeginPaint, and msgWinEndPaint.

Graphics Primitives

As indicated previously, there are two categories of shapes for which Pen-Point defines primitives: open and closed. There are two other types of graphics primitives as well. One relates to displaying text and the other to copying rectangles of bits. We will look at each of these categories of graphics primitives in turn.

Open Shape Primitives

PenPoint includes primitives for drawing lines, curves, and arcs.

You use msgDcDrwPolyline to draw a line that can consist of multiple line segments. Each segment is a straight line joining two points on the display. Figure 9-3 shows two sample lines that might be created with msgDcDrawPolyline. The longer line consists of several shorter line segments, each of which is a single straight line. The shorter line consists of a single straight line between two points. In both cases, msgDcDrawPolyline takes as an argument a pointer to an array containing the points through which the line is to be drawn, as well as a number that defines the number of points in the array .

Bezier curves can be drawn with the message msgDcDrawBezier. This command takes a pointer to an array of four points that act as control points for the curve. Figure 9-4 shows a sample Bezier curve drawn with this command.

The third type of open shape for which PenPoint defines a graphics primitive is the arc. As you can see from Figure 9-5, an arc is a portion of an ellipse. From PenPoint's perspective, an arc is defined by a rectangle enclosing the ellipse of which the curve is a part and the two points that form the end points of the arc. The message msgDcDrawArcRays produces an arc like the one shown in Figure 9-5. It takes a pointer to a structure called SYSDC_ARC_RAYS, which defines the enclosing rectangle and the two points that delimit the arc.

The Power of PenPoint

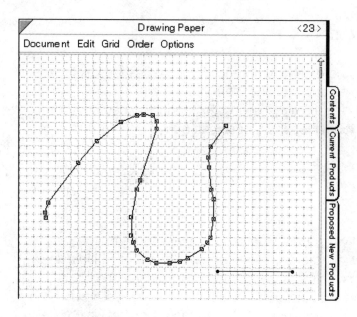

Figure 9-3 msgDcDrawPolyline Sample Line Output

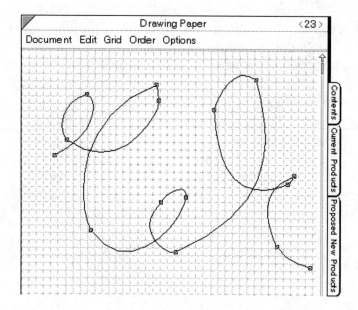

Figure 9-4 msgDcDrawBezier Sample Curve

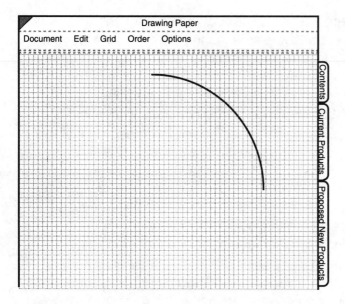

Figure 9-5   msgDcDrawArcRays Sample Arc

Closed Shape Primitives

There are six basic PenPoint graphics primitives that produce closed shapes, which may be filled with a pattern. More precisely, all closed shapes in PenPoint are filled, but you can make them appear to be "hollow" by using a transparent pattern as the fill pattern. There are also times when you want to produce only the filled portion of the rectangle rather than the filled portion and the line circumscribing the area. In those cases, you can set the width of the line to zero.

Rectangles are produced with msgDcDrawRectangle. It takes a pointer to a data structure that specifies the origin and size of the rectangle. Whether this message produces a square-cornered rectangle or a round-cornered rectangle depends on the setting of the value of the radius. Any value other than zero produces some rounding at the corners of the rectangle.

Ellipses and circles (which are a type of ellipse) are drawn with msgDcDrawEllipse. This message takes an argument that contains the rectangle within which the ellipse is drawn. If this rectangle is a square, then the ellipse is a circle.

You can draw an arbitrarily shaped polygon (regular or irregular) by sending the DC msgDcDrawPolygon. The argument to this message is identical in structure to that used for msgDcDrawPolyline. The only difference is that this structure defines an ending point that is equal to the starting point.

The message msgDcDrawSectorRays is similar to msgDcDrawArcRays except that it encloses the arc by drawing lines from its defining points to the center of the ellipse, creating an enclosed shape. This is a pie-wedge shape. This message takes the same arguments as msgDcDrawArcRays.

A chord ray can be produced by sending the DC msgDcDrawChordRays with the same argument set as you use with both msgDcDrawArcRays and msgDcDrawSectorRays. A chord ray encloses the arc by drawing a line between the two end points of the arc rather than from those points to the center of the ellipse. Figure 9-6 depicts the differences among an arc, a sector ray, and a chord ray using the same argument in all three cases.

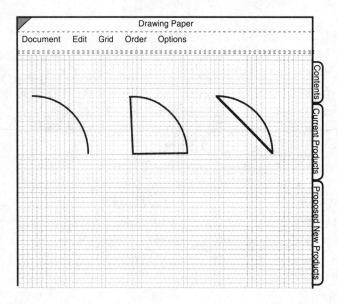

Figure 9-6　Three Figures Produced with Same Arc Argument

The last closed shape primitive is msgDcFillWindow. It draws a rectangle exactly the same size as the window to which the DC is bound. The enclosing lines fall partly within and partly outside the window (see Figure 9-7). You will most often use this message to erase everything inside a window. To draw a bordered window, you will normally use clsBorder (see Chapter 10).

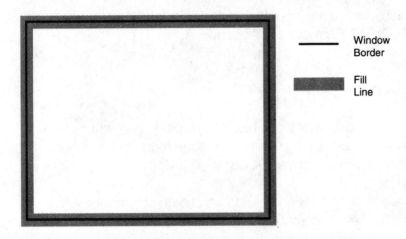

Figure 9-7 msgDcFillWindow's Line Position

Text Primitive

All text that appears on the screen of a PenPoint-based system is drawn using a font. Recall that when we discussed the default contents of the DC at initialization, we indicated that PenPoint does not supply an automatic font. If you fail to set the font before attempting to draw text, your text will be drawn using a default font.

The process of drawing text consists of four steps

1. loading the desired font with msgDcOpenFont
2. scaling the font with msgDcScaleFont
3. initializing SYSDC_TEXT_OUTPUT
4. drawing the text with msgDcDrawText

168

. . . .

The Power of PenPoint

With the font set, you can send the DC msgDcDrawText along with a pointer to a structure called SYSDC_TEXT_OUTPUT. This structure is defined in detail in the final section of this chapter, but for now you simply need to know that it contains styling information, a pointer to the string itself, the length of the string, the starting position for the string, and other information that helps PenPoint draw the text as you want it.

We will have much more to say about fonts and about the contents and use of a SYSDC_TEXT_OUTPUT structure in Appendix A.

CopyRect and CopyPixels Operations

ImagePoint provides two types of pixel copy operations which other systems sometimes call "bit blits." You may move the rectangular pixel images between image devices with msgDCCopyPixels and within a window with msgWinCopyRect.

Image devices are in-memory windows into which you can render your drawing operation. The resulting image can then be copied nearly instantaneously from memory to the actual screen with msgDCCopyPixels. This technique is, in essence, a method of caching the actual pixel image. If you are displaying an image repeatedly this can be a useful technique for speeding its display.

When you need to relocate a portion of your on-screen image to a different position on the screen, use msgWinCopyRect. This technique is most often used when your window has been repositioned on the screen due to the user dragging the window or scrolling its contents. Rather than completely redrawing your window, it is most efficient to copy the window contents from one place on the screen to another. ImagePoint's msgWinCopyRect not only performs the underlying "bit blit" operation of copying the pixels, but will also handle all window regions from the source. You can, therefore, think of msgWinCopoyRect as a window-aware bit-blit operation.

Color Graphics Interface

PenPoint supports the use of color on hardware platforms capable of displaying graphics in color. In fact, it treats even monochrome screens as color-capable by simply treating black, white, and optional shades of gray as if they were colors (which, of course, they are, even though we are accustomed to thinking of colors as being everything that isn't black or white or gray).

The PenPoint color metaphor uses the concepts of foreground and background. Most drawing takes place in the foreground as the pen creates lines using a color that contrasts with the color of the background and therefore produces visible output. It is possible that a single drawing operation can use both the foreground and background colors at the same time.

As you build PenPoint applications, you can rest assured that all platforms on which your programs will run support a minimum of four colors. Translation of programs that use more than four colors to appropriate shading on a four-color system is handled automatically by PenPoint. If you follow the instructions for handling color in your programs, they will run suitably on all PenPoint-based systems.

You can describe and set color values in two ways. You can use a palette of colors and index into it for the color you wish to use, or you can use RGB (red, green, blue) color combinations. We strongly recommend you use the latter method, for the following reasons:

- It is more compatible with printer support. If you use a palette and index into it, and the user connects to a printer that doesn't recognize the palette, output is likely to be less than acceptable.

- As we indicated earlier, PenPoint automatically handles the translation from RGB color values to appropriate and usable colors on a minimum-color system. PenPoint even dithers the colors in a color window before sending its contents to a printer that produces only gray-scale output.

- You can achieve device independence not only at the printer level, but also with various displays that might be connected to a PenPoint-based system.

If you use RGB values for your colors, you will use numbers from 0 to 255 to define the brightness of each RGB component.

Dealing with Prestored Images

By nature of their design and intended uses, many PenPoint-based computer systems must deal with a wide range of images. This includes not only images that are produced by the system on which PenPoint is running and by other PenPoint systems (generally using PicSegs as described previously) but also images produced in other standard formats as well as those that are for some reason incompatible with PenPoint's graphics operations.

An example of the latter is the digitized image of a facsimile that might be received via a fax modem built into a PenPoint-based computer system. Its resolution, aspect ratio, and other characteristics may make it impossible to work with directly as text on the PenPoint-based computer system.

But PenPoint includes powerful high-level support for dealing with such images, in the form of its Sampled Image Operator (SIO). These images are pixel-based. Even relatively straightforward translations (such as a resolution conversion that converts every pixel to four to increase its visibility on an incompatible platform) tend not to work very well. To display a pixel-oriented image at anything other than its original resolution and density requires image processing. PenPoint's SIO handles simulated analog image processing.

SIO performs relatively sophisticated mapping of source pixels into destination pixels and source gray levels into destination gray levels. It also supports run-length-compressed sources and allows easy scaling and rotation of pixel-based images.

Obviously, such pixel-based images are not editable in the same way as images constructed from PenPoint's graphics routines. However, you can design PenPoint applications that have an effect similar to editing. It is possible, for example, to simulate document markup with a prestored image by capturing and storing user ink separately and just OR-ing it onto the screen.

Fonts

PenPoint supports a sophisticated font model. But fonts can be extremely memory-intensive, and on a pen-based computer that relies on memory for most of its active storage, the system must find ways around this problem.

PenPoint addresses this problem in two ways. First, it synthesizes some font attributes to save memory. For example, rather than store a bold version of a font, PenPoint's DC defines a flag that the system uses to underline text as if it were a separate font. Second, PenPoint stores fonts as outlines, which are far more memory-efficient than the alternative bitmapped images of the font characters.

Using outline fonts has another distinct advantage. The outlines are easily scalable to any point size, which fits nicely with the fundamental graphics concept in PenPoint that everything is scalable. Because ImagePoint can render fonts in a wide range of point sizes, even PenPoint's system user interface takes advantage of scalable fonts by allowing the user to choose the size of the system-wide PenPoint font.

When a font is specified in a DC, PenPoint will always find the closest possible match to that font. Using font metrics described later in this section, PenPoint interprets your font request and determines which available font comes closest to matching those metrics.

If the system has a bitmapped font of the same name and/or ID as the font requested, it will use that font. Otherwise, it will examine its outline font library for the best match, transforming and simulating attributes as necessary.

All fonts have standard 16-bit IDs that are registered with GO Corporation and are valid on all PenPoint-based computer systems. Thus, moving applications from one system to another should not result in font display problems.

Table 9-2 summarizes the attributes of a font that describe its appearance in terms that PenPoint can understand in its efforts to match a font specification.

Table 9-2 Font Attributes

Attribute	Description
Typeface	Name of the family to which the font belongs (Roman, Old English, and so forth)
Character weight	Bold, normal, light, extra-bold, and so forth
Aspect	Condensed, normal, or extended
Italic	Indication whether or not font is italicized

172

. . . .

The Power of PenPoint

Note that the size of the character is not a font attribute. In modern typography it is understood, for example, that Helvetica is a different font from Helvetica Bold or Helvetica Bold Condensed, but 24-point Helvetica and 12-point Helvetica are the same font, with different character sizes.

Font attributes are stored, along with a great deal of other information, in a structure called SYSDC_FONT_SPEC. One of the fields in this structure defines the group to which the font belongs. In PenPoint, a group is a broad categorization that describes whether the font looks more like newspaper headlines, type set in a book, handwriting, or other basic types of font "looks." If you want to use the system default font, you can define this group as sysDcGroupDefault. In that case, PenPoint uses the current system font.

Opening a Font

Since, as pointed out in the previous section, all fonts have unique 16-bit identifiers, you might expect that opening a font would be a simple matter of passing that identifier as a parameter in a message to open that font. However, that simplistic approach would ignore the probability that the user of a particular system may never have installed the font in question or may have removed it for some reason. As a result, it is not sufficient simply to supply the ID of the font; you must also define its font attributes (see Table 9-2).

Once you have set up the font attributes correctly, you can open the font with msgDcOpenFont. PenPoint then uses the font whose ID you provide, if it has it available. If not, it uses the group to find the font that is closest to your request.

Because PenPoint's font system is flexible in matching font requests and because PenPoint can synthesize certain font attributes, both users and programmers are freed from being concerned with font management and determining exactly what fonts are currently loaded. For example, if you load a font that is not italic but specify in its font-attributes setting that it should be italicized, PenPoint will synthetically italicize the font as it opens it. The result is that the programmer should ask for the desired font; PenPoint will do the right thing.

Font Metrics and Character Geometry

Quite often when you are drawing text with a font, you need some information about the font. For example, the width of spaces differs from font to font and in some situations you may need to know precisely how wide a space is in a specific font. Similarly, the height of ascenders and the length of descenders can become important in vertically spacing text.

Such font information is stored in the structure SYSDC_FONT_METRICS, which is described in detail in Appendix A. You can retrieve the values in this structure by sending your DC the message msgDcGetFontMetrics.

Drawing Text

As you already know, you draw text in PenPoint with the message msgDcDrawText. This section provides additional details about the process of drawing text and how PenPoint handles it.

All of the text you draw in a window is drawn using the current foreground color. Note that you cannot pattern-fill text without appropriately setting the foreground color. Because all text you draw is simply more graphics content for the window, it unites with the rest of the images in the window and therefore will scale and rotate along with the rest of your drawing.

When you send msgDcDrawText, you supply the pointer to a SYSDC_TEXT_OUTPUT structure. While all characters appear on the display as bitmapped images, PenPoint actually stores most fonts in outline form. Font outlines are superior to bitmapped fonts because outlines are more device-independent and compact for larger point sizes.

When PenPoint needs to display a character in a particular font, it looks up the character in an internal bitmap character cache. If the character is present, it is copied to the screen. If it is not present, a fault occurs and Pen-Point will render the requested character into the bitmap character cache. The rendering logic uses an installed font, which can be either in outline form (most common) or bitmap (typically for very small point sizes). If the installed font is in outline form, the requested character is rasterized as an actual bitmap at the requested point size. Characters are rendered into the cache with all attributes (such as weight and aspect ratio) and rotation.

Text Calculations

You can control some aspects of the way text is displayed in PenPoint by performing certain calculations. PenPoint provides a number of messages that permit you to gain access to information about the font and text you are using and to perform useful calculations on those results. For example, you may want to customize the horizontal spacing to justify a line. Since information such as the width of characters in the font is available to you, this is relatively straightforward.

Another calculation you may need to perform is determining the length of the text to be displayed. Since it tends to vary with the font and size of text in use, PenPoint provides messages that help you calculate this value.

Printing

Application printing comes almost for free in PenPoint. The ImagePoint imaging model can be used by the application to print as well as to display to the screen. Since there's a single API used to render to both screen and printers, an application need only write display and layout code once.

Printed pages are collections of windows. Therefore, the printing process essentially consists of your application displaying itself to a different image device (a printer image device that PenPoint provides to you). All UI Toolkit components (see Chapter 2) print nicely, so you can use them freely at print time as well as on the screen (for example, if you embed a button in your application data that you are printing, you needn't worry that it might not print correctly).

PenPoint handles the user interface for printing and pagination issues. The Document menu for every application contains standard Print and Print Setup commands which bring up Option Sheets. The print sheet controls print-time settings such as which printer to use, number of copies, and the like. The Print Setup sheet controls page size, orientation, headers, and footers.

Under PenPoint, print commands may be given at any time, even if there is not printer connected to the PenPoint machine directly or through a network or

PC. PenPoint uses the Out Box to defer printing operations (see Chapter 16 for more information on the Out Box). The Print command copies the document into the Out Box.

When the targeted printer is available, six things occur

- PenPoint creates an image device for that printer (recall that image devices are the object onto which ImagePoint (SysDC) renders graphics) and creates a root window on this image device.
- The document in the Out Box receives a msgAppOpen, with one of the message's parameters set to indicate that the application is being opened for printing.
- The printer image device root window is laid out with the optional headers and footers and with the application's first page of data filling the bulk of the page. This root window is then dirtied to cause a msgWinBeginRepaint, which, in turn, causes the display to the printer by the application.
- If a bitmap-oriented printer (such as dot matrix) is being used, the fully rendered page image is then sent to the printer in bands. If a more intelligent printer is being used, ImagePoint downloads its outline fonts into the printer and uses the printer's imaging engine to render most ImagePoint primitives.
- The page layout and print process repeats for as many pages as the application has data to print.
- When the print job is successfully concluded, the Out Box deletes its copy of the document.

By default, the Application Framework prints a document exactly as it appears on the screen. For many applications, this is all that's necessary. Other applications, however, might want to format differently for the printer than for the screen. Report generators, spreadsheets and word processors are good examples of this class of application. Such applications should check their response to msgAppOpen and use print-specific formatting and layout logic when they've been opened to print.

Summary

This chapter has examined ImagePoint, the graphical heart of PenPoint. It explained that graphics in PenPoint involve the use of an object called a drawing context, or DC. All drawing messages are sent to this object rather than directly to the window or screen in which drawing takes place. Your application must create these DCs, bind them to windows, draw with them, and, under some circumstances, file the drawings they create.

PenPoint windows support clipping, to ensure that drawing stays within appropriate borders, and painting/repainting cycles to minimize screen flicker during refresh of window contents as windows are moved, resized, created, opened, closed, and changed.

There are several graphics primitives in ImagePoint, including those that create open and closed shapes, a text primitive, and image movement operations. Color graphics and prestored images can also be manipulated within ImagePoint.

ImagePoint supports a sophisticated font model that adapts to the needs of a pen-based computer that relies on memory for most of its active storage.

Drawing text and printing are also parts of the ImagePoint environment.

10
The User Interface Toolkit

. . . .

The User Interface Toolkit has the largest and most complex application programming interface (API) in the PenPoint Software Developer's Kit. It encompasses more than a dozen classes and hundreds of messages.

Broadly speaking, the User Interface Toolkit (which we'll refer to variously as the UI Toolkit or simply the Toolkit) has one main purpose: to help you construct the consistent, easy-to-use interfaces that users of PenPoint-based notebook computers will come to expect. In Chapter 7, we touched briefly on how to lay out a window. In this chapter, you'll see all the various items that can go into a window and how PenPoint assists you in laying out windows quickly and easily while allowing you to create visually pleasing interfaces.

The UI Toolkit: An Overview

The basic principle at work in the PenPoint user interface is that all of the elements that appear in a window can be (and usually are) themselves windows. Recall from Chapter 7 our discussion of parent and child window hierarchies. All the UI Toolkit-based design elements that you place into a client window of your application will be child windows to that window.

Laying out a window involves arranging these windows in such a way that when you display the window, all its child windows appear and are usable in

177

the way you intend and the way the user expects. Because some of the child windows in your application may also contain child windows, you can appreciate the complexity that would be involved in displaying a window if you had to handle all of these windows individually. PenPoint's UI Toolkit supports you so that you need only provide high-level directives that arrange the windows and then tell the parent window to lay itself out. The system takes care of the rest of the work for you, including the recursion involved in having child windows first lay out their child windows, and so on, arbitrarily deep into the tree hierarchy.

At the top level of the user interface classes are four basic categories or groups of classes with which you need to be concerned: border classes, layout classes, message dispatching classes, and presentation/interaction behavior classes.

Borders around a window are handled by clsBorder, which supports all of the many border styles defined by PenPoint.

You'll see that two related classes, clsTableLayout and clsCustomLayout, provide you with the tools for virtual automatic layout of your windows. These classes enable you to create windows as complex as your application needs (and your user can deal with) without being concerned about the complications of displaying such a window.

User interface events that take place within the elements of a PenPoint application's window are filtered and processed using messages defined in clsControl. This class plays a key role in the entire construction and management of a user interface.

The display of and interaction with the various types of controls are handled through clsLabel.

You can nest controls inside controls, enabling you to create arbitrarily robust interfaces from a relatively small number of types of controls. Controls are often collected in a Toolkit Table, a concept that is so central to PenPoint that it has its own class (clsTkTable). This approach facilitates your construction of interface components that contain many controls but that can be treated as an integral whole for many programming and user interface purposes.

All UI components can be filed using the same techniques that we discussed in Chapter 7 for filing other types of windows. Once again, the consistency of the PenPoint design means that there is less for you to learn about how to get things done so you can spend more time achieving your program's objectives.

Figure 10-1 is a class diagram for the UI Toolkit.

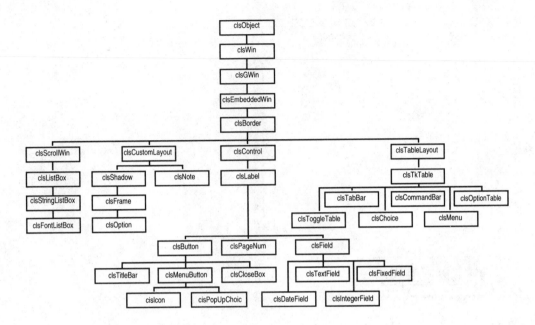

Figure 10-1 Class Diagram for User Interface Toolkit

Automatic Layout

The automatic layout of the user interface through layout windows is a major point of differentiation between PenPoint and traditional operating systems. Chapter 7 discusses this subject from a broad perspective. This chapter focuses on more of the implementation details of the layout process in PenPoint.

PenPoint provides both tabular and custom window layout support. It does this by means of two separate but related classes, clsTableLayout and clsCustomLayout. Both are descendants of clsBorder, as you can see in Figure 10-1. As their names indicate, clsTableLayout defines messages that enable you to lay out a window in a tabular form (see Figure 10-2 for an example of such a layout), while clsCustomLayout permits you to define an irregular layout. In both cases, you define how the parent window should lay out its child windows; the difference lies in the amount and kind of parametric data you supply to PenPoint.

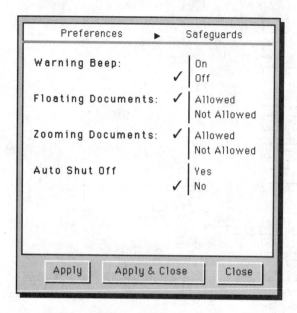

Figure 10-2 Sample Table Layout

If you are laying out a tabular window, you define the number of rows and columns, the height of each row, and the width of each column. You can also instruct clsTableLayout to adjust the size of each column to fit its members. This means you can specify layouts such as

- three rows by two columns
- ten-unit-tall rows, as many columns wide as will fit, with all columns as wide as the widest entry in each
- two columns of menu buttons sized so that all buttons in each column are the width of the widest button in the column

Menus are simple table layout windows that arrange their child windows (menu buttons) in a row (as in the case of the menu bar across the top of most main windows) or in columns (as in the case of the pull-down menus).

When you define custom layouts using clsCustomLayout, you must supply a layout description for each child window you insert into the parent window handling the layout. This description provides the parent window with a set of constraints for each child window. These constraints define such things as

- the x-y coordinate position of the child window
- the width and height of the child window
- an indication of the object to which relative values are to be calculated (for example, whether the x-y position is relative to the edge of the window or is an absolute position)

Frames are good examples of custom layout windows in PenPoint. They have a non-tabular appearance.

Types of UI Components

Earlier in this chapter, we divided the UI Toolkit classes into four groups, or categories. As we move into a deeper examination of the Toolkit and its contents, we will deal with twelve types of controls

- labels
- buttons
- menu buttons and menus
- list boxes
- scrollbars
- fields
- notes
- frames
- frame decorations
- Option Sheets
- icons
- Toolkit Tables

We will discuss each type of control in the order in which it is listed, except that we discuss frames and frame decorations in the same section because of their close relationship. But first we will discuss types of behavior that are common to all of these types of control.

Common Control Behavior

PenPoint controls are all created in nearly identical ways. In addition, most of them exhibit notification and preview behavior, which we consider together as responsive behaviors.

Creating Controls

All controls in a PenPoint application are instances of one of the subclasses of clsControl. As you can see from Figure 10-1, clsControl ultimately descends from a number of parent classes, including clsGWin, the class where windows that respond to gestures are defined. By extension, then, all controls respond to gestures by the user.

Controls respond to user input, in general terms, by sending themselves messages. You implement behavior for these messages that describes how you want the application to respond when the user activates a control with a gesture. Different controls respond to different gestures. For example, while you would expect buttons to respond to the tap gesture, some (such as the pop-up choice) also respond to flick gestures.

To create a control, you store descriptive information in two data structures, CONTROL_METRICS and CONTROL_STYLE. The former defines the control's client (that is, the object that will receive all notifications from the control when something, such as a gesture, causes it to provide such notification), and the latter defines the appearance and behavior of the control.

> **NOTE**
>
> There is no structure called CONTROL_METRICS. Rather, the name of the specific type of control is substituted for the word "CONTROL" in these pseudo names, which are used here simply to allow us to discuss control behavior generically. Thus we will encounter data structures called BUTTON_METRICS and BUTTON_STYLE, and similar data structures with appropriate names for the other eleven types of control previously defined. As we discuss each type of control in the remainder of this chapter, we will describe unique contents of these structures where they are appropriate.

Once you have defined these data structures for a particular control you want to create, you create an instance the same way you create all other PenPoint objects, that is, by sending msgNewDefaults followed by msgNew to the class you want to instantiate.

Responsive Behaviors

Each control can have only one client to which it reports user interaction taking place within its borders. The end result of the user interacting with a control is usually, but not always, an action-taking command. For example, if the user taps on a button indicating a desire to quit your application and you've defined msgMyAppQuit, that message is sent when the user activates the appropriate button.

This interaction is more complex than it sounds. Figure 10-3 shows the broad outline of the processing that takes place when the user interacts with a control.

Notice that when the user selects a control (by tapping or gesturing on the control and thereby creating a msgPenDown event) the control first enters a preview mode. Different controls respond to this mode in different ways. For example, most buttons simply invert themselves so that they provide the user with some visual feedback that they have been selected. Toggles may turn a checkmark or other decoration on or off, and scrollbars respond by inverting their scroll handles. We will describe the preview behavior engaged in by each control when we discuss the individual controls later in the chapter.

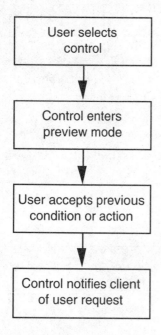

Figure 10-3 Interactive Process in Control

Labels

Labels are the simplest of controls. They display text strings or windows. Labels do not exhibit notification or preview behavior; they are passive design elements.

In the PenPoint class hierarchy, however, buttons, menu buttons, and frame title bars are all descendants of clsLabel. All these subclasses implement some notification and preview behavior; we will discuss those behaviors when we describe each of these types of control later in the chapter.

Labels can contain text or child windows as their visible "label." A child window might appear, for example, in a print Options Sheet to ask the user to enter the starting and ending page numbers to print. In that case, the "From __ To __" construct is a label with a Toolkit Table as a child window. The Toolkit Table comprises the two blanks the user must fill in.

The LABEL_METRICS structure provides the label's string or, if it is a child window, its window UID. It also includes information about the font to be used, the scale at which to draw the label, and the number of rows and columns in the label. Part of LABEL_METRICS is the LABEL_STYLE structure, which defines such parameters as

- whether the label is a string or a window
- alignment
- rotation
- text style (underline, strike-through, and so forth)
- decoration, if any
- method for determining number of rows and columns in the label
- style of boxes around label characters, if any
- word wrap
- whether the label's text is selectable

If a label's contents are a text string, the only behavior it exhibits relates to its need to lay itself out in a parent window. You can define whether the label is to have a constant size, a scaled size, or an application-controlled size that grows and shrinks as needed.

If a label is defined to have a child window, clsLabel merely inserts the window as a child of the label. From that point, the label is treated like any other child window for layout and repainting.

Buttons

A button is an instance of clsButton, a descendant class of clsLabel. You can think of a button as a label that responds to user activation.

There are three basic types of buttons in PenPoint, differentiated by how their on and off condition is changed

- Push buttons are momentary switch buttons whose value is changed from Off to On when they are activated and back to Off when they are released. Goto buttons are examples of this type of button (see Figure 10-4).

- Toggles are contact switch buttons whose value changes from Off to On and back again with each push. Checkboxes generally are toggles, but so are many other kinds of buttons. Figure 10-4 shows a collection of related toggles decorated with check marks.

- Lock-on buttons are turned on when they are pushed but cannot be turned off by pushing on them again. Many choices in Option Sheets are lock-on buttons. This type of button is used when you must have a value for a particular setting, but only one value is permitted. Figure 10-4 shows three lock-on buttons in a group forming a typical setting area in an Option Sheet.

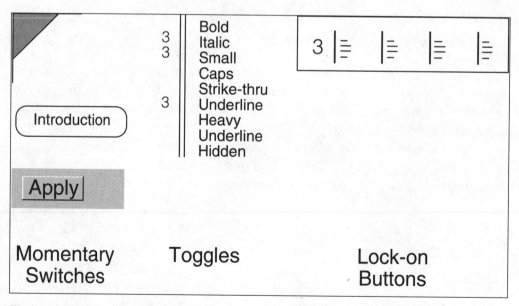

Figure 10-4 Three Types of PenPoint Buttons

The BUTTON_METRICS structure contains the message to be sent when the button is activated as well as possible arguments to accompany the message.

BUTTON_STYLE describes the following aspects of a button's appearance and behavior, among others:

- contact type (that is, push button, toggle, or lock-on, as previously described)
- how the value of a button is displayed
- the button's On-Off state
- type of message sending and handling expected
- button manager (none, parent, or client)

What constitutes "activation" of a button is directly dependent on button type. A push button, for example, is not activated (although it is previewed) if the user taps on it and then moves the pen away from the button while keeping the pen on the surface of the display. This allows users to change their minds about activating a button. Toggles and lock-on buttons, however, are activated when they are tapped. Actions dictated by such buttons usually take effect later rather than immediately; thus, users can easily change their minds by "undoing" the choice either by tapping on the button again in the case of a toggle or by selecting another alternative in the set of lock-on buttons.

Menu Buttons and Menus

A menu button is an instance of clsMenuButton, which is a descendant class of clsButton. When a menu button is activated, it receives a message and can take an action. Most top-level menu buttons display a pop-up menu. The menu, in turn, can contain other menu buttons, non-menu buttons (see previous section) or, less frequently, almost any other type of control.

Menu buttons are toggle switches. When you tap on a menu button, it turns on and displays its pop-up menu. It stays active until the pop-up menu is dismissed, which happens when the user either makes a choice from the menu that does not lead to another hierarchical pop-up menu or taps on the open menu's button or anywhere outside the menu. (See Figure 10-5.)

As you can see, menu buttons and menus are closely related. But they don't have all behavior in common, so we will discuss them separately.

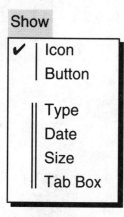

Figure 10-5 Typical Activated Menu Button

Menu Buttons

The metrics for a menu button are quite straightforward. It has the usual style fields (which we'll discuss shortly) and a single other field, which contains a pointer to the submenu if one is associated with the button. Most menu buttons do not have submenus.

The BUTTON_STYLE structure defines four main characteristics of a button and its submenu

- type of submenu (pull-down, pull-right, pop-up, or none)
- whether the submenu's width is determined dynamically
- whether the submenu contents are provided dynamically by the menu button's client
- whether the submenu should dynamically determine the activation status of its controls

There is one special type of pop-up menu called a pop-up choice menu button. This kind of button leaves its present value displayed when its submenu is closed. It also has another interesting behavior: The user can scroll through the available options without actually opening the submenu of choices by using scrolling gestures on the button.

Menus

A PenPoint menu is an instance of clsMenu, which in turn is a descendant of clsTkTable. (We discuss Toolkit Tables later in the chapter.) This is because menus are really tabular tables (see previous discussion about automatic layout), generally one column wide or one row deep, depending on whether the menu is vertical or horizontal. The menu across the top of most PenPoint windows is a horizontal menu that is actually a Toolkit Table one row deep and a variable number of columns wide. The pop-up menus that its buttons display generally are vertical Toolkit Tables one column wide and a variable number of rows deep.

Built-in behavior in clsMenu automatically positions pop-up menus optimally, taking into account where they appear on the display, the number of entries they contain, and other factors such as physical screen size. Figure 10-6, for example, shows how PenPoint positions the pop-up menu in the Preferences application differently, depending on the current choice.

The structure MENU_METRICS contains only style fields and in-line storage for a MENU_BUTTON_METRICS structure. The contents of the menu are specified in a TK_TABLE_ENTRY array, which we will discuss when we look at Toolkit Tables later in the chapter.

Scrollbars

PenPoint scrollbars have two primary purposes: to permit users to change the portion of a document they are viewing when that document is larger than the window and to allow users to see at a glance approximately how far into the document their current view is positioned. Together with the window itself, scrollbars give the user the illusion of moving the window around to look at different portions of the document.

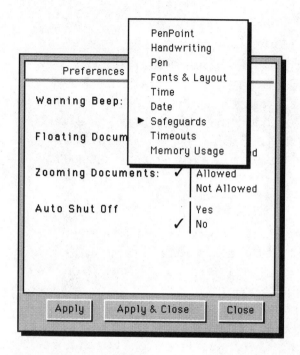

Figure 10-6 How clsMenu Positions Pop-Up Choices Optimally

Scrollbars are the only type of control in PenPoint that descend directly from clsControl rather than through clsLabel.

Figure 10-7 shows a typical vertical scrollbar in PenPoint and its constituent parts. The buttons at the top and bottom of the scrollbar are momentary switch buttons. The dotted line appears just inside the document frame. The thicker part of that line is called the scroll handle; it indicates the approximate location in the total document (the nearer the end of the document you are positioned, the nearer the bottom of the display the scroll handle appears).

Generally, the client of a scrollbar is the document that is being scrolled. When the user interacts with the scrollbar, the scrollbar sends a message to the document indicating that the user has requested a change in the view. The document responds by scrolling to show the appropriate new contents.

PenPoint scrollbars support a process known as normalization. You can avoid having the user's scrolling process clip off the tops or bottoms of characters or small portions of other kinds of images. This is handled by the simple expedient of permitting the client document to send back to the scrollbar an offset value that is different from the offset value sent to the document by the scrollbar. This can permit the scrollbars to fine-tune their position and make scrolling more aesthetically pleasing to the user.

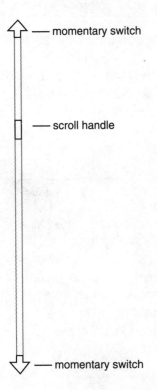

momentary switch

scroll handle

momentary switch

Figure 10-7   Vertical Scrollbar and Its Components

You can support scrolling in your application's documents without display-ing scrollbars. If you use clsScrollWin in your application to handle scrolling, the user can employ any of the gestures PenPoint recognizes as scrolling commands. The gestures are all flicks. Your application defines how to re-spond to each flick or multi-flick gesture, although GO Corporation's PenPoint User Interface Style Guidelines suggest that a single flick always reposition the object on the line on which the gesture occurs. Typical uses of these gestures are as follows:

- single flick repositions the line on which it starts (moving it to the top of the screen if the user flicks up, to the bottom of the screen if the user flicks down)
- double flick moves to the top of the document if the user flicks up, to the bottom if the user flicks down
- triple and quadruple flicks are available for application-specific interpretation

PenPoint also recognizes a quadruple-flick gesture for applications that may involve more complex scrolling (spreadsheets, for example). These gestures can be made on the scrollbar or in the document itself, assuming of course that the document window has as an ancestor clsGWin so that it recognizes gestures. Even if the gestures are performed on the document window, the resulting scrolling message comes from the scrollbar, which greatly simplifies application coding.

Why Scrolling Without Scrollbars?

PenPoint's support for scrolling without the need for scrollbars is unusual. There are two primary advantages to this approach to the architecture of the system. First, by permitting applications to omit the scrollbars without sacrificing scrolling ability, PenPoint allows more screen real estate to be available for the document. Second, users can scroll more conveniently because they can use reduced hand motions. They need not move the pen to the scrollbar to scroll; flicking anywhere within the document will have the desired effect.

You may often want to implement scrolling in your document by creating an instance of clsScrollWin, a descendant of clsBorder. This type of window is useful when the scrolling your application needs is relatively straightforward, requiring simply a shift in the portion of a single window the user is viewing. Although it can't handle line-by-line scrolling without your application's help, it can respond to page-up and page-down scrolling with no intervention on your part.

If you use an instance of clsScrollWin to implement scrolling, this instance inserts your window as its child, repositions your window in response to scrolling messages, and isolates your window from the scrollbar interface. All you have to do is repaint when you're requested to do so, and scrolling is automatic.

List Boxes

A list box is a scrolling window that can contain a large number of entries. It is most often used to provide the user with a way to choose from among many options. In fact, one type of choice the user often makes from such a window is a font. This need is so frequent in PenPoint that the system defines a special class for a list box that automatically handles font display and selection.

List boxes descend from clsScrollWin. They differ from instances of their parent class in that you need not supply the client window to be scrolled; PenPoint maintains that window for you, creating it from the choices you provide.

List boxes in most operating systems restrict their contents to strings. PenPoint's list box is a list of windows. Of course, windows can also display strings. But the windows could display any object the application wants to place in a list box. In fact, each element in the list can be of a different type and a different height.

Window List Boxes

Window list boxes contain a list of windows. Since windows can contain virtually any object or application, window list boxes can contain a list of any kind of object. Recognizing that lists of such object windows consume a large amount of memory, you can see how window list boxes can be great memory savers by dynamically updating during scrolling. In the process, they release memory no longer needed by windows that have scrolled outside the window's borders. Thus, you need not keep a separate window around for each of several dozen choices (for example, if you're only going to show the user a window with six choices at a time).

Each item in a window list box is called a list box entry.

The contents of the LIST_BOX_METRICS structure describe the client to which the list box sends messages, the total number of entries in the list, and the number of entries to be shown at one time in the window. Unlike most other controls, you don't supply the contents of the list box when you create it; it gets that information from your application dynamically.

Because a list box is not a layout window, you have little control over and no involvement in the appearance of the list box. The LIST_BOX_STYLE data structure contains only information about how the list box should be filed.

String List Boxes

A string list box is a much simpler type of control than a list box, from which it inherits directly. Only text strings can be placed into such a list box.

The data structure STRLB_METRICS contains an initial value, if the string has one. The STRLB_STYLE structure defines the overall behavior of the list box as well as how entries are displayed when they have been selected.

The behavior of a string list box can be set up so that it acts as any of the following types of controls:

- toggle table (zero, one, or more entries can be selected)
- choice (zero or one entry can be selected)
- choice (only one entry always selected)

You can instruct the system to highlight (invert) or decorate selected items (for example, with a check mark) in a string list box.

Font List Box

A special use of the string list box described in the previous section is to display strings that are the names of the fonts known to the system (that is, currently installed fonts). This is a simple class to use; you don't have to respond to any messages.

The FONTLB_METRICS data structure is the same as that for a string list box except that it adds a style field specifically for font list boxes. The only field in FONTLB_STYLE is a pruning control that determines whether your user will see all fonts or whether you will remove from the list of fonts all from the same family. You may also remove symbol fonts from the display.

Fields

A field is an instance of clsField, which in turn is a subclass of clsLabel. Fields are editable text fields that accept handwritten input from the user. The user enters text into a field either by writing directly into the field on the display or by popping up a special pad containing character boxes. Pads have specialized editing capabilities that fields lack. Because fields involve user input through handwriting, they are discussed more fully in Chapter 13.

FIELD_METRICS contains the name of the translator or template to be used for handwriting recognition in the field, as well as the maximum length of the text, in characters. FIELD_STYLE describes, among other things

- type of edit field (in-line, overwrite, or pop-up; see following paragraph)
- style of pop-up pad (character box or edit box)
- capitalization information
- whether translation is delayed until the user explicitly requests it
- how and when client notification occurs
- validation information

There are three types of edit fields. In-line fields permit the user to write directly into the document and appear as blank areas, generally labeled so it is clear that they are intended for input. The heading portion of a memo is an example where such a field might appear next to the "To:" label. Overwrite fields are segmented fields, with dividing lines between character positions. The user writes directly into these boxes. Option Sheets often use overwrite fields for entries such as the font size. Pop-up fields do not accept handwriting or recognize gestures directly in the field; instead, any pen stroke in such a field creates an insertion pad for editing the field's contents (see Figure 10-8). The first two field types permit the user to indicate by a gesture a desire to use an insertion pad rather than writing directly into the field.

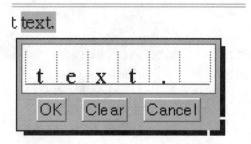

Figure 10-8 Typical Pop-Up Insertion Pad

Why the Diversity of Field Types?

PenPoint's provision of three field types, rather than one, is an example of how, in many areas, PenPoint provides expressive power for applications to fine-tune their user interfaces to the pen. GO Corporation's user interface research demonstrated that there is no best style of field interaction; different applications have different needs. For example, some form designers might want very small fields so that the form can be displayed entirely on one screen. They would use pop-up fields. Other form designers might want to optimize their forms for simplicity by using overwrite fields. GO's PenPoint User Interface Style Guidelines recommend the use of a single field type consistently throughout a single page of a form.

Notes

A note in PenPoint is functionally equivalent to dialog boxes and alerts used in other windowing systems. Notes are windows that appear, present information to the user, encourage or require the user to make some response, and disappear on command by the user. Notes are instances of clsNote, which inherits from clsCustomLayout.

Notes can be generated either by the system or by your application. Their appearances are, or can be, identical. We are concerned here primarily with application-generated notes.

You specify the contents of a note as an array of Toolkit Table entries (see the discussion of such tables later in this chapter). Alternatively, you can tell notes to get their contents from resource files.

PenPoint notes are either modal or modeless. Modal notes require the user to take some action before they go away, although you can design such notes to dismiss automatically after a certain amount of time. In either case, the user cannot perform certain actions while the note is displayed. Modeless notes permit the user to continue to work inside the application while they are displayed. In PenPoint, if you need to display information for the user but don't care if the user continues to use the application while the information is displayed and the user has not responded to the note, you can use either an Option Sheet or notes.

A system modal note stops the user from doing anything until the note is dismissed, either by user action or automatically. Notes asking the user to confirm actions that have system-level impact are examples of notes requiring user response. A note that informs the user that the battery is running low might not need user dismissal; instead, the note can be shown for a certain period of time or until the user dismisses it, whichever happens first. Despite their name, system modal notes are not generated only by the system; your application can generate these notes when it needs to force the user to respond to their contents and not take any other action before doing so.

Application modal notes, on the other hand, only prevent the user from performing actions within that application. The rest of the interface, including embedded applications in the same document, are available to the user while the note is pending.

There are two major differences between Option Sheets and notes. First, Option Sheets usually have multiple cards, each dedicated to managing a particular type of characteristic. Notes, on the other hand, are simple, single-message components. Second, Option Sheets feature a protocol that enables choices made in the Option Sheets to be applied to the selection.

You can use any kind of control in a note, including pop-up menus, choices, buttons, and fields.

The NOTE_METRICS structure includes several pieces of information. The three most important, other than the style flags, are

- the message the note returns or sends if and when it is dismissed
- the time before a note auto-dismisses
- the note's client

Note style flags contained in NOTE_STYLE describe the following characteristics of a note, among others:

- whether the note is a system modal note
- how to label the note (see following paragraph)
- how the note should be disposed of when it is dismissed

When a note is displayed (see Figure 10-9 for an example), it includes a label that tells the user its origin. You can tell the note to use the system name or the application's default document name in this label.

Figure 10-9 Sample Notes Showing Origin

Frames and Frame Decorations

As we indicated in Chapter 7, users often think document frames are windows. While its name may lead you to think of it as consisting of only the border of the window, the frame contains a number of child windows common to all windows by default. Your application can of course override this default behavior. Unless it does, however, the frame consists of the border that contains your client window, along with the following decoration windows:

- a close box (triangular corner at the left of the title bar that appears only in frames that do not occupy the entire display area)
- a title bar at the top
- a page number (unless your application is embedded inside another document, in which case it has no page number)
- a menu bar
- a tab bar to the right of the window

Figure 10-10 shows a frame with all of its constituent parts labeled. Frames receive messages only through their decorations, but they do not understand most messages that controls can send. It is therefore unwise to make the frame the client for your application's controls. Instead, make your application object the client. Frames can be selected, zoomed, closed, floated, and deleted.

Unless you need more than one frame in an application, you normally will not find it necessary to create a frame explicitly. The Application Framework (see Chapter 6) creates a frame for your application during initialization processing without additional effort on your part. The FRAME_METRICS structure contains fields for all of the UIDs of the child decoration windows it contains. FRAME_STYLE, on the other hand, is a compact structure containing a single bit for each such window indicating whether or not that window's frame is visible (recall that the user can control the visibility of window frames through the document's Options Sheet).

Frames file their state and all their windows in much the same way all other PenPoint windows are filed (see Chapter 7 for details).

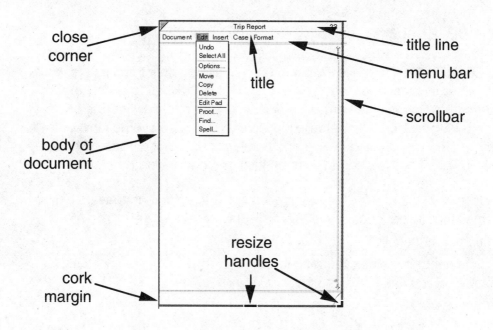

Figure 10-10 Typical Document Frame Components

Option Sheets

As we have seen in Chapter 2, the user interface in PenPoint relies heavily on the selection-oriented paradigm that involves the user selecting an object and then performing some action on that object. This approach lends itself well to the use of Option Sheets. Most objects in PenPoint have (or may have) Option Sheets associated with them. The user indicates with a gesture a desire to examine an object's Option Sheet. The user can then modify the appearance, location, behavior, and other information about the object by altering settings in the Option Sheet.

Option Sheets are a special type of frame, and clsOption is a subclass of clsFrame. Figure 10-11 shows a typical Option Sheet. You should notice several things about it.

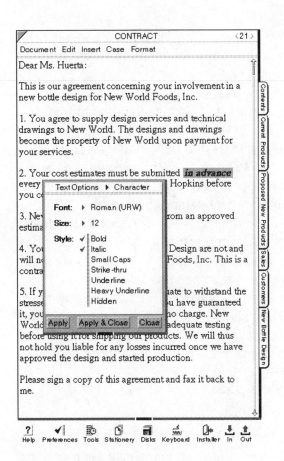

Figure 10-11 Typical Option Sheet

First, notice that this Option Sheet consists of more than one type of property the user can set. Each set of properties corresponds to a card and may be selected from the pop-up choice that appears in response to a user tap on the button next to the name of the current property type in the title bar. You could of course design and construct your own types of Option Sheets. But PenPoint's User Interface Style Guidelines encourage you to use clsOption, since that class already handles all layout necessary for your application's style to be consistent with the style of presentation of other PenPoint Option Sheets.

Second, an Option Sheet comes equipped with three buttons at the bottom: Apply, Apply & Close, and Close.

Finally, notice that any type of control can appear in an Option Sheet. Once the user makes a choice here, this floating window will disappear, and the choice will be listed in the option card.

Option Sheets can be left open while the user changes the selection to which they apply. This is a very powerful idea that permits the user to undertake a kind of property-copying process. For example, the user might select some text, open an Option Sheet, change the text to bold, and then scroll in the document to more text to be changed to bold. The Option Sheet need not be closed between such operations, as is often the case in other windowing systems that use a different type of paradigm for setting properties.

The OPTION_METRICS data structure contains, in addition to the style field in OPTION_STYLE, an optional pointer to descriptive information that overrides the default set of buttons contained in an Option Sheet. (If you do modify these buttons, the resulting user interface element is sometimes referred to as a Command Sheet rather than an Option Sheet.) OPTION_STYLE has two entries: one determines whether the Option Sheet should interact with the Selection, and the other gives the modality style of the sheet. A third data structure, OPTION_CARD, applies to each card in an Option Sheet. It contains

- a label to be used in the Option Sheet's pop-up choice
- the UID of the card's window
- a tag (which serves as a unique identifier for this card)
- the client of the card (that is, the object that processes messages regarding application of the Option Sheet's settings)

Icons

An icon (see Figure 10-12) is a square object that may act either as a button or as a menu button. Normally, an icon consists of a picture and some text drawn in a label, but icons can exist without a picture and/or without text. Icons are instances of clsIcon, which inherits from clsMenuButton.

Tools

Figure 10-12 Button Icon

You can specify whether the picture associated with an icon is a bitmap or a pixelmap. When you create an icon, however, you don't define its picture, only its type. The text label, if any, for the icon, is maintained by clsLabel, and you specify it in a label metric. The data structure ICON_METRICS specifies the style of the icon and its size. The style, contained in an ICON_STYLE structure, defines the type of background (transparent or opaque) and the type of picture, among other things.

If the picture is a bitmap, then you will probably store it as a resource and provide it to the application when clsIcon requests it from the icon's client. If it is a pixelmap, you can instruct clsIcon to create its pictures by copying the pixels of some window.

Toolkit Tables

As you have probably gathered by now, a Toolkit Table is a place where you can group other UI controls. Typically, such a table contains buttons or other descendants of clsButton. PenPoint creates all of the items in a table at once. The components of such a table can be from different classes and are even allowed to be tables themselves. This permits you to create many kinds of user interface elements.

In fact, PenPoint makes extensive use of Toolkit Tables. Menus, choices, option tables, tab bars, and command bars, for example, are all Toolkit Tables composed of collections of labels and buttons.

To create a Toolkit Table, you supply information that is common to all of the components, along with a pointer to an array structure containing data for each child. Common information stored in TK_TABLE_METRICS includes such descriptive detail as the table's client and manager as well as its style. Information describing each button or other component in the table is contained in an array of TK_TABLE_ENTRY structures. This information varies depending on the type of child involved. In the case of a button, for example, the first argument is the name of the button, the second is the message it sends when activated, and the third is optional data to accompany the message. These arrays also contain window tags, a set of flags that determine the style of the individual component (and which are dependent on the type of element involved), and an optional but recommended help ID for the object.

These structures can become somewhat complex since it is perfectly permissible to include within a Toolkit Table a control such as a choice that calls for a number of other arrays to describe its contents and behaviors.

There are several specialized types of Toolkit Tables, all of which are subclasses of clsTkTable. The two most important are toggle tables and choices. A toggle table has up to 32 independent toggle buttons, each of which may be turned on or off, and which act as a control panel. A choice is similar to a toggle table except that it is designed so that only one button can be on at a time.

Summary

This chapter has examined the User Interface Toolkit portion of the PenPoint development environment. This is the largest and most complex API in the SDK, encompassing more than a dozen classes and hundreds of messages.

As we saw, PenPoint includes the ability to lay out the user interface through layout windows almost automatically through behavior supplied in clsTableLayout and clsCustomLayout.

There are twelve types of controls in the UI Toolkit, each of which is represented by a class with related behaviors. These controls share some behaviors but have many unique capabilities as well.

11
The File System

....

The file system is a crucial component of PenPoint. Much of the functionality of the operating system is built around or depends upon it. A pen-based computer obviously must maintain data connectivity and compatibility with existing computers and networks. As a result, PenPoint's file system is designed for compatibility with existing file systems, particularly MS-DOS, and includes full support for reading and writing MS-DOS-formatted disks.

The PenPoint file system provides many of the standard features of traditional file systems, including hierarchical directories, as well as extended features such as 32-character file names; memory-mapped files; object-oriented application programming interfaces (APIs), and general, application-specific attributes for files and directories.

Throughout this book, you will notice the important role of the file system. For example, in Chapter 16, you can see how the whole process of remote file transfer is built integrally around the notion of a hierarchical system of directories and files. Similarly, automatic installation (see Chapter 6) and the interface to device drivers (see Chapter 15) are based on this file architecture.

A File System? On a RAM-Based Computer?

It might strike you as peculiar for a computer system based primarily in dynamic and static RAM to have a file system at all, much less one that closely resembles the MS-DOS and Macintosh file systems with which you may already be familiar. There are at least three good reasons for taking this approach: reliability, compatibility, and efficiency.

Since the file system area is administered by the operating system, PenPoint can guarantee that the file system will be highly robust against failures of all sorts. PenPoint does this by using hardware memory protection to guard the file system.

Existing desktop personal computers and servers are based on file systems, which makes the file the standard unit of transfer of information. By basing Notebook data storage on a file system, PenPoint is able to accept and generate files for exchange with existing computer systems and networks.

If PenPoint didn't use a file system "behind" the Notebook user interface, every application would be running all the time because there would be nothing else that could be done with them or their data. A 1,000-page Notebook would have 1,000 processes for 1,000 application instances. Since each process consumes 5–20 KB of memory, you can see how much memory PenPoint saves by supporting the ability of off-screen pages to file their data to the file system and shut down their processes.

Finally, because the Notebook's data is stored in a file system, disk-based notebooks are possible. Future versions of PenPoint will support Notebooks as the standard interface to hard disks, CD-ROMs, and file servers, for example.

PenPoint's file system is built around the notion of a volume. There are three types of volumes in PenPoint

- memory-resident
- local disks
- remote disks and servers

The memory-resident volume in a PenPoint system is named RAM. It is the only volume your application can be sure is always available, since the user cannot disconnect it.

(Note that on two-tier memory architectures, the RAM volume might actually reside on the second tier, possibly a hard disk. Think of the RAM volume as the always-present volume that is hidden from the user. It is always present on both one- and two-tier memory systems.)

Local disk volumes take advantage of PenPoint's chameleon-like nature as a file system. Because it defines no native disk format itself, the file system is designed to reside on a disk using that disk's normal volume organization. In its first release, PenPoint supports the MS-DOS disk format (with Macintosh HFS format under development as of this writing); other disk formats may be supported in the future and by other vendors building PenPoint-based systems.

Remote volumes are available over a network or a communications link. A computer that responds to a remote file access protocol is called a remote file server. This server can be any type of computer. See Chapter 16 for a more detailed discussion of this subject.

Why Multiple Volume Types?

New operating systems are usually designed to be worlds unto themselves. PenPoint, by contrast, was designed to be a highly mobile operating system with excellent connectivity capabilities. Rather than invent its own file system, PenPoint developed a file system that can interface with and provide rich access to other existing file systems. Multiple volume types are the heart of the PenPoint file system's ability to provide this access to data on other personal computers and networks.

All volumes have root directories. Generally speaking, PenPoint and applications built for this operating system take extensive advantage of the subdirectory tree structure of a hierarchical file system to position files in places where the operating system will be able to find and retrieve them.

To perform file system operations, you send messages to file or directory handles. Messages you send to file handles affect the file directly. Messages you send to directory handles usually include other information identifying the node the message is designed to affect.

You also use the file system to create data files for your application, to read and write data to and from those files, and to manipulate file and directory organization.

PenPoint itself uses the file system to store objects and application data.

Traditional File Activities Supported

PenPoint supports a number of file activities that it shares with traditional file systems. These functions include

- creating, opening, closing, and deleting files on any volume
- copying or renaming files or directories
- moving files and/or directories
- moving the read pointer to a new location with a seek operation
- modifying file and directory attributes

You can also use traditional C stdio library routines to access the PenPoint file system.

Unique File Activities Supported

As we have already seen, PenPoint adds the notion of a memory-mapped file to traditional file structures supported by pen-based computers using the PenPoint operating system. It also has a chameleon-like approach to its ability to coexist with other file systems and permits highly transparent user access to remote volumes. PenPoint supports several other unique file activities.

Every file and directory in the PenPoint system can have application-defined attributes. These attributes are completely free-form and subject to your program's management. There is no theoretical limit to how many attributes or what size attribute information can be associated with a given file or directory.

PenPoint handles the disconnection and reconnection of non-RAM volumes smoothly. The user can freely relocate the PenPoint-based computer from its base station (with a built-in floppy disk) to a network and even to more than one network during the course of a day or week. As we discuss in Chapter 16, activities that require access to volumes that are not connected at the time the user calls for them are simply stored until the volume is reconnected. At that point, the system, by observing what is happening in the environment, detects the presence of the required volume and, unless disabled by the user from doing so, simply carries out its assignment as if no time had elapsed. This notion of delayed execution is essential to the smooth and transparent use of a portable system like a PenPoint-based computer.

Another unique file system activity supported by PenPoint is automatic and dynamic file compression and decompression. To save valuable RAM space, all files in PenPoint, unless they are marked as exempt from the process, are automatically compressed when closed and decompressed when opened. You can determine not only whether your application's files will be compressed or not (we strongly recommend that you allow them to be), but what type of compression is to be used. Some types of compression work better with text files, others with graphic files. You can choose from several popular types of compression in PenPoint.

If all of this specialized behavior is not enough and your application needs some very specific file-related support, you can, of course, subclass the file system classes and extend their capabilities.

Installation

PenPoint's standard for application distribution is 3.5-inch, 1.44 MB MS-DOS disks. Every PenPoint-based machine has access to a floppy disk drive; it may be built in, attached via a base station, or through a desktop computer.

When you distribute your PenPoint application, the file hierarchy and contents it uses are important if you want PenPoint's installers to handle installation automatically for the user. If you follow the file structure depicted in Figure 11-1, you can be sure that when the user wants to install your application on a PenPoint-based system, the process will be as automatic as possible.

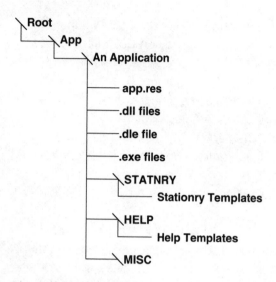

Figure 11-1 File Hierarchy for Application Installation

If you include a quick installer file on your distribution medium and the user inserts the disk containing your product into a disk drive connected to the PenPoint-based system, the operating system will not only detect the presence of the disk, but also determine that the user wants to install the application and handle all of the processing transparently and automatically.

The user also can choose to install an application starting from the Installer icon in the Bookshelf at the top level of the Notebook. In addition, users can simply drag objects around to install and deinstall applications and other installable objects, in which case PenPoint carries out at least basic verification of the correct placement and usage of these objects.

Application Framework's Default File System Usage

As we have intimated several times, the PenPoint Application Framework makes extensive use of the file system in several important ways. For instance, it uses the file system for installation, activation, and deactivation. See Chapter 6 for details of this usage.

Interaction with Other File Systems

The PenPoint file system is in many ways a superset of other systems. It is hierarchical, based on volumes and root directories, and ultimately contains documents. This nearly parallel architecture permits a high degree of interaction between PenPoint files and those of other systems to which a PenPoint-based system might be connected.

The superset information contained in a PenPoint file and not in other file systems includes the following items:

- longer file names than MS-DOS permits
- PenPoint-specific attributes
- application-defined attributes

When PenPoint stores its files in other systems, it can either keep this superset information or strip it.

If the process of storing a PenPoint file on another system retains PenPoint superset information, it stores this additional data in an extra file in each directory for which superset information exists in the PenPoint system. This approach is useful for storing PenPoint documents, sections, and notebooks on PCs and servers for later retrieval into and use by a PenPoint-based system.

If you store a PenPoint file on an external volume and retain its superset information, PenPoint will recognize this file and its extra encoding when the disk is mounted and the user opens a Disk Browser on it. It will show this extra information in the Browser in the form of a document.

When a PenPoint file is stored on a non-PenPoint medium without its superset information, that information is, of course, lost to that copy of the file forever. This approach is useful when you want to store a file or collection of files on a disk in native DOS or Macintosh HFS format, particularly if those files are intended to be subsequently manipulated from DOS or the Macintosh OS. These other operating systems would obviously not know what to do with the superset information.

Files and Compound Documents

One of the key ideas in PenPoint is that of the embedded application, which the user perceives as an embedded document.

PenPoint handles compound documents (that is, documents consisting of two or more documents composed in and managed by two or more applications) through the file system. It does so by storing embedded documents in subdirectories of their containing documents. This keeps the compound document together as a single directory in the file system, which makes it possible to move it and copy it without the user or programmer understanding the details of its contents.

See Chapter 8 for a complete discussion of this subject.

File Import and Export

The import and export of files is not strictly speaking a responsibility of the file system, but we discuss it here because of its obviously intimate involvement with the filing architecture.

If you have designed and built programs on traditional operating systems where you were required to support file import and export, you know how difficult this process can be. Generally, each application includes its own set of filters (routines that process data to convert it from one known format to another) to support the types of files with which it can exchange data. This requires a great deal of code, which is difficult to share because your own application's file format is at least potentially proprietary to it and certainly unknown to the rest of the system.

In traditional operating systems, the user who needs to import and export files to and from a system needs to understand the concept of file formats. For example, moving a document created in a word processing system to a different word processor, perhaps running in a different operating system, requires the user to know

- the file formats in which the creating word processor can store its files
- the file formats the target word processor can use as import formats
- what, if any, formatting and other information will be lost in the translation

PenPoint takes a different view of both files and users from this traditional approach. Files, for the most part, are transparent to users, who really see only documents (which are, from PenPoint's perspective, instances of applications). PenPoint does not require its users to understand deep-seated details of file structures and formats. As a result, PenPoint tries to achieve as much transparency as possible in this process.

The need for data connectivity and compatibility further influences the design of the import/export process.

PenPoint makes the file transfer process as transparent to the user and as efficient to the system as possible by two primary means

- It supports sharable filters for data so that each application need not create its own filters to move from its internal format to a standard or recognized external format.

- It uses a standard user interface for controlling these formats and their interactions.

File Import

Any file being imported into PenPoint must "belong" to an application when it is stored on the RAM volume. Files are not simply "there," as in traditional operating systems, existing on the disk but unowned. The connection between applications and files is essential.

As a result, the file import process is different in PenPoint from the way it works with other systems. When the user nominates a file for import by copying or moving a non-PenPoint file from a Disk Viewer window into the Notebook Table of Contents, PenPoint queries every application running on the system to determine whether it can handle the type of file being imported. It then presents a scrolling list of all candidate applications in a pop-up import dialog and asks the user to select the one with which the file is to be used.

Your application supports file import by knowing what kinds of files it can import and by responding to two messages defined in clsImport. When the user initiates an import, your application is sent msgImportQuery to determine if it can import the file involved. Your application simply checks the file import type, which is passed as a parameter to msgImportQuery, against its list of known file types and responds with True or False. If the user then chooses your application to be the target for the file import, your application is sent msgImport to start the import process. Your application creates a new document and then sends msgImport to that document, which in turn becomes responsible for reading and translating the data in the original file.

File Export

File export is of necessity less transparent to the user than file import. Since PenPoint cannot know about the file formats used in non-PenPoint files and systems, the user must supply information about the file format before the export can take place. Still, PenPoint makes the process somewhat more automatic than it is with traditional file systems.

When the user selects Export from the Document menu of a PenPoint document or selects the document in a Browser and chooses the Export option, PenPoint queries the document to determine the types of formats it can write. It then creates a scrolling list of these file formats and places this list in a pop-up export dialog. The user chooses the file format and a destination file and then initiates the transfer process. From that point, PenPoint handles the file export automatically.

To support file export, your application must know the file formats it can write and must respond to three messages defined in clsExport: msgExportGetFormats, msgExport, and msgExportName.

When your application receives msgExportGetFormats, it responds by providing a list of the formats it can write, along with some control information that is used by the translator when the export process is underway.

For each format you support, you will either use an existing translator object or define your own. In either case, part of that translator's definition is the ability to propose a file name for the exported file. When the user selects an export type from the Disk Browser, PenPoint sends msgExportName to the designated translator, which gives back the proposed name. The Disk Browser then displays this name. The user may, of course, either accept or change it.

Once the user chooses a format and instructs the system to start the file export, your application will receive the msgExport message. This message is accompanied by information about the source file, destination file, and translator to use.

Summary

This chapter has examined the file system in PenPoint. As we have seen, it is built on the long-established concepts of hierarchical file systems, but includes such extended features as

- 32-character file names
- memory-mapped files
- object-oriented APIs
- file attributes

The PenPoint file system supports multiple types of volumes to give users maximum flexibility in connecting to and using networks and external storage devices. In addition, we saw the roles played by the file system in installation and in the Application Framework.

File import and export are an integral part of PenPoint, freeing application developers from concern with the operational details of these frequently needed functions.

12

Resources and Their Management

Programs include various types of non-code data such as text strings for menus, prompts, and error messages, and images for icons. Traditional operating systems typically leave application developers to their own devices as to how to store and access this non-code data. Most often, it is compiled into the program code itself as static data declarations. However, this means that it is difficult to change the non-code data, and this is problematic. Foreign-language translations must be performed directly on the program source code, leading to errors and version control problems.

The Macintosh operating system took a step forward by introducing the concept of resources, which are a repository for all non-code data that a program or an application instance needs. PenPoint builds on this Macintosh innovation and has generalized it so that it is useful for a variety of tasks. The result is PenPoint's Resource Manager.

PenPoint resources are special files that contain resources and nothing else. The Resource Manager is used to create, find, access, and modify these resource files. Other parts of PenPoint, such as the Application Framework, count on and exploit the capabilities of the Resource Manager.

Types of Resources

There are two types of resources in PenPoint: objects and data. Any file can mix both types of resources, although different messages are used to read and write the two types of resources.

An object resource contains information needed to create or restore a PenPoint object. The object's class (and its ancestor classes) must be able to unite and read the object's instance data to and from a resource file. This capability is so important that it is defined in clsObject itself in the form of msgSave and msgRestore. Every class you create is responsible for reading and writing its object instance data in response to these Class Manager messages. The Application Framework maintains one instance data resource file for each application instance, or document.

All resources have a unique 64-bit resource ID that your application uses to locate the resource.

While the information saved in conjunction with objects can be quite varied in type and format, data resources contain information saved as a stream of bytes. Data resources are often used for such things as default Option Sheet settings, default prompt strings, and so forth. Using data resources for these objects leads to greater transportability and internationalization of your programs.

All resources are read and written through resource agents. Such agents, designed to deal with specific objects and data structures, help you manage resources by unpacking and interpreting the formats of the data they read from the resource file. PenPoint includes several such agents, including a default resource agent which simply treats a data resource as a stream of bytes where sequence and position have no particular meaning. There are also default resource agents to handle null-terminated strings singly and in arrays.

When Are Resources Created?

Resources can be created either at application program compile-time, or at runtime. You can think of compile-time as being appropriate for relatively static resources, and runtime for more dynamic resources.

Static resources change infrequently and can be completely specified ahead of time by the programmer. They tend to be part of an application, not of a document (although documents can override application resources; see the following section on locating resources). Static resources are used to define the non-code parts of an application such as user interface elements (option cards, menus), text strings, and icons. As previously mentioned, these are often stored as data resources, not as PenPoint objects in a resource file. Static resources are identified with predefined resource IDs that are declared by the programmer at compile time. Application resources reside in a file called App.Res.

Resources that cannot be specified ahead of time are inherently dynamic and therefore can be created only at runtime. They can be stored in resource files created for this purpose through the Resource Manager. Dynamic resources are identified with resource IDs allocated at runtime. The Application Framework provides a default file for dynamically created resources called DocState.Res. This is the default resource file for all objects belonging to a particular document (application instance).

Locating Resources

The Resource Manager insulates your application not only from having to know the precise location of a resource within a given file, but from knowing precisely the file in which the resource is located. The Resource Manager does this through Resource File Lists.

Resource File Lists are instances of clsResList. Entries in this list can be resource file handles or other Resource File Lists. When you send a read or a find message to such a list object, it sends the message to each object in the list until the message returns a value indicating the instruction has been carried out.

Every document class in PenPoint has a default Resource File List with three elements (see Figure 12-1). These elements are

- the PenPoint system resource file (PenPoint.Res)
- the application resource file (common to all application instances) (App.Res)
- the document resource file (unique to one instance of this application) (Doc.Res)

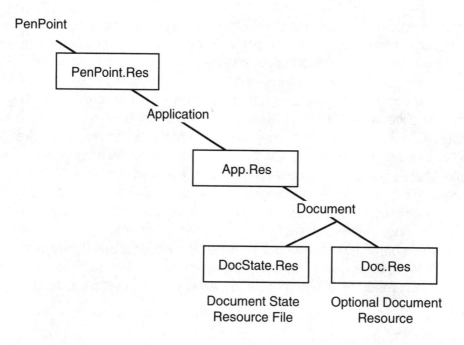

PenPoint

PenPoint.Res

Application

App.Res

Document

DocState.Res

Doc.Res

Document State
Resource File

Optional Document
Resource

Figure 12-1 Resource File Hierarchy

Since the Resource Manager automatically searches a Resource File List until it finds a resource or runs out of places to look, you can see that every PenPoint document's resources can come from one of at least three locations: the document, the application that implements that document, or the system.

This flexibility is invaluable in providing efficient sharing and overriding of resources. For example, applications can use some system resources unchanged (such as standard fonts, Option Sheets, or error messages) without the need to provide these resources in their application resource file. An application might override other system resources or create new applicationwide resources and place these in the application resource file. Finally, applications could allow a user to attach specific versions of resources to individual documents.

Figure 12-1 shows two resource files for a document. Since a document instance is represented as a directory in the file system, you could actually create more than two resource files for each document, if that was useful for your application. The two resource files DocState.Res and Doc.Res are PenPoint's default behavior, which is adequate for most applications.

As mentioned in the previous section, DocState.Res is the resource file that contains the document's runtime state — that is, objects belonging to that application instance. It is therefore a resource file that stores objects (not data), and that is created dynamically.

Doc.Res is an optional resource file. It is created by PenPoint only if the document overrides an application resource with a local, or tailored version. For instance, if an application provides the user with the option of customizing application menus on a document basis, the customized version of an application menu would be stored in Doc.Res, which PenPoint would automatically create the first time there was a need to store a document-specific copy of an application resource.

To find a resource and its agent, you send a message either to a resource file handle or to a resource file list. In both cases, the message returns a handle to the file and the location in the file of the resource for which you are searching unless, of course, it cannot find the resource. In that case, it returns a special status code.

When you need to process all available resources of a particular class (such as all font resources), you can use a special message that enumerates over all of the resources in a resource file or resource file list and returns two parallel arrays containing the file in which the resource was found and the resource ID of the located resource.

Resource File Formats

As we pointed out earlier, many resources can exist in a single file. The Resource Manager makes it relatively easy to locate a particular resource and then to read it, because the layout of the resource file is highly flexible, yet known to the system.

Many resources can coexist in a single file, all laid out as one long stream. In fact, they are implemented as a stream; I/O in such files is handled by clsStream. PenPoint keeps track of where each resource begins and what its size is and automatically prevents accidental overwrites of data while keeping the data elements next to each other in a file.

If you store all of your instance data in objects that respond to the standard clsObject messages msgSave and msgRestore from the Application Framework, then loading and saving files are handled automatically. You need not even be aware of the file system or how it handles this type of file management.

Figure 12-2 shows how a file containing objects and instance data could be structured in a typical layout.

UUID	length	object	UUID	length	object	. . .	UUID	length	object

Figure 12-2 Typical Resource File Layout

The Resource Manager also permits non-linear retrieval of resources. As indicated earlier, when you ask PenPoint to find a particular resource, it returns the file name and the location of that resource in the file. You can then use this information to retrieve the resource.

Managing Resources

Aside from reading and writing, there are two other resource-related tasks with which your application may have to deal: creating resources and compacting resource files.

Creating Resources

As we have seen, application instance data may be written as a resource file. The actual updating of the file occurs when the application instance receives msgAppSave. This behavior is included automatically with all applications as a result of the Application Framework and its default behaviors (see Chapter 6).

Some resources, however, are essentially static and don't need to be written out each time the application terminates. For example, user interface component resources seldom if ever change between runs of the program. For these resource types, you typically build resource files at compile time on your development PC using the resource compiler in the Software Developers Kit (SDK). This compiler creates a standard C Source file which you then compile and link. When the resulting MS-DOS program executes, it writes a complete resource file containing all the static resources you defined in the source code.

Compacting Files

Resources may be deleted during program execution. When they are deleted, they leave "holes" in the resource file. PenPoint provides a semiautomatic compaction facility to remove this unused space, which is important because such fragmentation can lead to reduced performance and wasted storage space.

You can explicitly compact a resource file, but it is more likely that you will simply design the file in such a way that it is automatically compacted. You can do this by specifying when you create a resource file handle that it is to be compacted on file closure. This compaction can be unconditional or it can be based on an assessment that reveals that the file is becoming fragmented. The latter approach uses a combination of determining the number of resources and the ratio of deleted resources to the file total. You specify the ratio beyond which you want the file to be compacted. This is probably the most-efficient use of the resource management system's automatic compaction process.

Application Instance Data

The PenPoint file system, discussed in Chapter 11, is the most obvious way for you to store application data. But it may not always be the most efficient or effective way to store and manage information. Resources afford you a higher-level interface that you may want to use rather than the more traditional, low-level access available through the file system.

If you store data in raw files, not only must you keep track of where the file is stored so that you can open it on demand, you must also invent the file format. If your data is at all repetitive or large, you must design compact file formats.

PenPoint's built-in compression (discussed in Chapter 11) relieves you of the undue effort required to minimize the size of your filed data. Furthermore, you have the programming responsibility of knowing precisely where in the file each piece of information is stored. If a new piece of data is to replace an existing one, you must take care that the new data doesn't grow beyond the size allocated to the data it is replacing and thereby corrupt the file. In a traditional operating system, this requires yet another layer of management from your code.

These and a host of other details mean that you may spend as much time coding the portion of your application that deals with the relatively mundane issue of file storage as you do on the functional parts of the program.

Resources solve these problems. As we've seen, all application objects automatically receive a msgSave when the application receives a msgAppSave. The result is automatic filing behavior for your application. If your application keeps all of its dynamic data as objects, think first of resources when you need file storage; resort to the file system only when resources are inappropriate for a specific reason.

Summary

This chapter has examined resources in PenPoint. Resources can include such things as menus, dialog boxes, application code, and other objects. They are stored in special files managed by the Resource Manager.

We have examined the creation, storage, location, and use of resources, as well as the typical file format for these special elements of PenPoint applications.

13

Input and Handwriting Recognition

Clearly, if you had to name one thing that sets PenPoint apart from earlier operating systems, your attention would tend to focus on the pen. Where other operating systems obtain their input — both in terms of data and in terms of command and control — from users via keyboards and mice, PenPoint is designed to work most smoothly with a pen. It will, as we have seen, support a keyboard for text entry, but its primary interaction takes place through the pen.

Designing an operating system to work primarily with a pen poses some interesting issues and imposes some unique requirements.

The most interesting and challenging of these issues relates to the observation that a pen is a two-way communications channel, unlike keyboards and mice, which are one-way devices. With a traditional input system, the device sends events to its operating system, which then deals with them. But with a pen-based system, ink patterns must be "recognized." A two-way channel is required. Whenever possible, the user interface provides context to guide the operating system's gesture and handwriting recognition algorithms. As you will see later in the chapter, applications do not literally pass text or numbers into the input subsystem. Rather, the input operations (called "scribbles") are given to the application's user interface code, which is in full control of whether and how to translate the scribble, including the context for the translation.

In PenPoint, the location of a gesture controls its intended meaning. This is made possible by the input subsystem's support for user interfaces to control the recognition process.

For example, a circular motion with the pen can mean any of the following, depending on its context (see Figure 13-1):

The Power of PenPoint

- the letter "O"
- a command to edit selected text
- a circle graphical shape

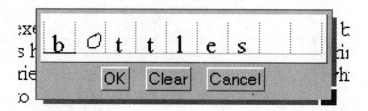

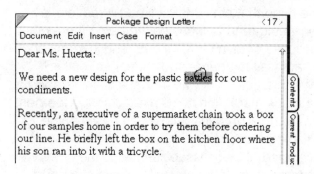

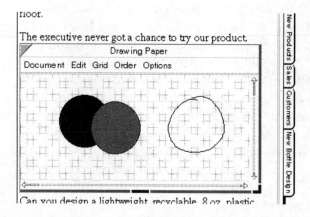

Figure 13-1 Three Interpretations of a Circular Motion

The operating system's interpretation of a circular motion, then, is context-dependent. There is therefore a two-way communication between the pen's actions and the operating system's reactions. An operation is triggered by a pen action, processed by the operating system based on the window in which the pen first touched down, and the resulting scribble is passed to the user interface owning the window for it to control translation. The application controls translation by passing the scribble and control parameters (context) back down into the handwriting recognition (HWX) portion of the input subsystem. Finally, the input subsystem passes recognition results back up to the user interface, where the user sees the results of the operation.

Another challenge involved in designing an operating system for pen-based input and control is that the pen must be able to dribble ink anywhere over the screen, but the system must support rapid cleanup and interpretation of the pen motions. It would not do to have the ink "spilled" all over the screen for a prolonged period while the operating system figures out what the user meant or laboriously repaints the screen to erase the ink.

We'll see later in the chapter how PenPoint responds to these and other challenges. For the moment, it's safe to say that the old computer adage "Easy to use is easy to say" was never more accurately said than it is in relation to pen-based operating systems.

Overview of Input

Input processing in PenPoint is the user's most visible contact with the operating system. This is because everything the user can do in PenPoint can be done with the pen. Compare this with traditional desktop operating systems, which use both keyboard and mouse but have a requirement that everything must be accessible to the user via the keyboard so that a mouseless environment can be supported. PenPoint relegates the keyboard to a secondary role; everything must be attainable via the pen, but the keyboard is an optional accessory.

Your applications can, of course, make more-extensive use of the keyboard. PenPoint provides full support for the user of physical keyboards for high-speed data entry. It can also use other device drivers to provide another kind of interaction where appropriate. But, ultimately, users will see PenPoint-based systems as pen-based systems. As a prelude to discussing the details of how input is processed in PenPoint, let's take a look at how input looks to the user and what advantages it provides.

What the User Sees

Users touch the pen to the screen and things happen. In fact, some things happen without the user touching the screen, when the pen is in close proximity to the surface of the display.

Direct input of data (via handwriting recognition and direct drawing), commands (through the interpretation of gestures), and control (such as the direct manipulation of objects on the screen) are all handled through the pen interface. The user sees the pen as the sole or primary means of interacting with the system.

In a portable computer, this has some powerful implications for the user's perception of computing. For example, it is unlikely that a portable computer could be built that would incorporate a full-page-size screen and a usable keyboard. It would simply be too unwieldy.

Another thing users come to recognize about pen-based computing is that the interface is not as nearly like a mouse interface as first impressions might indicate. Besides being more direct (and therefore much easier for many people who have trouble connecting mouse movements in a horizontal plane with cursor motion in a vertical plane), it involves different kinds of physical actions. Because the pen is controllable with a great deal of hand-eye coordination, accurate and direct manipulation, drawing, and gesturing are all the norm with the pen. These same operations tend to be imprecise and difficult with the mouse.

Terminology

In fact, it is not only the names of pen-related user actions that change in the transition from traditional operating systems to pen-based computing. There are a number of other terms, some of which users come to know and others of which are important for you as a designer to understand.

A "stroke" in PenPoint terms has two meanings. It is both a pen action that leads to the appearance of ink on the display and a data structure that holds information about that action. Collections of related strokes (where the meaning of the term "related" is application-dependent to a significant degree) are called scribbles. Like strokes, scribbles are data structures that can be stored and manipulated efficiently.

Scribbles that have some meaning in a particular context may be gestures, characters, or shapes. As we indicated previously, the interpretation of scribbles is the province of your application, consistent with PenPoint User Interface Style Guide recommendations.

When users move the pen across the display of a PenPoint-based system, they see what seems to be ink appearing on the screen. This process, as we have pointed out earlier, is called dribbling ink.

Finally, by "input focus" PenPoint refers to the question of where input from the keyboard will be directed. From PenPoint's perspective, there is always only one selection in the entire system. That selection becomes the input focus from the user's perspective; keyboard strokes are always sent to the current selection. Do not let this distract you from the fact that gesture commands typically target (in other words, go to) the data directly beneath where they are made.

Key Problems and Their PenPoint Solutions

As we mentioned at the beginning of the chapter, designing an operating system specifically optimized for pen-based computing poses some challenges. Three of the most intriguing from your perspective are

- eliminating flicker and slow response in dealing with pen input
- dealing with the issue of ink dribbles and the windows in the user interface
- providing for flexibility of handwriting recognition technologies

Pens are marking instruments; users expect them to flow ink. When the user is moving the pen across the surface of the display, the common result is to "echo" this "ink" that traces the pen's path, regardless of how varied or widespread the path becomes. As soon as the pen leaves the screen, however, the ink must be handed to the user interface and erased from the screen. If the echoed ink was displayed in the "real" (or normal) screen, considerable flicker would result from all the repainting.

To address this problem, PenPoint includes an acetate layer, a transparent overlay atop the display where ink is dribbled and strokes are collected into scribbles. The operating system can essentially ignore the intermediate movements of the pen between the time a scribble is started and the time it ends, then collect the data points and other information into a scribble data structure. All of the ink in the acetate layer can be quickly and easily erased because the system need not analyze the impact of such erasure or deal with the need to refresh the underlying display as it would if the ink were drawn directly on the user interface layer of the screen. Figure 13-2 depicts this design.

A related problem involves confining ink drawing to the window in which it originates. While a windowing system normally must contain or clip all display activities within a window's boundaries, ink display must be allowed to flow temporarily wherever the pen moves. If the operating system did not allow ink to echo outside the owning window, the user would find it difficult to draw gestures that overlap window boundaries or to handwrite a bit larger than the size of an input field.

PenPoint processes the pen scribbles to the owning window as a separate step to get around this problem. This is related to the fact that there is an acetate layer in which the ink dribbles can be displayed as the appropriate internal stroke and scribble data objects are generated from sampling points. There is no need for the system to worry about strokes that are drawn outside the boundaries of a given window; the system just lets the user draw such strokes, echoes them temporarily in the acetate plane so the user can see the ink, and then the system hands the scribble data to the application when the acetate layer is erased.

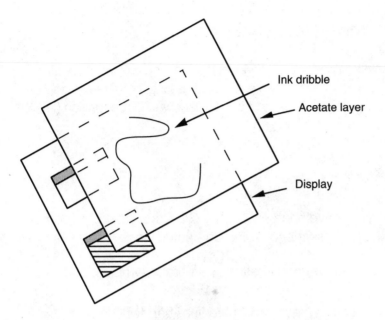

Ink dribble

Acetate layer

Display

Figure 13-2 The Acetate Layer in PenPoint

Finally, PenPoint must recognize two realities about handwriting recognition. First, the technology to support this aspect of pen-based computing is in a continual state of evolution. Better printing recognition and, ultimately, cursive handwriting recognition will undoubtedly emerge. Second, non-Roman (or script) alphabets, such as Cyrillic and Kanji, require entirely different recognition techniques from those required by Roman letters as used in English and, with minor modifications, in all Romance languages. If PenPoint were to lock in its handwriting recognition system, it would run the twin risks of obsolescence and reduced usability internationally.

To solve this problem, PenPoint's handwriting recognition subsystem is completely replaceable. This enables not only GO Corporation but hardware vendors incorporating PenPoint into their computers and third-party developers focused on specific markets to swap new translation subsystems into PenPoint as the need and opportunity arise.

Handwriting Translation in PenPoint

PenPoint's input subsystem generates low-level input event messages for all pen activity on the screen. These low-level events are grouped into higher-level aggregates (scribbles), which in turn are translated by the handwriting recognition (HWX) subsystem into either text characters or command gestures.

Characteristics of the HWX Engine

The current HWX engine, developed entirely by GO Corporation, recognizes hand-printed characters and has the following characteristics:

- handles mixed upper- and lowercase letters, numerals, symbols, and punctuation
- handles both "boxed" (segmented) and "ruled line" handwriting (at the user's option)
- operates in real time (three characters per second) on a 16-MHz 80286-based system
- occupies less than 100 KB of memory (plus another 100 KB for a general-purpose spelling dictionary)
- achieves 80 to 90 percent word-level accuracy, which is equivalent to 90 to 97 percent character-level accuracy
- runs in background mode
- accommodates multiple users with or without each user training the system to recognize his or her handwriting
- allows non-unique character forms (for example, the letter "O" and the number zero)
- tolerates inconsistency by the same user (that is, the user shaping the same character in different ways at different times)
- can accept optional context-sensitive translation aids (such as word lists, dictionaries, and character templates) provided by the application
- has memory requirements of 64 KB for code, less than 128 KB for static data

How Handwriting Recognition Works

The handwriting recognition system is based on a blackboard model from the world of artificial intelligence. Data from multiple knowledge sources is combined and sorted using a dynamic programming algorithm. These knowledge sources include predefined information (for example, specific word lists for a specific input field). One of these knowledge sources is the character-shape recognizer built into PenPoint.

Strokes are examined as they are received by the recognition engine. Character recognition is performed by comparing character shapes with a set of character "prototypes" for each character. PenPoint comes with a preinstalled set of hundreds of such prototypes that work well for many writers. Users can train PenPoint's prototypes through brief handwriting training sessions in which PenPoint builds additional prototypes for each user's unique style of shaping characters.

The Pen and Data Entry

PenPoint's handwriting recognition is powerful enough to open up major new markets for both skilled and inexperienced typists. The first version of PenPoint provides excellent recognition of neatly printed random English-language text containing mixed upper- and lowercase letters, numerals, symbols, and punctuation. After a small amount of training, users typically experience recognition accuracy rates of four out of five words translating completely correctly and the fifth word having an easily correctable error. For many people, this results in data entry rates faster than they can type.

Clearly, then, under PenPoint, the pen is a respectable data entry device. With time it will only get better. Because PenPoint provides standard programming interfaces to all PenPoint applications and insulates them from the specifics of any particular handwriting recognition algorithm, PenPoint's algorithms can be continually improved without disturbing the growing base of applications.

Although PenPoint is designed primarily for pen-based input, an optional physical keyboard may also be attached for high-volume data entry. In addition, a pop-up "virtual keyboard" can be displayed on the screen and used for text input by tapping with the pen.

How Input Is Processed

While the actual detailed flow of the input subsystem's handling provides for sophisticated filtering and routing (all explained later in this section), it is helpful to take a step back and examine the simple steps involved in the normal case of the user touching the pen down on an application. When that happens, the following occurs:

1. The input subsystem sends a "pen down" message to the application.
2. The input subsystem looks at the application's window data structures to determine its appropriate responses (for example, whether to echo ink or not). Applications will have set up these data structures when creating their windows.
3. Once the user has finished drawing this event (determined by a combination of time and distance thresholds), the input subsystem hands the resulting scribble to the application.
4. The application determines what to do with the scribble (for example, store it as pure ink or translate it).
5. To translate the scribble, the application packages it with control parameters that describe a context for the scribble, and then sends a translate message to a handwriting or gesture translator object.
6. The translator object returns a ranked list of translations to the application, which then determines what to display to the user.

The Processing Pipeline

You can think of input processing in PenPoint as taking place through a pipeline. Figure 13-3 depicts this pipeline, which is discussed in detail in the remainder of this section. The portion of the pipeline to the left of the dashed line corresponds closely to the input processing in traditional operating systems, while the rest of the diagram focuses on concepts and actions that are new to PenPoint. For the most part, applications hook into and use the activities in the left portion of the diagram while they either reimplement, modify, or use unmodified the functions in the right portion of the diagram.

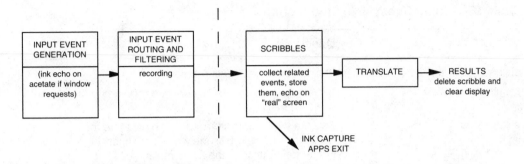

Figure 13-3 The Input Processing Pipeline

Events

Input events can be created in three ways in PenPoint

- by software synthesis (that is, by using a message designed to simulate the event), a process that can be used to replay pen or key strokes in demonstrations, macro playbacks, and tutorials, for example
- by device drivers such as keyboards and other input devices
- by the pen under control of the user

The input subsystem maintains an event queue. Each event is placed into this queue. The type of information stored depends on the type of event. You can think of events as being divided broadly into two groups: XY events (those which take place in the borders of the screen and have a coordinate associated with them) and non-XY events (such as keyboard events, which do not relate to a specific point on the display). All events post at least their associated message name. Optional information includes the coordinate, a specific listener object, and/or other event-specific data.

When an event is processed by the input subsystem, a return status code determines what step takes place next. Table 13-1 summarizes and explains these codes.

Table 13-1 Input Subsystem Status Codes

Status Code	Description
stsInputTerminate	Stops processing the current event
stsInputContinue	Allows input subsystem to continue processing the current event normally
stsInputGrab	Sets the input subsystem's grab object to be the one to which the original message was sent, effectively terminating further distribution of the event message
stsInputGrabTerminate	Terminates the current event, then sets the input subsystem's grab object
stsInputGrabContinue	Sets a new grab object and permits processing of the current event to continue

In response to a pen input event, ink is dribbled on the acetate layer. As we have seen, these dribbles are seen as individual strokes, which are ultimately collected into scribbles. As you can see in Figure 13-3, it is these scribbles that are ultimately processed by your application.

Because of the spatial nature of window-based input, PenPoint incorporates a sophisticated distribution mechanism for event processing. It uses a leaf-to-root (child-to-parent) model of XY distribution so that when an event occurs in a window, the parent chain is followed back to the root window. Each window in the chain can either process the event or not. It then has the choice of passing the event to the next window or terminating the event.

Among other advantages of this model, it permits a "penetration" mode, whereby a pen event on the screen appears to penetrate through a child window and is processed by a parent window as if it had occurred at the same position in the parent window, conceptually behind the child window.

Each window can turn on and off its interest in each type of pen event. There are messages to handle these status changes, so a window's behavior with respect to any given pen event can be changed depending on the context.

Although it is possible in PenPoint for you to intercept and handle low-level pen events directly, this is not a recommended practice. In a cooperative multitasking environment such as PenPoint, this could be an unfriendly way for your application to behave. Instead, PenPoint provides several ways in which you can cooperatively process and pass on input events.

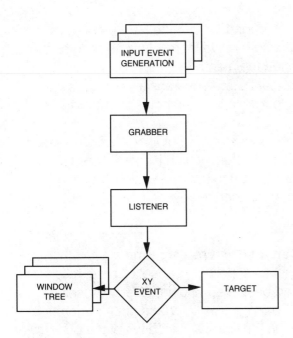

Figure 13-4 Input Registry

Filters, Grabbers, and Listeners

At the second stage of processing shown in Figure 13-3, the pen event is passed to the Input Registry, where all known objects that have expressed interest in receiving input messages are identified. Figure 13-4 shows this portion of input event processing schematically.

An input event is routed through the Input Registry starting with any filters that might exist in the application or system. Filters carry priority ratings from 0 to 255 so that they can avoid conflicts with each other. Normally, filters deal with low-level events. Sometimes, they remap the event by modifying the data structure accompanying the message that sends the event into the Input Registry. You might use a filter, for example, to remap a keyboard event to emulate a 3270 display terminal.

Grabbers are the next level of Input Registry entry. These objects handle all subsequent input messages until they release control. Modal Notes and menus (see Chapter 10) are examples of grabbers in the PenPoint environment; by grabbing pen input, menus can remove themselves as soon as the user touches the pen anywhere outside the menu.

Refer again to Figure 13-3. Notice that before any translation occurs, processing stops if the application's only purpose at this point is to capture ink and not translate or interpret it.

As you can see in Figure 13-4, if an input event is not filtered or grabbed, it goes to the window hierarchy if it is an XY event (which is most of the time). Non-window (that is, non-XY) events are sent to a target (which is defined as the point where the input focus is located when the event is processed).

The Unique Problem of Gesture Targeting

While the mouse is inherently a pixel-level pointing device, GO user research has determined that the pen is often best used to point to larger, user-significant objects. Therefore, the PenPoint user interface often performs a certain amount of "targeting" logic on the literal X-Y location of the pen-down event. For instance, in PenPoint's text editor, most commands act on words, not characters. (The user "explodes" a word into a pop-up edit pad to edit individual characters.) The result is a more powerful user interface in which the user can draw gestures very quickly and know that they will affect just the data the user intended.

The application is responsible for whether to handle gesture targeting and the actual mapping of the XY coordinates into user-significant objects.

Translation

There are four types or classes of translation in PenPoint

- text
- numbers
- gestures
- word

You can even call for repeated translations. For example, the Drawing Paper application created by GO Corporation as a demonstration of PenPoint looks at scribbles passed to it to determine if there are more than four strokes. If so, it requests word translation. If the number of strokes is four or fewer, it requests gesture translation first, and then looks at the same scribble through a geometry translation. If it doesn't match at either of these translations, it simply displays a polyline. Note that it is important here that you pay attention to the order in which you ask for repeated translations because you may want a match at any one level to preclude the processing of the others.

Summary

This chapter has examined the input and handwriting recognition systems in PenPoint. The context dependence of pen motions has led to the need for a two-way communication process between pen actions and the operating system. This contrasts with the one-way linkage between older input devices (keyboards and pointing devices) and their operating systems.

We have seen how PenPoint deals with user input via the pen to avoid such problems as excessive flicker, the need for windows to be able to maintain their own contents, and the need for flexibility in handwriting recognition. The acetate layer is the key to PenPoint's solution to these problems.

The handwriting recognition (HWX) subsystem translates scribbles, groups of related pen actions gathered into data structures. We saw how handwriting recognition works with strokes and scribbles that are compared against prototype characters.

14

Text Editing and
Related Classes

. . . .

The text component of PenPoint displays editable text. It is a fairly powerful formatted-text editor available to all PenPoint application developers for inclusion in their applications because the text classes are bundled with PenPoint. It is also available to PenPoint users because PenPoint includes MiniText, a small application that delivers the text editor subsystem's functionality. Its classes allow

- display and storage of plain and formatted text
- user editing of characters and their attributes
- user-directed transfer of all or part of text to and from other objects
- filing of text data objects
- application monitoring of user interaction with text data objects
- embedded objects

This subsystem has another virtue for PenPoint programmers: It serves as a good example of why and how to implement the view/data observer model (see Chapter 8).

> ### The Value of a Text-Editing Component
>
> Designing and implementing pen-based text editing is a challenge. It involves a host of problems and concepts that don't confront the designer of a text editor in a more traditional environment. For example, just the issue of targeting pen gestures (that is, where do they really start and end, and what are they designed to do in the appropriate context?) requires significant thought and experimentation. With the built-in text-editing component in PenPoint, application developers are freed from the significant effort building such a text editor requires; they simply use the text component as provided by PenPoint, modifying by subclassing where they need slightly different behavior.
>
> You would probably not use the PenPoint text component to create a full-featured word processor. But you should consider using it in almost all other applications, such as in a comments field in a form where its word-wrap and direct editing capabilities would be attractive features.

Editable text, of course, differs from text displayed in the graphics subsystem (see Chapter 9). That text cannot be modified by the user because it is completely under control of the program making the display calls to the graphics subsystem (unless, of course, that program implements the text editing).

Basic Approach to Programming

All instances of the text component consist of paired instances of text data objects and text views.

A text data object is a block of text from zero to approximately 65,000 characters in the Developer's Release. The Commercial Release supports much larger text blocks. Like all PenPoint objects, text data objects are identified by UIDs so that they can be unambiguously referenced in any context. Views display text data objects and permit the user to modify them. In other words, text data objects handle the storage of the characters and attributes they contain, while text views provide a user interface that permits the user to modify the characters and attributes.

To create a new text view with an empty text data object, you send msgNewDefaults and msgNew to clsTextView without any initialized object. This is the normal way of starting an editing session with a blank editing area. (Actually, you could create an empty text object by sending those messages to clsText but you wouldn't be able to see the object because it would not have a view.)

If, however, you want to create a text component instance with existing text (for example, text selected by the user with the pen), then you send the same messages to clsTextView, this time accompanying the messages with an identifier of the text data object to be edited. PenPoint then creates the editing context with the indicated text available for immediate direct editing.

Text Data Objects

You create text data objects by creating instances of clsText. You are then responsible for making these objects visible by creating text views on them.

A text data object has default attributes for the formatting of characters, paragraphs, and entire documents. There are two types of attributes for text data objects: default attributes and local attributes. Local attributes apply to contiguous ranges of characters or paragraphs within the document, while default attributes apply to whatever ranges of characters or paragraphs don't have local attributes. Therefore, a text data object has only one set of default attributes but may have a theoretically unlimited number of local attributes within the limits of the size of the data object and the number of characters and paragraphs it contains.

When you create a new text data object, PenPoint uses the system resource file to determine the current default attributes unless your application redefines this default resource in its own resource file (see Chapter 12).

Character attributes include display and font attributes. The former include such display characteristics as underlining, small capital letters, and size. The latter define a character's typeface and weight. Paragraph attributes include alignment, leading, space before and after, margins, and tab settings.

Text Views

A text view is a special case of an embedded window. In fact, clsTextView inherits from clsView, which in turn descends from clsEmbeddedWin. Text views behave quite differently from other views defined as instances or subclasses of clsView; as a result, clsTextView overrides much of the behavior of clsView.

When you create a text view, it displays the initial portion of the data (as much as will fit in the view) beginning at the first character of the text data object. If the text data object contains more characters than can be displayed in the view, then you are responsible for placing the text and its view into a scrolling window so that it will have scrollbars. The text component defines a special function to allow you to create such a view.

Like all views, text views support the saving of their contents. When a text view receives a msgSave message from the Application Framework, it sends filing messages to its text data object. Your application must implement behavior to save the data in a plain text file (see Chapter 11) or in a resource file (see Chapter 12). This may require little or no work depending on your specific needs; the default filing behavior in PenPoint is often adequate.

Text Insertion Pads

By default, when you create a text view, PenPoint creates an insertion pad so that the user can enter new text into the view. You can, of course, override this behavior.

Insertion pads are part of the PenPoint input subsystem, which is discussed in detail in Chapter 13.

Summary

This chapter has examined text editing in PenPoint. As we have seen, PenPoint includes a special application called MiniText that incorporates all of the text editing behavior available in the system.

All instances of the text component in PenPoint consist of paired instances of text data objects and text views. The former contain the text itself and the latter permit it to be displayed on the screen.

15

The Service Manager

. . . .

In PenPoint, a service is a program that enables applications to communicate with a hardware device or to access a software function or service of some kind. Software functions that do not have or require a user interface but rather run as background processes can be implemented as services. PenPoint's Service Manager makes these services accessible to any application in the PenPoint environment.

Traditional operating systems usually invent separate, special-purpose solutions for device drivers, networking software, background processes, and the like. Application developers must learn different mechanisms for each new class of special system service, and none of the classes works very well with the others.

Under PenPoint, each of these areas is unified under the Service Manager architecture, which generalizes common application operations such as enumerating, finding, observing, binding to, owning, and opening services. All these operations work in an environment in which services can be dynamically installed and deinstalled and in which the underlying hardware connections can be made and broken by the user at will. In addition, services are defined in such a way that they can use each other, allowing layering and a high degree of code sharing.

How do you know whether your software should be written as a service? Typically, all non-application functionality under PenPoint should be a service. Remember that PenPoint has a stringent definition of what an application is: It must subclass clsApp, follow the document model, support multiple instances via the Stationery menu, and so forth. Service architecture is the alternative to structuring your software as an application. Examples of services include device drivers, the In Box and Out Box as well as their transfer agents (see Chapter 16), network protocol stacks, and databases.

Layering Services

The most basic services are those that communicate with a hardware device. Examples of hardware devices accessed by services include serial and parallel ports and network adaptor cards. These base services represent a hardware device; they are similar to device drivers in other operating systems.

PenPoint must obviously provide for a variety of installation, configuration, and access mechanisms for hardware device services. Where other operating systems have treated these as a special case, PenPoint's Service Manager generalizes these operations well beyond the specific needs of hardware device handling. The result is an important class of services that don't represent hardware devices, instead providing a pure software service.

The most common style of a pure software service is one that accesses another service. The referenced service is called the target service. When one service targets another service it is, in essence, layering some added functionality and abstraction on top of the targeted service. Services may target other services to any depth. The resulting targeting relationships can be thought of as a pipeline or target chain. PenPoint provides a great deal of support for this pipelining method of invoking services.

Pipelining is an excellent way to layer architectures, with services farther up the chain from the hardware device providing higher levels of abstraction. For example, networking protocol stacks can be implemented with each protocol layer corresponding to a service. Alternatively, your application might open a service designed to interact with an electronic bulletin board. That service may in turn need to open a serial port service. Your application can safely ignore all but the service it must open.

Some services reference neither a hardware device nor another service: These services can be thought of as "the end of the line"; they typically provide specialized data-handling or reconciliation services. A background database service is a good example of this class; it doesn't access other services but just stores its data in PenPoint's file system. You can think of it as targeting a data file rather than a hardware port.

PenPoint's Service Manager provides a common architecture and implementation to allow a variety of services to be accessed by application programmers consistently and modularly. The Service Manager consists of two key classes: clsService, which defines a service, and clsServiceManger, which provides access to services.

clsService is of interest only to programmers defining a new service; new services are implemented by subclassing clsService. Services can belong to one or more service managers.

clsServiceManager groups together a set of services and provides access to them. Each of these provides a common core API that is consistent across each service in that group. clsServiceManager is of interest to any application programmer who is a client of a service; most PenPoint application developers will need to use it.

Internally, services are implemented as non-application dynamic link libraries (DLLs). A single Service Manager handles a group of related services. For example, there may be multiple serial ports on a PenPoint-based system, but they will all be handled by one Service Manager.

Your application is likely to use rather than create services. But if your application is or contains routines (such as a database engine, for example) that could be isolated from the main application code and that might be useful to other applications, you may want to consider implementing these modules as services.

Standard Service Managers

PenPoint predefines a number of service managers that are guaranteed to be available on all PenPoint-based systems. Some examples include

- theAppleTalkDevices
- theSerialDevices
- thePrinterDevices
- thePrinters
- theSendableServices
- theTransportHandlers
- theLinkHandlers

The names of most of these service managers are self-explanatory. The last three merit at least a brief explanation. A sendable service in PenPoint includes such things as facsimiles and electronic mail. These will appear to the user in the Send menu option of the Document menu. (See Chapter 16.) Anything that embodies the idea of being transmitted outside the PenPoint system is a sendable service. Transports and links are part of the networking API described in Chapter 16.

If you want to create or add a service to the system and none of these predefined Service Managers is suited to its management, then you must build a new Service Manager. You do this by subclassing clsServiceMgr.

Service Managers provide the following basic functions:

- finding a particular service (for example, the service for a particular printer or a specific serial port)
- binding to a service (which allows a client to receive notification messages from that service)
- becoming the exclusive owner of a service
- opening a service for data transfer
- closing a service

Installing and Using Services

Services are dynamically installable and deinstallable. They can be explicitly installed by the user, by an application, or by another service. The system Installer ensures that only one copy of a service is stored in the machine. The system Installer also keeps track of how many clients have asked to install a particular service and only deinstalls it when the last client is deinstalled.

Your application must be bound to a service before using it. To bind itself to a service, your application sends a special message to the appropriate Service Manager. Once this binding connection is established, the service adds your application to the list of objects it notifies when its status changes. This permits your application to be constantly aware of the availability of the service.

PenPoint supports the concept of delayed binding. This means that if Service A targets Service B, they can be installed in any order and everything will work out correctly. Without delayed binding, Service B would have to be installed before Service A could be installed. This would force the user to understand the dependency relationships between services and to install services in exactly the correct order.

Obviously, a service can be bound to a theoretically unlimited number of applications. Some services only permit one application to own and open (access) them at a time. Once you have ownership rights to a service, you can open it for your application, thereby gaining control over it, which means you can send it messages. You should open a service when you need to use it and close it as soon as possible so that lower-level services can be freed.

Since PenPoint is a multitasking operating system, the Service Manager must support multiple clients sharing the same service. In other words, shared simultaneous access should be allowed when the service can support it, and access must be clearly arbitrated (that is, clients take turns) for those cases in which services cannot be accessed by more than one client at a time.

Services are available to clients either exclusively or shared. If they are exclusive, clients must gain ownership rights to the service before being allowed to open it. Exclusive ownership makes particular sense for entities that cannot be shared, such as a physical serial port. The Service Manager provides protocols for clients to transfer ownership among themselves cooperatively.

When a service can be shared, it can have many clients at a time. A good example of a service being shared is a networking protocol. Such a service could be used by several applications simultaneously.

Once a client is bound to a service and has ownership of it (if it's an exclusive service), the client must open the service. Clients should only open a service instance when they are ready to send or receive data. Opening a service provides the client with access to the service object. Open status indicates that the service is in use and blocks certain other operations. For instance, an opened service cannot be deinstalled by the user. Clients should close a service once they have completed data transfer.

Like all installable PenPoint objects, services can be deactivated or deinstalled whenever they are not in use. This destroys all a service's objects and removes all of its code.

Connecting and Disconnecting

Unlike desktop computers, mobile, pen-based computers do not have their phone line, network and printer connections plugged in all day long. They must therefore gracefully tolerate the connections frequently being made and broken by the user. You can think of the presence or absence of a particular physical hardware connection as a connection status. The Service Manager architecture is where connection status is managed and communicated among interested PenPoint software parties.

Hardware device services are responsible for determining whether the hardware is connected. Some hardware provides this information to the software (for example, they may provide hardware ports or values that indicate the connection status). Other hardware must be polled to determine whether it is present.

Non-hardware services automatically change their connection state when their targets change connection state. Thus, connection state propagates up from the hardware to all services that are bound to that hardware. The end result is that the users win; they are freed from having to perform additional steps to initiate and terminate software activities before they make and break connections. A good example of the elegance of this architecture is the In Box and Out Box architectures described in Chapter 16; they both will automatically fill and empty their queues whenever the appropriate connections appear. There is no need for the user to initiate queue filling or emptying.

User Interfaces for Service Managers

A key role of a Service Manager is to allow clients to obtain a list of available services. Clients often need to do this before they can choose a particular service and proceed with binding, owning, and opening it. To see this clearly, imagine a printer Service Manager: If more than one destination printer is available, a particular one must be chosen as the destination of a print job.

Service Managers support interrogation by enumerating all the available service instances. This list is often made available to the end user via a simple user interface that maps directly onto the Service Manager in question. For example, PenPoint's printing user interface provides a simple "chooser" style user interface to allow the user to indicate to which available printer a particular document should be sent.

Designing Services

If you design a new PenPoint service, it will be an instance of a subclass you create from clsService. Remember that it must also have a service manager unless one of the existing service managers provides the needed behavior. Service managers are instances of clsServiceManager.

Should You Develop a Service?
You would typically consider designing a new service to handle new devices or protocols or to build an application that will share data via a background client-server model. A database-oriented application (such as a Personal Information Manager, or PIM) can be designed so that each page in the Notebook is a view of the data in the database service. Each application instance would bind and open the database service, allowing multiple pages to look at the same data and present it differently to the user. The database service would be a shared service, allowing multiple clients

The PenPoint service architecture is ideally suited to providing transparent access to databases, whether they reside locally on the PenPoint system or remotely (for example, on an SQL server).

Summary

This chapter has examined the Service Manager, an element of PenPoint that coordinates operations of applications that facilitate communication with hardware devices or some types of software functions. PenPoint includes several standard services.

The Service Manager deals with the installation, deinstallation, binding, and operation of services in the system. It also supports a common user interface for access to these services.

16

Connectivity

....

Connectivity is an inherent part of PenPoint's design. By nature, a PenPoint-based system will usually coexist with other computers and peripheral devices. Recognizing this, PenPoint includes full support for a connectivity interface that is not only robust enough to deal with complex interactions with other systems, but is also customizable and therefore extensible.

Overview of PenPoint Connectivity Support

PenPoint is designed for mobile connectivity. Not surprisingly, it builds in standard connectivity APIs so that applications can count on a strong foundation of connectivity.

PenPoint connectivity is provided by three key layers: remote file systems, transport interfaces, and link interfaces.

Any kind of connectivity must be built on top of some form of communications protocols, conventions that two computers agree to follow to communicate over a physical link. The link is often a wire such as a serial or network cable, but it could also be a wireless link such as infrared or radio-wave communications.

PenPoint allows true networking protocols to be used for its communications protocols. These reside in PenPoint's transport and link interfaces. They allow PenPoint to use a variety of industry-standard protocols to communicate with other computers and networks. These protocols are also available to applications that want to communicate.

Networking protocols are insufficient, however, for widespread connectivity at the application and user levels, because they require some expertise in networking protocols. A higher-level, more convenient interface to remote systems is needed. This is where PenPoint's Remote File system comes into play.

Remote File System

Many key aspects of PenPoint are implemented on top of PenPoint's file system. For instance, all documents in the Notebook are actually stored in the file system, and when the user moves, copies, deletes, or imports/exports a document, these operations are actually performed in the underlying file system representation.

Because the PenPoint Notebook is based on a file system, all PenPoint operations based on the file system can extend into the remote environments.

PenPoint's file system is designed to work with a variety of file system types. Not only can PenPoint file systems reside in the PenPoint computer, they can also be on locally attached disks (for example, in a base station), and on devices (that is, on another computer system). Examples of remote file systems include the floppy drives and hard disks in a desktop PC or Macintosh, and the file server on the network in an office.

A remote file system is accessed through APIs running on the PenPoint computer that use the networking transport interfaces to communicate with the computer on which the file system resides. Other software on the host computer implements file system operations under the "remote control" of the remote file system APIs on the PenPoint computer. The result is that the remote file system appears to PenPoint clients to behave identically to all other PenPoint file systems.

The Remote File system, therefore, provides the higher-level API PenPoint needs to make connectivity easy for application programmers and transparent to the user. It's easy for application programmers because they are familiar with how to use file system APIs: The same messages will read and write files whether they are local or remote. It's transparent for end users because they can use the same Table of Contents Browser and Disk Browser to exchange files with remote file systems as they use for local file operations.

Other Types of Remote Connectivity

Remote file system access typically meets the bulk of remote connectivity needs, since it provides a powerful and transparent method for data files to be uploaded and downloaded. However, there are two other important classes of connectivity: remote printing and program-to-program communications.

Remote printing is conceptually similar to remote file systems. PenPoint must make remote printers just as accessible to PenPoint applications and users as directly attached printers. Whether the printer is attached to your PenPoint computer, to your desktop PC, or to the network, its location should be transparent. PenPoint does this via a Remote Printing interface that removes the need for its clients to know the exact location of the printer.

Program to program communication takes place when a PenPoint program communicates with a program running on another computer. The other computer might be any type of system: a PenPoint computer, a PC, a Macintosh, or some other system. The two systems typically communicate to establish some form of live data connection. Two examples of this would be calendar programs running on two machines that need to reconcile their calendars, and a database front-end on the PenPoint machine that needs to send SQL queries to a database back-end on another machine (and get data back from it). PenPoint's networking interfaces offer program-to-program communication through standard techniques such as remote procedure calls.

The flexibility of network connectivity in PenPoint extends to support for multiple file system volume types and multiple network protocol stacks, in a single PenPoint system. As part of its extensibility, you can even define your own remote file system, transport, or link, completely refashioning the networking interface to suit a specific need. A user can take a PenPoint-based computer from one network configuration to another (for example, from one field office to another where the two networks are incompatible) and simply connect to the network with no special configuration effort.

Key principles involved in PenPoint connectivity include the following:

- a volume connectivity strategy that enables users to install and configure volumes from many other different file systems on the fly
- use of the Service Manager to enable users to connect, disconnect, install, deinstall, and configure devices, device drivers, and network protocol stacks on the fly

- multiple network protocol stacks that can coexist
- a general-purpose document import/export architecture (see Chapter 11), including a standard interface to file format converters
- In Box and Out Box support (discussed later in this chapter) that allows deferred document I/O for printing, filing, electronic mail, faxing, and similar operations

Since PenPoint gives your application such extensive connectivity support for free, you need to understand this chapter only if you are interested in creating new remote file systems, transports, or links. If your application is simply one that intends to make use of PenPoint's inherent connectivity support, you can safely ignore the rest of this chapter.

Remote File Systems

In its initial configuration, PenPoint includes remote file systems to support several of the most-popular networks and most-popular file access protocols. It also supports a straightforward file import/export model that permits a PenPoint-based system to communicate virtually transparently with an IBM PC or compatible, for example.

Among the networks supported by the early release of PenPoint is TOPS. In fact, the initial Developer's Release of PenPoint uses TOPS as the primary means of moving software developed on the PC using the PenPoint Software Developer's Kit to a running PenPoint-based system for testing and evaluation. We will look briefly at TOPS and the IBM PC as a networking system using remote file access, but keep in mind that this is only one of several possible connectivity configurations for the system.

You can connect a PenPoint-based system to a desktop machine running TOPS in four different ways

- a direct serial connection between the PenPoint-based system's high-speed serial port and a PC serial port
- AppleTalk between a PenPoint system and an Apple Macintosh

- FlashTalk between a PenPoint system and an IBM PC with a TOPS FlashCard installed
- slower serial connection using modems

Once you connect a PenPoint-based system to a desktop computer using one of these methods, the PenPoint computer can access any printer or file system available to the PC or Macintosh.

Transport Layer

The transport API provides access to layers 3 and 4 in the standard seven-layer Open Systems Interface (OSI) network model. (If you are not familiar with this model and are going to be developing remote file systems, transports, or links for the PenPoint-based system, you should consult an authoritative book on the subject. Explanation of that model is beyond the scope of this book.)

Well-established industry-standard transports such as ATP, IPX/SPX, or TCP can be developed under the transport API by GO Corporation or third parties.

Link Layer

Link protocols are the software layer closest to the physical networking hardware. PenPoint provides built-in support for both of these as well as several others.

By nature, links are the closest interface to the hardware of all network components, residing at Layer 2 of the OSI model.

You can create new links for PenPoint with the Link API, which is explained in detail in the SDK documentation.

Connectivity-Related Facilities

PenPoint incorporates several subsystems that support the central ideas behind connectivity. The three most useful and unique of these services are In and Out Boxes, a Send user interface, and Send address lists. We will take a look at each of these.

In Box and Out Box

As we explained in Chapter 1, it is essential that a mobile, pen-based operating system provide support for deferred data transfer. The computer should allow the user to issue a variety of data transfer commands whenever the user wants to, regardless of whether there's a connection present. Data transfer commands should be loosely construed to include printing, sending electronic mail, faxing, file transfers, and the like.

PenPoint's In Box and Out Box provide support for deferred data transfer. They work with all data in PenPoint, with no special programming on the part of application developers. (In traditional operating systems many application developers go to great lengths to build special electronic mail and FAX commands into their applications.)

At the bottom of the Notebook (see Figure 16-1) screen is a collection of icons residing in the Bookshelf. The two icons highlighted in Figure 16-1 are the In Box and the Out Box.

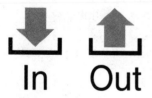

Figure 16-1   In Box and Out Box Icons

The In Box and Out Box are specialized, floating PenPoint notebooks that act as queues for incoming and outgoing documents. They are not capable of performing a transfer operation themselves; rather, they provide a common user interface and architecture in which application specific transfer services are grouped and provided to the user. The kinds of transfer operations they support can be extended by third parties writing new transfer-related services.

There are two halves to a transfer-related service: its implementation and its user interface. Its implementation is a special service (see Chapter 15) typically called a transfer agent. Its user interface is a section in the In Box or Out Box notebook called a service section (these sections can provide specialized user interfaces for configuring the service).

As the user buys and installs transfer-related services, the In Box and/or Out Box gains new sections. A typical Out Box might contain sections for the two printers typically prints to, a section for outbound MCI mail, and one for outbound facsimiles.

Service sections queue documents awaiting a transfer operation by that service. Because normal documents are queued, PenPoint applications need not be aware that this queueing is occurring. It takes place at the file system level using a simple copy of the document (or, if memory is a concern, a virtual copy of the document in the form of a pointer).

To send a document using a service (a process described in the next section), the user does not need to know if the service is connected and available. Instead, the user simply issues the Send or Print command to the document. A copy of the document is made into the appropriate Out Box service section; in effect, it is queued. Whenever the connection is available (including immediately), the transfer agent responsible for that service section is notified of the connection and it processes each document waiting in its queue.

It is important to recognize that the queue contains documents, not print or facsimile jobs, which would contain a bitmap image of the document. This approach would consume too much memory. The document itself tends to be quite compact. When the Print and Fax transfer agents empty their queues, they alert each queued document and send it messages requesting that it print or send itself.

The user is always in ultimate control of the documents in the Out Box, of course, until they are sent and removed from the Out Box. The user can decide not to send a document simply by deleting it from the Out Box.

Any connection that can transfer data can have an In Box transfer agent so that it can place documents in PenPoint's In Box. When the PenPoint system is connected to a network or remote file system, it may also receive documents from other nodes on the network. These documents are transmitted to the Pen-Point-based system's In Box, where the user can dispose of them as desired.

The Send User Interface

PenPoint's Standard Application Menus (see Chapter 2) provide a standard Send command on every document's Document menu. The Send command allows the user to use PenPoint's Send User Interface to place the document into the Out Box.

Like the Out Box itself, the Send User Interface is extensible by third-party developers. Whenever a new Out Box transfer agent is installed, it will typically extend the Send User Interface so that the user can use this single, standard user interface for addressing documents, no matter what transfer technology is used.

To understand the Send User Interface, let us first consider what occurs in traditional operating systems. Each electronic mail and facsimile application provides its own user interface and its own address list. To send something to John Doe via one electronic mail program, it's done one way. If you choose another program, the interface is different. In addition, John's name must appear in multiple address lists.

It would be better if the operating system provided a single address list in which John's name would only appear once. If John were available via a facsimile number, an MCI mail box number, and a local network mail name, all three of these addresses would appear next to John's name in this single list. To send to John you would choose the appropriate method of transfer.

PenPoint's Send User Interface is built around just such an address list, called the Send List. It is a miniature address book containing all the people and places the user might wish to send documents. When new transfer agents are installed, they extend the Send List by adding to it a new field type for their particular type of addressing.

Users choosing the Send command are presented with a list of the currently installed sendable services. Once they choose a service, it presents its own special send user interface (typically based on the Send List name list). They then choose to whom they want to send the document. A few taps of the pen, and the user is done; PenPoint has queued the document into the appropriate Out Box section.

PenPoint has a built-in interface to permit the user to manage the address book, which is actually a database. The user can transfer this database to another system, send it to another user, and generally treat it like any other document.

Summary

This chapter has examined the highly integrated connectivity of PenPoint. Many key features of connectivity are implemented through the remote file system, which in turn is built on the PenPoint file system.

Networking connectivity in PenPoint can be looked at as divided into transport and link layers.

Deferred connectivity, an important concept in PenPoint, is supported via the In Box and Out Box interfaces. These elements, in turn, make use of the Send User Interface which includes a built-in address book database.

Appendix A: Important Data Structures, Classes, and Messages

....

This Appendix includes useful technical information regarding the PenPoint Operating System and how it is programmed. This data is useful only to programmers interested in developing applications for PenPoint-based systems. Material in this Appendix is arranged in chapter order as the related topics are discussed in the main body of the book. For each class, this Appendix describes key metrics and data structures as well as the most important messages and their uses.

Full documentation of the PenPoint programming interfaces is included in the Software Developer's Kit (SDK). This Appendix provides only key data and is designed to provide you with a sense of the scope and depth of the programming issues involved in PenPoint rather than with a complete reference to the system.

The Class Manager (Ch. 5)

clsMgr Protocols

Because of its position at the root of the hierarchy and its unique role in the system, clsMgr differs from other classes in PenPoint. The primary difference is that in addition to object-oriented messages, it also contains a reasonable amount of procedural interface code.

Table A-1   Important clsMgr Functions

Function	Description
ObjectCall	Sends a synchronous message call
ObjectCallAncestor	Passes a message to an object's immediate ancestor class
ObjectPost	Posts a message to an object by placing the message in the input subsystem's event queue rather than sending directly to the object itself
Object PostAsync	Posts a message asynchronously
ObjectSend	Sends a message to an object across task or process boundaries (that is, to another application) and waits for a reply
ObjectSendUpdate	Same as ObjectSend, but returns changed data

Table A-2   Important clsMgr Macros

Macros	Description
Cls	Extracts the class code from a message or status value to determine the class to which message was sent
ObjCallChk	Returns True (1) if an error is reported by the target object
ObjCallJmp	Branches to a Goto label if an error condition arises during message processing
ObjCallOK	Evaluates to True (1) if no error condition is reported by the target object
ObjCallRet	Returns the status value from a called object if an error occurs
Sts	Extracts the error code from a status value
WKNVer	Returns the version number of a well-known UID

Table A-3   Important clsMgr Messages

Message	Description
msgAddObserver	Adds an observer to the receiver object's observer list
msgCan	Returns the state of the requested capability or capabilities in the receiver
msgClass	Returns the class of the receiver
msgDisable	Removes capabilities from receiving object
msgEnable	Adds capabilities to receiving object
msgGetObservers	Returns a list of observer objects in the receiver
msgIsA	Tests if a class appears anywhere in the inheritance hierarchy of receiving object
msgNew	Creates an object
msgNewDefaults	Initializes msgNew arguments to default values
msgNotifyObservers	Sent to self to cause object to notify all of its observers of a state change
msgNotUnderstood	Sent to self when a message sent to an object was not handled anywhere in its inheritance hierarchy

Table A-3 Important clsMgr Messages (continued)

Message	Description
msgNumObservers	Returns the number of observer objects defined in the receiver's observer list
msgObjectVersion	Returns the version of a well-known object and checks it against the current version
msgRemoveObserver	Removes an observer from the receiver object's observer list

The Application Framework (Ch. 6)

clsAppMgr

The application manager class clsAppMgr defines messages to keep track of application classes after installation and to create, activate, and destroy instances of an application.

From your application's perspective, clsAppMgr provides messages to create new application classes and to obtain information about any installed class.

clsAppMgr Metrics

Metrics that pertain to an application class in general are stored in a clsAppMgr data structure called APP_MGR_METRICS. Among its more important contents are

- the shared application directory for the installed application
- the resource file used by the application documents
- the default position of its window
- the application name

- your company's name
- the default name for a document the application creates

In addition, APP_MGR_METRICS contains a structure called APP_MGR_FLAGS, consisting of eight Boolean values. The most important of these tell PenPoint whether to

- put the application into the Stationery Notebook
- put the application into the Tools Palette
- allow the user to embed child applications in its documents
- ask the user to confirm an attempt to delete the document
- permit the user to deinstall the application

Table A-4   Key clsAppMgr Messages

Message	Description
msgAppMgrActivate	Activates an instance of an application
msgAppMgrCreate	Creates a new instance of an application
msgAppMgrGetMetrics	Retrieves the contents of the APP_MGR_METRICS structure for the class

clsApp

You can think of clsApp as picking up in the PenPoint application life cycle where clsAppMgr leaves off. Once a document has an application object and is ready for the user to manipulate, clsApp becomes the important class.
The messages defined by clsApp handle such tasks as

- instance data initialization, saving, and re-creation
- opening and controlling the instance's windows
- beginning message dispatching to the application instance

- determining various behavioral characteristics of the application instance (including floating and zooming, for example)
- deleting application instances

clsApp Metrics

The data structure associated with clsApp is called APP_METRICS. Among other things, it includes

- the document's unique ID
- the document directory
- the document's parent document
- the UID of the main window
- identification of the floating windows, if any
- a list of resource files associated with the document
- a set of flags called APP_FLAGS, discussed below

Within APP_METRICS is a set of flags that determine if the document

- is in hot mode
- is floating
- is read-only
- can be deleted
- can be moved
- can be copied

Table A-5   Key clsApp Messages

Message	Description
msgAppAbout	Displays information describing the application
msgAppActivate	Activates an application instance
msgAppClose	Closes the main window of an application instance

msgAppCopySel	Prepares to copy the selection into this application
msgAppCreateClientWin	Creates a standard application client window, an instance of clsView
msgAppDelete	Deletes the instance from the system
msgAppDeleteSel	Prepares to delete the selection from this document
msgAppGetMetrics	Retrieves the application's metrics from the APP_MGR_METRICS structure
msgAppHelp	Displays help for the selection if help is available
msgAppInit	Creates the resource file and main window for an application instance
msgAppMoveSel	Prepares to move the selection into this application
msgAppOpen	Opens the main window of an application instance, making its contents visible to the user
msgAppOptionShow	Shows or hides an Option Sheet
msgAppPrint	Prints the application using the selected graphic imaging device
msgAppPrintSetup	Asks the user for information to prepare a document for printing
msgAppRestore	Retrieves the application's objects from the resource file named in APP_MGR_METRICS for the class
msgAppRestoreFrom	Retrieves the application's objects from the resource file supplied as an argument
msgAppRevert	Replaces the current document and its instance data with the filed copy of the application
msgAppSave	Saves the application's instance data in the resource file with which the instance was opened
msgAppSaveTo	Saves the application's instance data in the resource file supplied as an argument
msgAppSearch	Searches the application for a specified string, including options the user can set and options your program can determine
msgAppSelectAll	Selects all objects in an application instance
msgAppSelOptions	Prepares to display an Option Sheet for the selection
msgAppSetTitleLine	Turns the title line of the application's main window on or off
msgAppSpell	Invokes the spell-checking logic for the application instance
msgAppTerminate	Terminates an application, making it dormant
msgAppUndo	Reverses the effect of the msgAppTerminate

clsEmbeddedWin

Table A-6 Key clsEmbeddedWin Messages

Message	Description
msgEmbeddedWinBeginCopy	Puts an embedded window into copy mode so that it is prepared to be copied by the user
msgEmbeddedWinBeginMove	Puts an embedded window into move mode so that it is prepared to be moved by the user
msgEmbeddedWinCopy	Copies an embedded window to a new destination at the completion of a user's copy operation
msgEmbeddedWinDestroy	Destroys an embedded window and removes all references to it
msgEmbeddedWinGetDest	Determines the destination point for a move or copy operation
msgEmbeddedWinGetMetrics	Retrieves an embedded window's metrics from a structure called EMBEDDED_WIN_METRICS
msgEmbeddedWinMove	Moves an embedded window to a new destination at the completion of a user's move operation

Table A-7 Key clsView Messages

Message	Description
msgViewGetDataObject	Retrieves the ID of the object related to a view
msgViewSetDataObject	Sets or changes the ID of the object related to a view

clsAppWin

clsAppWin is a descendant of clsEmbeddedWin that wraps an embedded application and provides the interface between the application and the Application Framework layer. The purpose of clsAppWin is to provide fundamental gesture behavior for an embedded application window.

clsAppWin Metrics

clsappWin defines a data structure called APP_WIN_METRICS that contains basic information describing an application window. This includes the following data

- the UID for the application
- the icon and label used for the Open button
- a Boolean value indicating whether the window is open or closed
- a Boolean value indicating whether the window is floating or not
- a Boolean value indicating whether the window is the current selection

In addition, it contains a contains a pointer to an APP_WIN_STYLE data structure, which contains values describing the title bar and document icon characteristics for the application.

Table A-8   Key clsAppWin Messages

Message	Description
msgAppWinClose	Closes the application window instance
msgAppWinGetMetrics	Retrieves the metrics for the application window from the APP_WIN_METRICS data structure
msgAppWinOpen	Opens the application window instance
msgAppWinSetStyle	Places values into the APP_WIN_STYLE data structure

The PenPoint Windowing System (Ch. 7)

Window Metrics

Much of the state of a window is stored in its WIN_METRICS structure. This structure contains fields that define such things as

- parent window
- child window
- size and origin of window (bounds)
- device on which window's pixels appear
- window tag, which you define
- various style flags

Table A-9   Key Window Flags

Flag	Comments
wsCaptureLayout	This window must be laid out each time children are moved or resized
wsClipChildren	Drawing in this window will not paint over child windows
wsClipSiblings	Drawing in this window will not paint over sibling windows
wsLayoutDirty	This window must be laid out each time its contents have changed or have been revealed after being obscured
wsPaintable	This window can be painted
wsSendLayout	This window must be laid out each time it is resized
wsVisible	This window is not hidden

Table A-10 Important clsWin Messages

Message	Description
msgWinBeginPaint	Sets up a window for painting a "dirty" region
msgWinBeginRepaint	Sets up a window for repainting a "dirty" region
msgWinDelta	Moves and/or resizes a window
msgWinEndPaint	Informs the window system that the window has finished painting
msgWinEndRepaint	Informs the window system that the window has finished repainting
msgWinEnum	Enumerates a window's children
msgWinGetFlags	Retrieves only the flag values in the WIN_METRICS data structure
msgWinGetMetrics	Retrieves the WIN_METRICS data structure's contents
msgWinInsert	Inserts a window into the hierarchy as the child of a parent
msgWinInserted	Advises a window that it has been successfully inserted
msgWinInsertOK	Informs a parent that a child has requested to be inserted into it in the tree hierarchy
msgWinLayout	Instructs a window and its subwindows to lay themselves out
msgWinLayoutSelf	Instructs a window to lay out its children
msgWinMoved	Informs a window that it or an ancestor window has been moved
msgWinRepaint	Tells a window to repaint itself (see Chapter 9 for more details)
msgWinSetFlags	Sets window flags in WIN_METRICS as well as an input-related flag structure described in Chapter 13
msgWinSetVisible	Turns window's visibility bit on or off and returns its previous value
msgWinSized	Informs a window that it or an ancestor window has been resized
msgWinUpdate	Forces a window to repaint immediately, if any portion of it requires repainting

Recursive Live Embedding Protocol (Ch. 8)

Three classes that define metrics and messages are important to your support of recursive live embedding and traversal: clsEmbeddedWin, clsTE, and clsTraverse. A fourth class, clsStdTE, is a convenient package class that combines support for clsTraverse messages with the creation of a traversal context.

clsEmbeddedWin

This class's purpose is to support common application window behavior such as responses to gestures and child embedded window actions. We looked briefly at this class in Chapter 7. As we have indicated, your application is most likely to be an instance of a subclass of clsEmbeddedWin.

Table A-11 Important clsEmbeddedWin Messages

Message	Description
msgEmbeddedWinBeginCopy	Requests initiation of a copying process
msgEmbeddedWinBeginMove	Requests initiation of a move process
msgEmbeddedWinCopy	Carries out the copying process
msgEmbeddedWinGetDest	Gets the destination of a move or copy operation
msgEmbeddedWinGetMark	Returns the mark of an embedded window
msgEmbeddedWinGotoChild	Goes to a child embedded window whose UID is furnished as an argument
msgEmbeddedWinGotoMark	Goes to the embedded window whose mark is supplied as an argument
msgEmbeddedWinMove	Carries out the move process
msgEmbeddedWinMoveCopyOK	Authorizes the move or copy operation to proceed
msgEmbeddedWinExtractChild	Extracts a child window
msgEmbeddedWinInsertChild	Inserts a child window
msgEmbeddedWinMoveChild	Changes the position of a child window
msgEmbeddedWinRestoreChild	Restores a child window from its file

clsTE

clsTE is the traversal engine class. It is a generalized traversal engine that implements the protocols defined in clsTraversal.

Table A-12 Important clsTE Messages

Message	Description
msgTEApply	Applies the message to the item at the current position
msgTEGetCreateCtxResponse	Gets the embedded response from the current context's Create processing
msgTEGetCtxData	Get client data for the current context
msgTENext	Moves the current position to the next item
msgTESetCtxData	Changes client data for the current context
msgTEUp	Moves the current position up to its parent

clsTraverse

The purpose of clsTraverse is to supply the basic protocol for class traversal engine creation.

Table A-13 Important clsTraverse Messages

Message	Description
msgTraverseApply	Applies the current action to the item at the current position
msgTraverseCreateChildCtx	Creates a traversal context over the specified child
msgTraverseCreateDocCtx	Creates a traversal context for a document
msgTraverseCreateGestureCtx	Creates a traversal context at the specified gesture
msgTraverseCreateSelCtx	Creates a traversal context for a selection
msgTraverseCreateWordCtx	Creates a traversal context for the word under the specified gesture
msgTraverseGetParent	Retrieves the UUIDs of parent
msgTraverseNext	Advances the position to the next item

ImagePoint: Graphics and Imaging System (Ch. 9)

Graphics Metrics

There are one key object and four important structures connected with graphics in PenPoint. The drawing context itself is the object; the four structures relate to fonts and text.

SysDC

A drawing context defines all of the essential characteristics of a graphic environment. Among its more important instance data are those defining

- units to be used (pixels, points, inches, and so forth) in measurements
- the matrix that defines what scaling and/or rotation is needed
- type and extent of clipping to be performed (normally defined to clip to the window boundaries)
- plane mask (whether the window can or does draw on the acetate layer where pen ink gets dribbled)
- line characteristics (how a line is capped, how two lines are joined, and how thick the line is)
- radius value for round-cornered rectangles
- foreground color
- background color
- fill pattern
- line pattern
- font
- miscellaneous flags

SYSDC_FONT_ATTR

The attributes of a font include the following characteristics:

- font group (sans serif, roman, and so forth)
- stroke weight
- aspect ratio
- italicized flag
- monospaced flag
- type of encoding used

SYSDC_FONT_SPEC

When you combine the 1A-bit font ID with its SYSDC_FONT_ATTR structure's values, you get a 32-bit quantity called a SYSDC_FONT_SPEC. You can file this value along with the text to indicate its formatting. When a font is opened, if the exact font ID is not currently installed, the SYSDC_FONT_ATTR is used to find the best matching installed font.

SYSDC_TEXT_OUTPUT

A SYSDC_TEXT_OUTPUT structure defines the parameters to draw a single string of text in the current font. Its most important fields describe

- alignment
- underlining
- a pointer to the text itself
- the length of the text
- where to place the string (x,y)
- justification metric data (such as width of normal space, how much to add to it, and so forth)

Table A-14 Key clsSysDrwCtx Messages

Message	Description
msgDcClipRect	Sets or clears clip rectangle
msgDcCopyPixels	Copies a range of pixels from an image device
msgDcDrawArcRays	Draws an arc using the rays method
msgDcDrawBezier	Draws a Bezier curve using four points
msgDcDrawEllipse	Draws an ellipse
msgDcDrawChordRays	Draws a chord
msgDcDrawImage	Draws an image from sampled data
msgDcDrawPageTurn	Draws a page-turn effect over the bound window
msgDcDrawPolygon	Draws an arbitrarily shaped polygon
msgDcDrawPolyline	Draws a potentially multisegmented line
msgDcDrawRectangle	Draws a rectangle
msgDcDrawSectorRays	Draws a pie-wedge shape
msgDcDrawText	Draws text in the current font in the current window
msgDcDrawTextRun	Same as msgDcDrawText, but draws using run spacing
msgDcFillWindow	Draws a rectangle the size of the window and fills it with a specified pattern
msgDcGetBackgroundRGB	Returns current background color as RGB value
msgDcGetFillPat	Gets the pattern in use for filling closed shapes
msgDcGetFontMetrics	Gets font metrics for the current font
msgDcGetForegroundRGB	Returns current foreground color as RGB value
msgDcGetLine	Gets all line attributes if argument is a pointer to a SYSDC_LINE structure; otherwise, gets only the line's thickness as return value
msgDcGetLinePat	Gets the pattern in use for drawing lines
msgDcGetMode	Gets drawing mode flags
msgDcGetWindow	Gets which window the receiver is bound to
msgDcHitTest	Turns hit testing on or off
msgDcInitialize	Resets all fields in the DC to their default values
msgDcInvertColors	Swaps background and foreground colors
msgDcMeasureText	Computes size of text and advances counter pointer as needed

msgDcOpenFont	Opens a font, finding the one nearest that specified if system doesn't have specified font
msgDcScaleFont	Scales font matrix
msgDcSetBackgroundRGB	Sets background color using an RGB specification (number)
msgDcSetFillPat	Sets the pattern to be used in filling closed shapes
msgDcSetForegroundRGB	Sets foreground color using an RGB specification (number)
msgDcSetLine	Sets all line attributes
msgDcSetLinePat	Sets the pattern to be used in drawing a line
msgDcSetLineThickness	Sets the thickness of the line
msgDcSetMode	Sets the drawing mode
msgDcSetWindow	Binds DC to a window

The User Interface Toolkit (Ch 10)

clsButton

Table A-15 Important clsButton Messages

Message	Description
msgButtonGetMsg	Determines the message sent by the button when it is activated by the user
msgButtonNotify	Sends appropriate message to button's client if one is specified, with optional arguments
msgButtonSetMsg	Changes the message sent by the button when it is activated by the user

clsControl

Table A-16 Important clsControl Messages

Message	Description
msgControlEnable	Forces control to re-evaluate whether it should be enabled
msgControlGetClient	Returns the identification of the client of the control
msgControlGetDirty	Determines whether the control has changed since its dirty condition was last set to False
msgControlGetEnable	Determines whether the control is presently enabled or not
msgControlSetClient	Changes the control's client
msgControlSetDirty	Resets the control's dirty condition to True or False
msgControlSetEnable	Enables or disables a control

clsCustomLayout

Table A-17 Important clsCustomLayout Messages

Message	Description
msgCstmLayoutGetChildSpec	Returns the specification for a child window in a custom layout
msgCstmLayoutSetChildSpec	Defines the specification for a child window in a custom layout

clsField

Table A-18 Important clsFieldMessages

Message	Description
msgFieldAcceptPopup	Accepts the insertion pad's contents and dismisses it
msgFieldActivate	Activates a field for user input
msgFieldActivatePopup	Displays the field's pop-up insertion pad
msgFieldCancelPopup	Dismisses the insertion pad without altering field contents
msgFieldDeactivate	Deactivates a field
msgFieldFormat	Formats text on the screen
msgFieldGetMaxLen	Retrieves the field's maximum text length
msgFieldGetXlate	Retrieves the field's input translator or template (see Chapter 13)
msgFieldModified	Processes a new input value for a field
msgFieldSetMaxLen	Changes the field's maximum text length
msgFieldSetXlate	Sets the field's input translator or template (see Chapter 13)
msgFieldTranslateDelayed	Translates delayed pen input

clsIcon

Table A-19 Important clsIcon Messages

Message	Description
msgIconGetPictureSize	Returns the size of the picture
msgIconGetRects	Returns the bounds for the label and the picture
msgIconSetPictureSize	Defines the picture size

clsLabel

Table A-20   Important clsLabel Messages

Message	Description
msgLabelGetCols	Returns the number of columns defined for the label
msgLabelGetRows	Returns the number of rows defined for the label
msgLabelGetString	Returns the string defined as the label's content
msgLabelSetCols	Changes the number of columns defined for the label
msgLabelSetRows	Changes the number of rows defined for the label
msgLabelSetString	Changes the string defined as the label's content

clsMenuButton

Table A-21   Important clsMenuButton Messages

Message	Description
msgMenuButtonGetMenu	Returns the pull-right or pull-down menu or null if none is defined
msgMenuButtonProvideMenu	Provides content of menu to be displayed if metrics call for dynamic menu generation
msgMenuButtonSetMenu	Sets the pull-right or pull-down menu
msgMenuButtonShowMenu	Puts up or takes down the menu

clsNote

Table A-22 Important clsNote Messages

Message	Description
msgNoteCancel	Dismisses note and cancels processing
msgNoteDone	Indicates that the application modal note has been dismissed
msgNoteShow	Displays and activates the note

clsOption

Table A-23 Important clsOption Messages

Message	Description
msgOptionAddCard	Adds a card to the Option Sheet
msgOptionApply	Tells the Option Sheet to apply its top card to the selection
msgOptionApplyAndClose	Tells the Option Sheet to apply its top card to the selection and close
msgOptionClose	Tells the Option Sheet to close itself
msgOptionGetCard	Retrieves information about a card
msgOptionShowCard	Displays a given card, making it the current card
msgOptionRefreshCard	Resets card settings based on selection

clsScrollbar

Table A-24   Important clsScrollbar Messages

Message	Description
msgScrollBarHorizScroll	Indicates client should perform a horizontal scrolling operation
msgScrollbarProvideHorizInfo	Indicates client should provide horizontal document and view information
msgScrollbarProvideVertInfo	Indicates client should provide vertical document and view information
msgScrollbarUpdate	Forces the scrollbar to repaint with the most-recent information about position and offset
msgScrollBarVertScroll	Indicates client should perform a vertical scrolling operation

clsScrollWin

Table A-25   Important clsScrollWin Messages

Message	Description
msgScrollWinGetClientWin	Returns current client window
msgScrollWinSetClientWin	Changes client window
msgScrollWinAddClientWin	Adds a new client window to the scrolling window
msgScrollWinRemoveClientWin	Removes specified client window from the scrolling window
msgScrollWinGetVertScrollbar	Returns the value of the vertical scrollbar
msgScrollWinGetHorizScrollbar	Returns the value of the horizontal scrollbar

clsTkTable

Table A-26 Important clsTkTable Messages

Message	Description
msgTkTableAddAsFirst	Inserts a specified window as the first child window in the Toolkit Table
msgTkTableAddAsLast	Inserts a specified window as the last child in the Toolkit Table
msgTkTableAddAsSibling	Inserts a specified window in front of or behind and existing child
msgTkTableAddAt	Inserts a specified window at a specified index position in the window list of the Toolkit Table
msgTkTableGetClient	Returns the client of the first child in the Toolkit Table
msgTkTableRemove	Removes a specified window from the Toolkit Table
msgTkTableSetClient	Sets client of each child in the table from an array of arguments

The File System (Ch. 11)

The File System Protocols

Because of the nature of directories and files in a hierarchical file system like PenPoint, there are a number of activities (such as copying, moving, and deleting) that can apply in nearly identical ways to both files and directories. As a result, several messages are defined in both clsFileHandle and clsDirHandle.We discuss these shared messages first, then look at messages that are unique to each class.

Shared Messages

Table A-27 describes the important messages shared by clsFileHandle and clsDirHandle.

Table A-27   Important Messages in clsDirHandle and clsFileHandle

Message	Description
msgDestroy	Destroys a directory or file handle (note that it does not affect the file or node itself, only its handle)
msgFSCopy	Copies a directory (and all its children) or a file to a new destination, leaving it in its original position as well
msgFSDelete	Deletes a file or a directory and all of its children
msgFSGetAttr	Returns one or more attributes of a file or directory
msgFSGetPath	Returns the path of a directory or the name of a file
msgFSMove	Relocates a directory or file to a new destination. In the case of a directory, moves all children as well
msgFSSetAttr	Changes one or more attributes of a file or directory

clsDirHandle

Table A-28   Important Messages in clsDirHandle

Message	Description
msgFSReadDir	Reads the attributes of the next entry in a directory
msgFSReadDirFull	Reads all entries in a directory into a buffer
msgFSReadDirReset	Resets the position for directory reading to the beginning of the directory

clsFileHandle

Table A-29 Important Messages in clsFileHandle

Message	Description
msgFSFlush	Flushes any buffers associated with the file
msgFSGetSize	Returns the size of the file
msgFSSeek	Changes the current byte position value
msgFSSetSize	Changes or establishes the size of the file
msgStreamRead	Reads data from the file
msgStreamSeek	Moves to a new position in the file
msgStreamWrite	Writes data to a file

Resources and Their Management (Ch. 12)

Resource Class and Messages

All resource file activities are handled by clsResFile, which inherits from clsFileHandle. The class includes messages to handle location, reading, writing, updating, and deleting of specific resource objects; enumerating over lists of resource files; and compacting resource files.

Table A-30 Important clsResFile Messages

Message	Description
msgResFind	Locates a resource in a file or file list
msgResReadData	Reads a data resource from a file
msgResWriteData	Writes a data resource to a file
msgResUpdateData	Updates an existing data resource in a file
msgResReadObject	Reads an object resource from a file
msgResWriteObject	Writes an object resource to a file
msgResUpdateObject	Updates an existing object resource in a file
msgResGetObject	Reads an object resource from the current file position
msgResPutObject	Places an object resource at the current file position
msgResDeleteResource	Deletes a data or object resource from a file
msgResCompact	Forces compaction of a resource file

Text Editing and Related Classes (Ch. 14)

Text-Editing Metrics

TD_NEW

When you create a new text data object, you must supply a TD_NEW structure. This structure's most important components are:

- a set of metrics for the text data object that define whether the text object is modifiable and whether editing operations can be undone
- the expected size of the text data object

TV_NEW

The TV_NEW structure associated with creating a new text view has a number of elements, the most important of which are

- a flag that determines whether the view will be filled with an insertion pad
- the UID of a text data object to view (NULL creates a new, empty data object)
- a pointer to a TV_STYLE structure that defines the style for the view

The TV_STYLE structure, in turn, includes:

- behavior flags defining such things as whether it is permissible to embed applications in the view, how text is to be formatted for printer output, whether word wrap is turned on or not and whether hidden text is to be displayed
- a character size adjustment, or magnification, value
- a flag indicating whether special characters (line break and paragraph break, for example) should be shown
- the UID of the destination printer

clsText

Table A-31   Important clsText Messages

Message	Description
msgTextChangeAttrs	Modifies either default or local attributes of a text data object
msgTextClearAttrs	Removes all local attributes for a defined span of characters in the text data object
msgTextEmbedObject	Embeds an object at the specified position in a text data object
msgTextExtractObject	Removes an object from the specified position in a text data object
msgTextGet	Retrieves a specified character
msgTextGetAttrs	Retrieves default or local attributes in effect at a given index in the text data object
msgTextGetBuffer	Retrieves multiple characters
msgTextInitAttrs	Initializes attributes in preparation for changing them
msgTextLength	Returns the number of characters in the text data object
msgTextModify	Inserts, deletes, or replaces characters in a text data object
msgTextRead	Imports from a file or stream of text
msgTextSpan	Computes the starting and ending character indices of the specified span of characters
msgTextWrite	Exports to a file or stream of text

clsTextView

Table A-32 Important clsTextView Messages

Message	Description
msgTextViewAddIP	Adds an insertion pad to the text view
msgTextViewEmbed	Adds an embedded object to the text view
msgTextViewGetEmbedded- Metrics view	Returns the metrics for an embedded object in a text
msgTextViewGetStyle	Returns the style settings for the text view
msgTextViewResolveXY the x-y coordinates of a pen tap	Determines the character index in a text view based on
msgTextViewScroll	Scrolls the text view
msgTextViewSetSelection which an operation can be performed	Converts the current selection to a span of characters on
msgTextViewSetStyle	Changes the style settings for the text view

The Service Manager (Ch. 15)

Table A-33   Important clsService Messages

Message	Description
msgSvcBindRequested	Responds to an attempt to bind the service to an application
msgSvcCloseRequested	Responds to an attempt to close the service
msgSvcDeactiveRequested	Responds to an attempt to deactivate the service
msgSvcDeinstallRequested	Responds to an attempt to deinstall the service
msgSvcGetConnected	Returns the connection state of the service
msgSvcGetFunctions	Returns a list of the function entry points for the service
msgSvcGetName	Returns the name of the service
msgSvcGetOwner	Returns the UID of the owner of the service
msgSvcGetStyle	Returns the style of the service as stored in the SVC_STYLE data structure
msgSvcGetTarget	Attempts to access the target device
msgSvcOpenRequested	Responds to an attempt to open the service
msgSvcSetConnected	Changes the connection state for the service
msgSvcSetStyle	Changes the style of the service
msgSvcSetTarget	Defines or redefines the target device
msgSvcUnbindRequested	Responds to an attempt to sever the bind between an application and the service

clsServiceManager

Table A-34 Important clsServiceManager Messages

Message	Description
msgSMBind	Binds the application to a service managed by the manager
msgSMClose	Closes a service
msgSMConnectedChanged	Indicates that the connection state of a service managed by the manager has changed
msgSMGetOpenList	Returns a list of all objects that have opened the service
msgSMGetState	Returns the activation and in-use states of a service managed by the manager
msgSMOpen	Opens a service
msgSMOwnerChanged	Indicates that the owner of a service managed by the manager has changed
msgSMSetOwner	Changes the owner of a service managed by the manager
msgSMUnbind	Severs the bond between an application and a service managed by the manager

Appendix B: Things to Keep in Mind

....

Memory Is Tight

You cannot squander memory. Your application should use little memory when active. It must be able to reduce its memory usage further when off-screen. An application that is packed with functionality but consumes a lot of memory is less likely to be successful than one that covers 70 percent of the problem while requiring very little memory.

Think Small

Most PC programs stand alone as large monolithic programs that attempt to do everything. In the cooperative, multitasking PenPoint environment it makes more sense to provide programs that present a facet of functionality or that orchestrate other applications and components. Use existing classes and components where possible in preference to writing your own from scratch.

Modular Components

Consider writing your application as a set of separable *components*. A component is a separately loadable module (a DLL) providing software functionality. It has a well-defined external interface so that other software can reuse it or replace it. Thus your application becomes an organizing structure that ties together visible components that can be embedded in other objects. For example, an outliner application might use a drawing component, a charting component, and a table entry component; you can license these components to or from other developers. GO is working to develop a market for third-party components, and itself offers two components: GrafPaper and the Table Server.

Everything's in Memory

The GO Computer's memory file system coexists with running applications in the same RAM. Most of the time most GO Computers will **not** be attached to any kinds of external media. You should be aware of the occasions when data in your application's memory space needlessly duplicates data or code that is also present in the file system. One way to avoid duplication is to use memory-mapped files for your application's data.

There's Only Memory

Because the GO Computer has a memory-resident file system, many of the trade-offs appropriate to traditional software design no longer apply. For example, the decision to read a start-up file "into memory" makes sense when memory access is several orders of magnitude faster than file access, but the GO Computer's memory file system **is** memory.

Your Application Must Recover

A user may go for weeks or months without backing up his or her GO Computer's file system. If your application goes wrong, PenPoint will try to halt it rather than the entire computer, but it is your responsibility to ensure that a new invocation of your application will be able to recover cleanly using whatever information it finds in the file system. This precept sometimes conflicts with avoiding data duplication, since the memory file system is more bullet-proof than the address space of a running application, hence filed state will usually survive a process crash.

Moreover, most of the time most users will not have the GO Computer boot disks on hand. You cannot rely on the user being able to press the reset switch in a jam. PenPoint uses hardware and software protection techniques to secure against applications unintentionally corrupting the kernel and/or file system, but it is not foolproof.

Object-Oriented or Else

You don't get to vote on using object-oriented techniques. You have to write a *class* for your application which *inherits* from *clsApp*. The windows your application displays on the screen must be *instances* of *clsWin* (or some other class inheriting from *clsWin*). Of course, there are tremendous payoffs from PenPoint's object-oriented approach in program size reduction, code sharing, application consistency, programmer productivity, and elimination of boilerplate code (large chunks of setup/housekeeping code that appear unchanged in every application).

Who Runs the Code? Who Owns the Data?

Think about what other parts of PenPoint need to access your classes, what tasks need to run the code in them, and who maintains their data. If your application has a client-server architecture, a separate back-end, or a core engine you'll need to have the picture in mind when choosing local versus global memory, dynamic versus well-known objects, process versus subtask execution, protecting shared data with semaphores and queued access, and so on.

Tip

PenPoint is a rich operating system with all these traditional kernel features available to applications. But a straightforward application may not need to concern itself with any of these issues. It just interacts with PenPoint subsystems, which make careful use of these features. For example, none of the PenPoint tutorial programs really gets involved with any of this.

User Sees Documents, Not Separate Programs and Program Files

Every document on a page is the conjunction of data and a process running an application. This leads to a document-centered approach to application design in place of a program-oriented approach. On a Mac or PC the user tends to fire up a program and work on a succession of files: under PenPoint, the user jumps from document to document, and the system unobtrusively starts up the right program for that document.

There are many ramifications of this: there are typically no *Open...* or *Save As...* commands in your application; PenPoint, not the user, saves data and quits programs; you present application templates and defaults to the user as stationery; and so on.

File Format Compatibility Is Important

The PenPoint environment is different from a PC (or Macintosh), and there are good reasons for many applications to take a different form on a GO Computer than their PC-based counterparts. However, some GO Computer users will transfer data to PC's where they and others will access the data with PC applications, so it is important to provide compatible file formats or file import/export support for your PenPoint applications.

Exploit the Pen

Graphical user interfaces built around mice and other pointing devices lead to flexible program architectures that respond to the user's actions instead of requiring the user to perform certain steps. The pen-oriented notebook interface of PenPoint is even more free-form. Just as with a mouse, the user can "point" to and manipulate (click, drag, stretch, wipe) entities on-screen, but on a GO Computer the user can also make gestures and handwrite characters "on" the visual entities. Taking advantage of the pen is a challenge and a tremendous opportunity.

The Good News

This list of cautions and additional concerns may sound like an intolerable burden on the developer, especially if it comes on top of learning C and object-oriented programming techniques. The good news is that the software architecture of PenPoint shoulders much of the load for you. The *Class Manager* supports the pervasive use of classes and objects throughout PenPoint not only in the user interface area, but also in areas such as the file system and the imaging model. This provides you with ready-made components that you can use as is or customize in your applications. These objects already conserve memory, exploit the pen interface, cooperate with other processes, and so on. In particular, nearly all of the work your application needs to do to be a first-class citizen in the GO Computer Notebook is already implemented by pre-existing classes that comprise GO's *Application Framework*.

Appendix C: Evaluating Pen-Based Computers and Handwriting Recognition Technology

This appendix was written by Bob Vallone, manager of User Research, GO Corporation.

Pen-Based Computing Does Not Equal Handwriting Recognition

Handwriting recognition technology is only one component of a pen-based computer operating system. Although it is a critical enabling technology, it is important to put it in context—many other attributes of a pen-based operating system are important and should also play a significant role in any comparison or evaluation of pen-based operating systems. Other important areas to evaluate are the quality of the user interface of the system, the sophistication of a wide array of traditional and novel operating system functionality, and the power of the development environment used by application programmers. In addition, a wide array of very powerful and useful applications are being developed for pen-based computers that either do not depend at all on hand-writing recognition technology, or use it for only limited, constrained input.

User Interface

A good place to start is to consider the metaphor used to help users organize their knowledge of the system. Some developers of pen-based systems
have chosen to extend metaphors invented decades ago for desktop computers. PenPoint features a notebook user interface (NUI) which presents users
with the familiar elements of a three-ring binder with pages of a notebook
organized into sections with tabs for easy access. The familiar notebook
metaphor, the gesture language, and other features of the user interface which
make it possible to avoid presenting users with the difficult concepts of files
and applications combine to make PenPoint computers exceptionally easy to
learn and use—significantly more so than even the most celebrated of today's
mouse-based graphical user interfaces (GUIs). The body of this book contains
a great deal of information about PenPoint's new user interface.

Operating System Functionality

It is sometimes easy to forget, especially when focusing on handwriting
recognition technology, that a pen-based computer operating system is first
and foremost an operating system—in particular, one that allows the pen to be
used as an input device in new ways. Potential users, developers, and licensees of a pen-based computer operating system should spend at least as
much, if not more, energy understanding and evaluating the design and
functionality provided by the operating system itself, as they do in evaluating
how well the system makes use of the pen, and how good its handwriting
recognition technology is. Operating system functionality grows in significance
especially when one considers that if the handwriting recognition subsystem is
replaceable (as PenPoint's is), the highest quality handwriting recognition
system available at any point in time can be easily integrated into the system.
The body of this book contains a great deal of information about PenPoint's
functionality.

Applications That Don't Rely on Handwriting Recognition

Many applications with broad horizontal appeal do not require users to enter significant amounts of handwriting that needs to be recognized (or translated) by the system. For example, *communications* applications such as receiving, marking-up, and sending faxes, or receiving, reviewing, and sending structured replies to electronic mail messages. A wide range of applications can all be characterized as *information access* and retrieval (query, sort, search, and display data from databases and large text documents or manuals). *Drawing*, painting, drafting, and layout applications do not require handwriting recognition, nor do applications designed to give computer based interactive *presentations*. Applications designed for *notetaking*, that do not require recognition, but rather focus on storing handwriting in a raw form that allows it to be organized, rearranged, moved, copied, edited, and hyperlinked to other data are also under development. This type of application also lends itself to group brainstorming and *meeting facilitation,* especially when combined with screen projection and shared screen networking.

Another key set of applications with broad appeal involve enabling users to review and *edit* files created on other systems, with rounC-trip data integrity—providing the power and use of use of the gesture commands for editing with the convenience of the mobility and portability of pen-based computers. Finally, one should consider that many additional horizontal computer applications may only require a limited amount of handwriting recognition. For example, some applications can make heavy use of highly constrained fields (like numbers only fields, fields with templates, or word lists) where recognition rates are very high, or multiple choice fields or pick-lists for choosing frequently used input. Examples of applications of this type include spreadsheets, calendaring and scheduling, contract management, and a wide variety of forms-based applications.

What Dialog between Applications and the Handwriting Recognition System Is Supported?

When evaluating a Pen-Based Operating System and its Handwriting Recognition System, it is important to understand what level of communication between applications and the Handwriting Recognition System is supported. Are applications in control of the raw input (strokes)? Can they perform their own analysis or recognition of strokes? When applications pass the raw input to the Handwriting Recognition System, can they pass along additional information that the system can use to aid in the recognition process? If so, what information can be passed to the handwriting system, what can the handwriting system do with this information, and what impact does it have on the recognition accuracy?

Looking at the subject of communication from the other direction, it is also important to know what information the Handwriting Recognition System can make available to applications in addition to the best guess at recognizing the input. Finally, it is important to understand whether the functionality to support this dialog between applications and the Handwriting Recognition System is a feature of the operating system, or is a feature of the particular Handwriting Recognition System. If the Handwriting Recognition system is replaceable, must every system provide this functionality, or can a new Shape Matching Engine be integrated and inherit this functionality from the operating system?

PenPoint applications are in control of the raw input; they can process it themselves, or they can utilize a very rich set of APIs that support a dialog with the Handwriting Recognition System. These APIs are a feature of PenPoint and its Context Management Subsystem—this means that the same dialog will be supported even if a new shape matching engine is integrated into the system.

The following is a brief overview of what information applications can provide to PenPoint and the Handwriting Recognition System to aid in the recognition process:

- Choice of Input UI (Boxed versus ruled input pads, size of boxes, line height, and so forth.)
- Choice of Editing UI (direct to application's client area with gestures to bring up edit pads, choice lists, etc., or direct to edit pads, choice lists)

- Choice of context aids or rules which aid the recognition process (e.g., spelling dictionary, personal dictionary, lists of acceptable characters, lists of acceptable words, templates similar to those used in database applications, case heuristics, punctuation rules, spacing rules)
- Level of Influence that context aids and rules should have in the recognition process (four levels: enable, propose, veto, and coerce)
- Choice of post-processing aids to the recognition process (e.g., spelling correction, case correction, space correction)
- Lists of acceptable gestures to aid in gesture recognition
- Choice of where to send strokes (gesture engine, text engine, both, or neither)
- Choice of when to process strokes or send them to a recognition engine (applications can store raw input and process them at any time)

In addition, PenPoint applications can manipulate strokes independently of the Handwriting Recognition System. They can: 1) filter strokes before sending them to any recognition engine, 2) perform their own analysis or recognition of the strokes, or 3) perform their own post-processing on the output of the recognition system. They can do any or all of the above in any combination. It is this flexibility which enables GO's Draw Demo Application to determine whether a circle should represent a circle, the edit gesture, or the letter o.

PenPoint's Handwriting Recognition System is also capable of providing a great deal of information to applications that they can use to help interpret handwriting input. The recognition system can provide to applications:

- lists of possible characters for single character input, not just a best guess character
- lists of possible words for word input, not just a best guess word
- weightings or probabilities when lists of multiple characters or words are provided
- size and boundary information per chararter or word (this information can be used by applications to determine what to do with the input, where to place the result in its client area, or how large the result should be—especially important for free-form applications like drawing, notetaking, or outlining)
- size, boundary information, and hot point of gestures

PenPoint also provides several components in the UI Toolkit that exploit this rich communication functionality with the Handwriting Recognition System by providing a higher level set of APIs that support specific application functionality. For example, one component greatly facilitates the process of developing forms fields with a set of APIs that tie together functionality of the input system, the handwriting recognition system, and the windowing system. Other UI Toolkit components facilitate the common uses of gestures, and ruled line input pads. PenPoint's object-oriented architecture encourages the development of such higher-evel components, and more will undoubtedly be developed over time.

Is the Handwriting Recognition System Replaceable?

Some pen-based computers have integrated handwriting recognition technology so tightly that it is not feasible to replace the system with one from another independent or third party developer. PenPoint is designed with a clean application programming interface (API) that enables the Shape Matching Engine in GO's handwriting recognition system to be easily replaced with engines from other vendors. Since the Shape Matching Engine is implemented below the level of Context Management Subsystem, any engine that replaces it will still benefit from all the powerful functionality that the Context Management Subsystem provides to applications. In much the same way that some desktop computer operating systems today can support different manufacturers' printers by installing printer drivers, PenPoint will allow handwriting recognition systems from independent third party developers to be installed.

This is important because handwriting recognition technology is still evolving and improving. Systems currently under development are based on radically different technologies ranging from neural networks to fuzzy logic algorithms. It is possible that one of these technologies may be significantly better than others at any given point in time over the coming years. The marketplace that PenPoint computers will create for handwriting recognition systems will stimulate competition among developers, which will inevitably lead to the development of more powerful systems.

The capability of replacing GO's handwriting recognition system with other systems will also enable computer manufactures to bring PenPoint computers to market in countries that require different character sets (for example, systems that support various European or Asian language character sets). It is also possible to add support for different symbol sets, enabling applications to be developed that recognize handwritten mathematical symbols or musical notation.

Users of PenPoint computers need not worry that they will be locked in to obsolete handwriting recognition technology. GO has an active program to recruit and support the efforts of independent thirC-party developers of handwriting recognition systems. Several developers are currently in the process of modifying the interfaces of their systems to be installable in PenPoint.

What Capabilities or Features of Handwriting Recognition Systems Are Important?

Symbols Recognized

Does the system recognize only uppercase characters and numbers (36 symbols), or does it also recognize lowercase characters (a total of 62 symbols)? How many punctuation characters does it recognize? GO's handwriting recognition system recognizes at least 20 punctuation symbols in addition to upper- and lowercase letters and numbers for a total of at least 82 symbols.

Segmented versus Unsegmented Input

Is the system capable of computing breaks between letters or are users required to write in boxed or combed fields to indicate letter spacing? Is the system capable of computing spaces between words, or is the user required to write a special space character or skip a space in a boxed or combed field to indicate word spacing? GO's handwriting recognition system is capable of computing both letter and word spacing—users do not need to write a special space character or write in boxes or combs to indicate letter and word spacing. However, users can choose to write in boxed or combed fields, to help maintain consistent spacing.

Flexibility of Writing Style

Is the system capable of recognizing a wide variety of printed forms for each character, or are users required to print characters in one or more standard ways? Are script forms of characters recognized? Can characters overlap or connect to each other without the pen being lifted? Can script handwriting be recognized (all characters connected)? Can a mixture of disconnected and connected characters (script and printed characters) within a word be recognized? GO's handwriting recognition system is capable of recognizing a wide variety of printed forms for each character (in addition users can train the system to recognize new shapes, see below). It is also capable of recognizing script forms of characters. GO's system is also capable of tolerating some overlapping as well as connected characters, although better recognition is obtained if characters are clearly separated. GO's current system is not capable of recognizing continuous script or mixed script and printed forms of writing.

Customization of Prototypes

Can users customize the handwriting system to recognize their particular idiosyncratic shapes or methods of forming characters? If the system is customizable (sometimes called trainable), is this required before the system can be used, or is it optional? What is the user interface for this customization process? Can more than one user store their individually customized prototypes on the system at the same time? GO's handwriting recognition system can be customized by users to recognize their idiosyncratic shapes or forms. This is optional, not required, as the system is usable for most people prior to using the customization application. The user interface for customization prompts users to write specified sentences, and learns how the user writes individual characters in the context of words and sentences. In addition, users can choose to focus on customizing only specific individual characters. More than one customized prototype set can reside on each computer, and users can easily switch between them.

Gestures

Is the handwriting recognition system capable of recognizing a wide variety of symbols and shapes as gestures, or command accelerators? GO's handwriting recognition system is capable of recognizing at least 50 gestures.

Flexibility in writing size. Can users write in different sizes, or is the system limited to recognizing characters written within a narrow range of heights and widths? GO's handwriting recognition system is capable of recognizing writing over a broad range of height and width.

Stroke Order Independence

Is the system capable of recognizing strokes out of sequence? For example, can users dot their i's and cross their t's at the end of a word, or on a previous word, or must they complete each character before writing the next? GO's handwriting recognition system is capable of recognizing strokes that are added to characters out of sequence, either at the end of a word, or even on any previous word in the entire input line.

Flexibility of Handwriting User Interface

Does the system allow users to vary the features of the input pads that they write into? Can users choose between ruled lines and boxed or combed fields? Can users vary the line height or the height and width of boxes or combs? Can users write in multiple lines? Can users vary the number of lines or rows in the writing pads? GO's handwriting recognition system allows users to vary all of these features of writing pads.

Gesture Recognition in Writing Pads

Is the system capable of recognizing and responding to gestures in writing pads (in the same space and at the same time that characters are also being recognized)? GO's handwriting recognition system is capable of recognizing certain gestures in writing pads and distinguishing them from text. For example, users may "scratch-out" handwriting prior to initiating recognition in order to avoid having the system translate letters or words that the user doesn't wish to be recognized for whatever reason. In addition, characters in boxed or combed fields may be deleted, or extra boxes or combs added with gestures.

Flexibility of User Interface for Error Correction

Does the system allow users to determine when to recognize or translate handwriting? Can users defer the recognition process indefinitely? Can multiple writing pads or input fields be simultaneously left in such a deferred translation mode? When the user does initiate recognition, does the system provide choices for how the results of the recognition are presented for verification and correction, or is there only one user interface that all users must use regardless of the accuracy rate that they achieve? Does the system enable users to choose the glyph that will be displayed when it is unable to recognize a particular character? GO's handwriting recognition system provides a flexible user interface for error correction in each of these respects.

Support for Uppercase Only Writers

Does the handwriting recognition system enable users to write in all upper case letters and automatically convert the characters to lower case after recognition? If so, does it do so intelligently, taking into account which characters should remain uppercase, or does it force all characters to lower case? GO's handwriting recognition system uses heuristics to enable users to write all upper case characters and have them intelligently converted to lower case, preserving uppercase when appropriate.

Speed

How fast does the handwriting recognition system recognize characters? Does the recognition proceed in the background, or does a majority of the computation take place after the user initiates the recognition process? GO's handwriting recognition system recognizes characters at about the rate of up to three characters per second. The recognition proceeds in the background in multiple line writing pads, so users rarely experience delays of more than the time required to recognize one line (2-4 sec), regardless of the amount of writing in the pad.

Interface with applications

See the Section, "What Dialog Between Applications and the Handwriting Recognition System Is Supported?" earlier in this appendix.

Recognition accuracy

See the Section, "What Metrics Are Available..." later in this appendix.

Measuring the Accuracy of Handwriting Recognition Systems

Before the widespread availability of personal computers in the mid 1980s, handwriting recognition systems existed primarily in research settings at major universities and a few corporate laboratories. In the mid 1980's the first low cost, interactive recognition systems built around opaque digitizing tablets connected as peripherals to Macintosh and IBM compatible PCs appeared on the market. Both the research systems and these early products typically characterized their accuracy simply in terms of the percentage of characters written that were translated correctly. This seemed to be sufficient, because

312

. . . .

The Power of PenPoint

the applications these devices were intended for were typically the collection of short strings of characters such as those required for entry into fields on simple forms.

The late 1980's saw the introduction of several personal computers that combined a digitizer with the viewing screen so that users could "write" on the glass surface of the screen with an electronic pen that appeared to dribble electronic ink (e.g., Linus and GridPad). The accuracy of the handwriting recognition systems used by these computers continued to be evaluated primarily in terms of simple character accuracy because the computers were being marketed for the purpose of gathering data on electronic forms in the context of specific vertical market applications.

GO Corporation's vision of Pen-Based Computing is much broader than simple data capture on electronic forms. GO has invested heavily not only in the development of a powerful general purpose handwriting recognition system, but in a research program chartered with developing real-world metrics and methods to evaluate the performance of the system for a wide variety of tasks. GO's research has discovered that there are four topics that are very important to enC-users of pen-based computers that have not previously been systematically measured or reported by vendors of handwriting recognition systems. The User Research Group at GO has worked extensively with the engineering team for over a year to design and implement improvements to the performance of the system in each of the following areas.

First, users are concerned about the acceptability of the handwriting recognition system's performance when *writing sentences and paragraphs of text* (as opposed to just short strings of characters in form fields). Second, users want the methods used when gathering data to characterize the system's performance to be realistic and representative of *typical (not ideal) performance.* Third, users are concerned about the acceptability of the total *time (including error correction)* it takes to complete a writing task. Fourth, developers of applications making heavy use of data entry fields like those found in forms need to know how the handwriting recognition system will perform when users are given various constraints on valid input (e.g., fields that accept numbers only, or fields that accept only certain uppercase characters).

Metrics for Writing Sentences and Paragraphs of Text

Users' acceptance of handwriting recognition accuracy in this context is related much more to *word level accuracy* (the percentage of words translated correctly) than it is to the percentage of characters translated correctly. Figure 1 shows a paragraph of text with some recognition errors. When asked to rate whether this level of accuracy would be acceptable, no users say that it would be, and most guess the character accuracy rate to be between 60 and 75%. Compare this to Figure C-2 which almost all users rate as acceptable, and most guess that the character accuracy is between 90 and 95%. In fact the two paragraphs have exactly the same character accuracy rate (300/333 = 90% correct) but widely different word level accuracy. Figure C-1 has a 50% word accuracy rate (28/56 words correct) because the individual character errors are distributed almost evenly over many words. Figure C-2 has a much higher 91% word accuracy rate (51/56 words correct) because the errors tend to cluster together in words. The difference between character level and word level accuracy is important when evaluating handwriting recognition systems because two systems that have similar levels of character accuracy can have widely different levels of word accuracy.

> Mg bvss at Wilcox Resegrch spoke rery kighly of yoyr cofpany and hecomkended that I aet in tuuch with yau. I am cuvrently looktng for a senior marlceting position in a grouth ofiented hign teoh somqany. I dould be very tnterested in kearpng your pefspeytive on the ibdustry tnd which negmehts are vffering good carefr oploortunities.

Figure C-1 A Sample of Handwriting Recognition with Errors Distributed over Many Words

My boss at Wilcox Rcseaneh spoke very highly of your company and recommended that I get in touch with you. I am cnenerfig looking for a senior marketing position in a growth oriented high tech company. I would be very ehfoncofca in hearing your perspective on the industry and ynlan segments are offering good ednoon oppor-tunities.

Figure C-2 A Sample of Handwriting Recognition with Errors Clustered Together

Figure C-3 illustrates the relationship between word accuracy and character accuracy for 75 samples of handwriting recognition that GO has observed in measuring early versions of its handwriting system and other systems currently available (each of the 75 samples represents a different user writing over 1300 characters). It is clear that high character accuracy rates do not guarantee high word accuracy rates. Many times, systems with approximately 90% character accuracy rates produced low word accuracy rates (between 50 and 70%). This level of performance is typical of handwriting recognition systems that focus primarily on the recognition of individual isolated characters and do not make effective use of dictionaries and/or other information about the relative frequencies of combinations of letters.

GO's User Research program has also determined that users' acceptance of handwriting recognition systems is strongly affected by how easy it is to correct words. GO's recognition system is capable of providing users with a list of alternatives for each word, so many words can be corrected simply by tapping on the correct word in a list. Other words can be corrected simply by writing over one or two characters. When users are faced with more than one or two errors in a word, and can't choose the correct word from a list, they typically choose to re-write the entire word. Another important metric therefore is the percentage of words that users will *re-write* vs. the percentage of words that can be corrected with a *simple edit*.

Appendix C: Evaluating Pen-Based Computers and Handwriting Recognition Technology

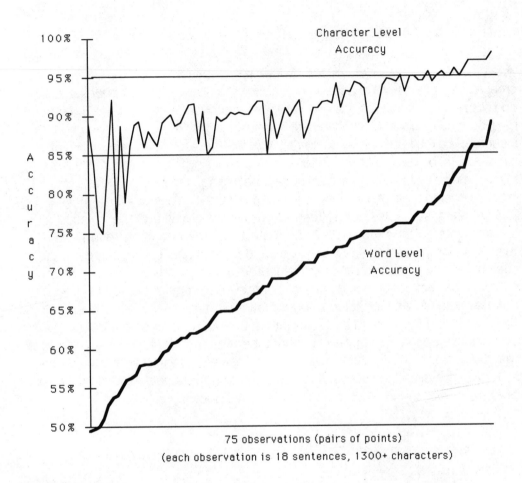

Figure C-3 The Relationship Between Word Level Accuracy and Caracter Level Accuracy in 75 Samples of Handwriting Recognition

Finally, it is important to measure and report the *variance* in users' accuracy rates. How much better than average do some users do, and how much worse than average do others do? It is useful to know the standard deviation of the mean (a statistical measure of variance) or to know what the average of the top 50% of users is as well as the average of the bottom 50%.

Methods for Measuring Typical Performance

Users' acceptance is determined by their own experience with the system. In order to predict the level of acceptance a system will have, it is important to test it and obtain metrics that are representative of typical users' experiences. The three most common ways in which handwriting recognition systems are measured with inappropriate methods are by using test *subjects* that are not representative of typical users, by using test *materials* (samples of writing) that are not representative of the material that typical users will usually be writing, and by using levels of *practice* prior to measurement that are not representative of typical use.

Samples of subjects used to test handwriting systems are often biased towards younger and more highly educated users. When interpreting test results, it is important to know the ages and educational backgrounds of the subjects. Sometimes systems are measured with samples of writing that contain only dictionary words, or that contain little if any punctuation. However, normal business writing includes punctuation and many words not usually in a dictionary, and this should be taken into account. Sometimes the accuracy of systems is measured after subjects have been practicing for weeks or months with the system, or only after they have extensively adapted their handwriting style. When evaluating results, it is important to understand exactly how much practice and/or training subjects in a test have had.

Metrics for Total Time to Write (Including Error Correction)

Users' acceptance is affected greatly by the total amount of time it takes to write a given amount of text. Thus, research data should include the time to write, the time for the system to translate the handwriting, and the time it takes the user to correct any recognition errors. The user interface for writing pads (areas of the screen that accept handwriting) has a large impact on writing time. For example, pads that require writing characters in segmented boxes typically result in increasing writing time by about 25 to 30%. Similarly, the user interface for error correction has a large impact on the time required to correct errors. One system may have a lower accuracy rate than another yet be strongly preferred by users if the total amount of time to enter, translate, and correct text is lower. A complete suite of metrics should include these time measurements in characters per second and words per minute.

Metrics for Writing in Fields with Constrained Input

Character level accuracy data should always be reported in conjunction with the size of the symbol set the recognition was being constrained to. These metrics are important to understand when designing applications involving large amounts of data entry into fields. What is the accuracy rate for numbers in a field that accepts numbers as well as uppercase and lowercase letters (62 symbols)? What is the rate in a field that accepts only numbers (10 symbols)? Similarly, what are the accuracy rates for upper- and lowercase letters in fields where 62 symbols are valid, and how does it compare to fields in which only 26 symbols are valid?

How Accurate Is GO's Handwriting Recognition System?

The following data was obtained from a study done on internal releases of PenPoint and GO's handwriting recognition system in October and November of 1990. This data reflects improvements made to the system after the Alpha release of PenPoint but prior to all improvements that will be made to the system in the Developers Release (currently scheduled for the first quarter of 1991). The latest available data will be presented at the GO Developers Summit in January 1991. Work on GO's handwriting recognition system will continue in between the Developers Release of PenPoint and the first enC-user release of the system (currently scheduled for fall 1991). The latest test data and results will be available from GO throughout 1991.

Subjects

Twelve subjects were recruited by a temporary employment agency in the San Francisco area. Half were male and half were female; about 1/3 were between the ages of 20 and 25, one third between 25 and 35, and one third between 35 and 45; about one third had 0–1 yrs post secondary education, one third had 2–3 years, and one third had 4 or more years.

Materials

For word level metrics, subjects wrote sentences of text that had been randomly selected from letters to the editor of a major business daily newspaper. The sentences contained punctuation and names of people, companies, and products that are not in the system dictionary. For field data entry metrics, subjects wrote name, address, and part number fields to obtain metrics for various levels of constraint (size of symbol set).

Practice/Training

Subjects spent three consecutive half days in a group training session (1 instructor, 6 students) that was modelled after a typical corporate training session. About 3 hours were spent on Handwriting Customization (customizing the recognition system to a particular user), 3 hours were spent practicing writing, 3 hours were spent gathering test data, and 3 hours were spent on other non-writing tasks to provide rest breaks for subjects.

Results: Word Level

In a test sample of 12 sentences (144 words) the average user achieved a word level accuracy rate of 78.3% (sd = 8.5%). The average character accuracy rate was 94.0% (sd = 3.3%). Most words with errors could be corrected with a simple edit (19.1%, sd = 6.8%) by either choosing an alternative word from the proof pad, or by overwriting 1 or 2 characters. An average of only 2.5% (sd = 2.5%) of words were categorized as needing to be re-written (this is an overestimate because it counts errors in one and two character words as re-writes, and because some users will in fact only re-write incorrect characters and not the entire word even when there are more than two errors).

The average of the top 50% of users was 84.6% word accuracy, 96.3% character accuracy. 14.1% of words could be corrected with simple edits, and only 1.4% were categorized as needing to be re-written. The average of the bottom 50% of users was 72.0% word accuracy, 91.7% character accuracy. 24.3% of words could be corrected with simple edits, and only 3.7% were categorized as needing to be re-written.

Results: Time to Enter/Correct

GO's handwriting recognition system accepts handprinted characters on ruleC-line input pads (boxed input is optional). As a result, the initial text entry rate averaged about 17 words per minute, or about 1.5 characters per second. GO's unique user interface for error correction enables words to be corrected in an average of under 9 seconds per incorrect word. This resulted in an average total net throughput including writing time, translating time, and editing time, of about 10 words per minute, or about .8 characters per second.

Results: Field Data Entry

Because of the relatively small sample sizes of our studies, the average character accuracy rate under various constraints can easily vary up or down by several percentages from one study to the next. For this reason, and because a great deal of fine tuning is currently under way prior to completing the Pen-Point Developers Release, we will report the range of accuracy achieved in our last several studies to provide a sense of the variance we encounter. The average accuracy rate for numbers in fields constrained to numbers ranged from 92 to 95%; the accuracy rate ranged from 90 to 93% when numbers were written in fields that could accept any uppercase characters, lowercase characters, or numbers (62 symbols).

The average accuracy rate for uppercase characters in fields constrained to uppercase characters ranged from 85 to 90%; the accuracy ranged from 82 to 88% when uppercase characters were written in fields that could accept any of uppercase characters, lowercase characters, or numbers (62 symbols).

The average accuracy rate for lowercase characters in fields constrained to lowercase characters ranged from 89 to 93%, the accuracy ranged from 86 to 92% when lowercase characters were written in fields that could accept any uppercase characters, lowercase characters, or numbers (62 symbols).

Results: Level of Acceptability for Various Tasks

Subjects were asked whether the level of accuracy and the effort required to correct errors that they experienced was acceptable for the task of filling out several forms a day. Subjects were also asked whether the level of accuracy and the effort required to correct errors that they experienced was acceptable for the task of writing several memos, letters, or notes a day. Typically about 75 to 85% of subjects rated the system as acceptable for these tasks. Subjects rating the system as unacceptable were not simply those subjects experiencing the lowest handwriting recognition accuracy, although accuracy was an issue for some of them.

The majority of users experiencing lower than average recognition accuracy still rate the system as acceptable for these tasks. Reasons cited by subjects who experience good recognition accuracy yet rate the system unacceptable seem to be idiosyncratic. For example, we recorded such diverse concerns as the speed of handwriting compared to typing for skilled typists, the physical strain of printing large amounts of text by hand, relative unfamiliarity of printing compared to script, legibility of the screen, etc. To summarize, although 15 to 25% of users rated their experience of the recognition system as unacceptable for certain tasks, it is important to understand that further improvements in the recognition accuracy will not guarantee that the system is acceptable by all users for all tasks.

To place these findings in perspective, we should ask what percentage of the population would rate today's computers, user interfaces, and input devices acceptable for a wide variety of tasks? We're not aware of any research indicating that it is as high as 75 to 85%. Of course the best way to do this type of research is to have users directly compare the ease of performing a series of tasks on a PenPoint computer to the ease of performing the same tasks on keyboard/mouse computers. GO's User Research Group has only recently begun to conduct this type of comparative research. Preliminary data from studies focusing on the user interface indicate that for a wide variety of basic operations most users rate PenPoint computers as easier to use than keyboard/mouse computers. Details of these studies will be available from GO in the spring of 1991.

Summary

PenPoint is currently available with GO's handwriting recognition system. This system is highly accurate as measured by a wide array of real-world metrics and methods, and is rated as acceptable for a wide range of tasks by most users tested. GO has had an ongoing serious research effort to focus on real-world use of handwriting recognition systems since the beginning of 1990. GO's User Research group will continue performing research to improve the effectiveness of GO's handwriting recognition system over time, as well as evaluating systems from other independent developers. PenPoint users, Independent Software Vendors, and licensees can be assured that the best handwriting recognition system for their application will be available to them because it is a feature of PenPoint that handwriting recognition systems can be replaced. GO has an active program of supporting third party developers' efforts to port their recognition systems to PenPoint.

Finally, it is important not to exaggerate the significance of the performance of the handwriting recognition system when evaluating an operating system for pen-based computers. Many applications don't require any (or only very limited) handwriting recognition. PenPoint is a new operating system that offers developers and users a great deal of valuable, innovative functionality and significant benefits in addition to handwriting recognition.

Glossary
of PenPoint Terms

This Glossary defines terms that are used in this book or that are important to an understanding of PenPoint.

abstract class	A class that defines messages or provides useful functionality, but is not useful as is; you wouldn't create instances of it.
accessory	An accessory document floats on the desktop when active, appearing over pages in the Notebook. Most accessories appear in the Tools auxiliary notebook.
acetate plane, acetate layer	The window system maintains a global, screen-wide display plane; called the acetate plane, which is where ink from the pen is normally dribbled by the pen-tracking software as the user writes on the screen.
activation	The transition of a document to an active state, with a running process, an application instance, and so forth.
activation	What happens when the user actually operates a control, often by lifting the pen up. The user can preview a control without activating it.
ancestor	Every class has one immediate ancestor. When a class receives a message, the class can elect to pass the message on to its immediate ancestor, and in turn the ancestor may pass on the message to its own ancestor. Hence a class can pick up, or inherit the behavior of its ancestors.
API	Application Programmer's Interface—The programmatic interface to a software system. The PenPoint API is covered in depth in the Architecture Reference; the functions and messages comprising the PenPoint API are listed in the API Reference and in the header files in \penpoint\sdk\inc from which the API Reference was derived.

323

application class	A PenPoint class that contains the code and initialization data used to create running applications.
Bezier curve	A curved line formed from two end points and two control points, supported by SysDC.
bind	You must bind a DC to a window (and hence a pixel device) before you can draw using it.
binding	The process that joins a device driver to a port or another device driver; for example, a client binding to a service makes the client known to that service.
bitmap	An array of pixels, with an optional mask and hot spot.
Browser	A component that displays file system contents to the user; used in disk viewers, installers, and TOCs.
button	Buttons are labels that the user can activate.
child window	A window that is a child, or grandchild, of another in the window tree.
choice	A table that displays several alternatives and allows the user to pick only one.
class	A special kind of object that implements a particular style of behavior in response to messages. Most classes act as factories for objects: you can create instances of a class by sending that class the message msgNew. In the PenPoint Class Manager, a class has a method table. The method table tells the class which messages sent to objects of that class to respond to. A class's processing of a message often involves passing the message to the class's ancestor in order to inherit appropriate behavior.
Class Manager	The code that supports the object-oriented, message-passing, class-based programming style used throughout the PenPoint operating system and in all PenPoint applications. The Class Manager itself implements two classes, clsObject and clsClass.
client	(1) The general term for any software using some feature of PenPoint (2) The object that receives messages from Toolkit components notifying it of important user actions and events.
client window	Frames and scrollwins manage a window that is supplied by, or of interest to, the client of the frame or scrollwin.
clipping	The process by which drawing operations in a window are prevented from affecting certain pixels on the windowing device, for example because those pixels are part of another window.
clsApp	Class for all applications; provides a head start framework by responding to the PenPoint Framework's protocol of messages.

component	A piece of system or application software functionality with a well-defined external interface, packaged as a DLL, which can be used or dynamically replaced by a third-party developer. Some components are unbundled and must be licensed separately from PenPoint.
component layer	The component layer of PenPoint consists of general-purpose subsystems offering significant functionality that can be shared among applications.
connected	A file system volume that is accessible from a PenPoint computer is connected: a volume may be known yet disconnected.
constraints	Specifications for the sizing and positioning of child windows during layout. The UI Toolkit includes clsTableLayout and clsCustomLayout, which implement tabular layout and relative positioning respectively.
context	(1) Information maintained by the driver and slave in a traversal engine episode. (2) Information maintained by the Class Manager to keep track of messages passed up and down the class hierarchy during message processing. (3) The PenPoint Source Debugger maintains a context indicating the current procedure body, which controls the lexical scope of variables.
cork margin	An optional thin strip in the default application frame which knows how to embed applications.
current directory entry	Each directory handle maintains a reference to the next directory entry it will use when the directory is read one entry at a time.
current grafic	A picture segment maintains an index in its set of grafics which is the grafic relative to which the next operation will take place.
data object	An object that maintains, manipulates and can recursively file data. Any descendant of clsObject can do this. Often used in Applications together with a view that observes the data object.
data resource	Contains information saved as a stream of bytes; see also object resource.
DC	Drawing Context—An object that implements, an imaging model; it draws on the device of the window to which it is bound. GO's SysDC is the imaging model used by all PenPoint's visual components.
deactivate	Deactivating an application removes its code from the user's PenPoint computer, but the Installer still keeps track of the application's UID and its home.
descendant class	A class that inherits from another, either directly or through a chain of subclasses.

. . . .

directory handle	An object that references either a new or existing directory node in the file system.
dirty layout	A client can mark a window's layout dirty to indicate that it needs to be laid out.
dirty window	The window system marks regions of a window dirty when they need to be repainted. Dirty windows later receive msgWinRepaint telling them to repaint their contents. You can mark windows as dirty yourself to make them repaint.
document	A filed instance of some application. A document has a directory in the application hierarchy, but at any given time it may not actually have a running process and a live application instance. These usually are destroyed when the user turns the page. Most documents live in the Notebook, but running copies of floating applications such as the Calculator and Installer are also documents.
dribble	The ink from the pen when the user writes over windows that support gestures and/or handwriting.
driver	The object requesting the traversal (such as the traversal engine or the search and replace application); see also slave.
DU4	Device Units 4th quadrant—The coordinate system of pixels on the PenPoint-based screen. Usually you perform window operations in LWC and specify drawing coordinates in LUC.
embed	The PenPoint Framework provides facilities for applications and components to display and operate inside other applications and components without detailed knowledge of each other. For example, every page in the Notebook is actually a document embedded in the Notebook's window. As another example, a business graphic document or component can be embedded within a text document.
embedded document	An embedded document is a document contained within another document.
embedded window mark	clsEmbeddedWin provides an embedded window mark that indicates the location of an embedded window.
entries	The items in a list box. List boxes are scrolling windows that support very large numbers of items, not all of which need to exist as windows at all times.
event	The occurrence of some an activity, such as the user moving the pen or pressing a key.
extract	The removal of a window and its children from the tree of windows on some device. It makes the window invisible but does not destroy it.
fields	Labels in which you can handwrite.
file export	A mechanism of the browser that presents the user with a choice of file format translators to export the selection.

file handle	The object with which you access a file node and its data (the handle is not a file itself).
file import	A mechanism of the browser that presents the user with a list of available applications that can accept the imported file.
filing	Objects must ordinarily file their state in the file system so that the user is not aware of documents activating and terminating on page turns.
filter	A means of restricting the kinds of messages an object or process receives.
fixed-point numbers	A 32-bit number composed of an integer and fractional component.
floating	A floating window appears above the main Notebook; unlike documents on pages in the Notebook, the user can move and resize a floating window.
font cache	After ImagePoint renders a font glyph into a bitmap, it keeps the bitmap in a font cache to speed future drawing of the character at that size.
frame	The border surrounding documents and Option Sheets, which often includes a title bar, resize corner, move box, and so forth.
gesture	A simple shape or figure that the user draws on the screen with the pen to invoke an action or command. (See also scribble.)
global memory	Memory accessible from all tasks—you can pass pointers to objects in global memory between tasks.
glyph	A symbol or character in a font.
grab	Getting exclusive notification of events in the system, for example when tracking the pen.
grafic	The individual figure drawing operations stored in a picture segment.
graphics state	The current scale, rotation, units, foreground and background colors, line thickness, and so on, maintained by a SysDC object.
heap	A pool of memory; individual chunks of memory in it aren't protected, but it's cheaper than allocating a segment.
hot mode	A state in which the PenPoint Framework will not terminate (shut down) an application.
image device	A windowing device the image memory of which is under the control of the client (instead of on a screen or printer).
in-line	In-line fields provide full handwriting and gesture recognition, allowing the user to write with the pen directly into the field itself.

In Box	PenPoint's In Box and Out Box services allow the user to defer and batch data transfer operations for later execution; they appear as iconic notebooks.
inheritance	A class inherits the behavior of its immediate ancestor class. Through inheritance, all classes form a tree with clsObject at the top.
insertion pad	A window that supports character entry. It may contain windows supporting different kinds of character entry such as character boxes, ruled paper, and a virtual keyboard.
installation	Usually refers to the process of installing some item onto a PenPoint computer, especially an application, but also fonts, handwriting prototypes, and services.
instance	Every object is an immediate instance of the class that created it. It is also an instance of that class's ancestors. For example, a button is an instance of clsButton, but it is also an instance of clsLabel, of clsWin, and of clsObject.
instance data	Data stored in an object; it is normally only accessable by the object's class, which uses instance data in responding to messages sent to that object. The class defines the format of the instance data. Classes often choose to have instance data include pointers to instance information stored outside the object.
kernel	The portion of the PenPoint operating system that interacts directly with the hardware; the core memory and task management code that is the first code loaded when PenPoint boots. Most system services are implemented in the kernel.
label	A window that displays a string or another window.
layout	The process of sizing and positioning a tree of windows. Windows and Graphics implement a protocol through which a client can tell windows to lay out, and windows can ask each other for their desired sizes. Instead of specifying the exact position and size of all windows, you need only supply a set of constraints on their relative positions.
list	An object that holds an ordered collection of items.
list box	A scrolling window that displays a subset of entries from a potentially very large set.
local memory	Per-process memory; pointers to objects in local memory can only be passed between tasks in the same task family.
local volume	Volumes on hard or floppy disk drives attached to the PenPoint Computer through its built-in SCSI port.
locator	Specifies a node in the file system; it is a directory handle:path pair, in which the path is the path from that directory handle to the node.

LUC	Local Unit Coordinates—Arbitrary coordinates associated with a DC. You can specify different units, scaling, rotation, and transformation for LUC.
LWC	Local Window Coordinates—The coordinates of a window in pixels, with the origin at the lower-left corner of the window.
main window	The window of an application that the PenPoint Framework inserts on-screen in the page location or as a floating window. An application's main window is usually a frame.
installation manager	An installation manager is an instance of clsInstallMgr that manages the installation, activation, deactivation, and Update from Home of a set of similar items.
memory-mapped file	You can map a file into memory so that you read and write to it simply by accessing memory.
menu bar	A frame has an optional menu bar below its title bar. The PenPoint Framework defines standard application menu items (SAMS) for an application's main window frame.
menu button	A button that displays a pop-up menu when the user taps on it.
message	A 32-bit value you send to an object requesting it to perform some action. Messages are constants representing some action that an object can perform. The type message is a tag that identifies the class defining the message and guarantees uniqueness. When you send a message to an object, if that message is mentioned in the class's method table, then the Class Manager calls a message handler routine in the class's code which responds to the message.
message argument(s)	The information needed by a class to respond to a message. Often the message argument parameter is a pointer to a separate message arguments structure: this is the only way a class can pass back information to the sender.
message handler	A function in a class's code that implements appropriate behavior for some message or messages; called by the Class Manager in response to message associated with it in the class's method table.
method	Synonym for message handler.
method table	An array of message-function name pairs (plus some flags) that determines which message handler function (if any) will handle messages sent to objects of that class.
Method Table Compiler	DOS program that compiles a file of method tables into an object file that you link with your class's code.
metrics	Information made public about instances of a class is often called metrics, and many classes provide a pair of messages to set and get metrics.

node	A location in the File System; can be a directory or file. The PenPoint file system is organized as a tree of nodes.
note	A window that presents transient information to the user.
Notebook	The main notebook on-screen, usually the user's personal notebook.
notebook metaphor	The visual paradigm in PenPoint of a physical notebook containing pages, documents and sections, with tabs, a page turn-effect, and so on.
object	An entity that maintains private data and can receive messages. Each object is an instance of some class, created by sending msgNew to the class.
object resource	Contains information required for creating or restoring a PenPoint object; see also data resource.
observer	An object that has asked the Class Manager to notify it when changes occur to another object. Objects maintain a list of their observers.
open	A document currently displayed on-screen.
Option Sheet	A floating frame displays attributes of the selection in one or more card windows.
owner	The process that creates a subtask owns that subtask and any sibling subtasks created by it.
parent window	Every window in the window tree but the root window has a parent window. Conversely, when you extract a window from the window tree, it no longer has a parent and so it and all its child windows are no longer visible on-screen.
PenPoint Framework	Both the protocol supporting multiple, embeddable, concurrent applications in the Notebook, and the support code that implements most of your application's default response to the protocol for you. The protocol and code provide a head start for building applications in the pen-based, document-oriented Notebook environment.
picture segment	An object in which you can store and replay sequences of drawing operations.
pixel	A picture element with a value.
pixelmap	A rectangular array of pixels.
point	1/72 of an inch.
pop-up	A window (usually a menu or field) that temporarily appears on top of all other windows.
previewing	The feedback provided by a control while the user is manipulating the control, before the user chooses whether to activate the control.
process	An operating system context with its own local memory.

prototype	A shape template with which sets of strokes are compared in handwriting recognition.
proximity	A state reported by the pen hardware on some PenPoint computers when the user has the pen near the screen. It's independent of the pen tip being down. Using a mouse, you simulate this by pressing the middle mouse button to go out of proximity.
PWC	Parent Window Coordinates—The Local Window Coordinates of a window's parent.
recognition	Matching a set of user strokes with the most likely prototype(s) during handwriting translation.
remote volume	Volumes available over a network or other communication channel.
repaint	The pixels of a window need to be repainted in various circumstances: when the window first appears on screen, when the window is covered by another window and then exposed, when the window changes size, and so on. When a window needs repainting, the window system marks it dirty. When you repaint a window, the pixels affected are the visible portions of the dirty region.
resource	A uniquely identified collection of data. Resources allow applications to separate data from code in a clean, structured way.
RGB	Red, Green, Blue—A means of specifying colors by the amount of these primary colors.
root directory	Top-most node of the file system hierarchy on a volume.
root window	Top of the window tree on a windowing device.
row	A Table Server table has a fixed number of columns and a variable number of rows.
sampled image	An image made up of pixels.
SAMS	Standard Application Menus—The PenPoint Framework supplies a set of SAMS (the Document and Edit menus), to which applications can add their own menu items.
scribble	A collection of strokes that translators can translate into either text characters or command gestures.
SDK	Software Developer's Kit—A development package to assist developers in writing applications for a system. The PenPoint SDK provides the code required to develop applications, and documentation and tools to assist development.
selection	PenPoint maintains a system-wide selection, which is the target for all editing operations. The Notebook UI lets users select applications and icons; applications and components may allow users to select words, shapes, and other entities within their windows.

self	The object that originally receives a message. Code that processes a message is passed the UID of self.
service	A general, non-application DLL that enables PenPoint clients to communicate with a device or to access a function, such as a database engine.
service section	A section in the In Box or Out Box; each is associated with a specific service and represents a queue to or from that service.
shut down	The PenPoint Framework shuts down a document to conserve memory by destroying its application object and terminating its process. Thereafter the document only exists as a directory and files in the application hierarchy.
standard message	A procedural interface to put up standardized notifications, warnings, and requests to the user in the form of notes. The text of standard messages is stored in resources.
stationery	Application-specific template documents.
status value	Most functions and messages in PenPoint return a value of type status, indicating success, an error of some sort, or some other status. Status values are constant tags in order to indicate the class (or pseudo-class) returning the status, and to guarantee uniqueness.
stroke	Data structure that stores the path traced by the pen when the user holds it against the screen and writes with it. Note that the pen hardware supplies stroke coordinates at much higher resolution than that of the ink dribbled by the pen on-screen.
subclass	To create a new class that inherits from an existing class. You subclass a class in order to pick up its behavior, while modifying or extending its behavior to do what you want.
subtask	A task that shares the address space (local memory as well as global memory) of its parent process.
SysDC	System Drawing Context—PenPoint's standard DC, which implements the imaging model used by all of PenPoint's visual components. It supports polylines, splines, arcs, outline fonts, arbitrary units, scaling, transformation, and many other features. It unifies text with other graphics primitives in a single, PostScript-like imaging model.
system layer	The system layer of PenPoint provides windowing, graphics, and user interface support in addition to common operating system services such as filing and networking.
system privilege	A high level privilege associated with executing code; particular segments may only be accessible by tasks running at this level. Only PenPoint code executes at this level.

tag	(1) A unique 32-bit number that uses the administered value of a well-known UID to ensure uniqueness. (2) An arbitrary 32-bit number that you can associate with any window. You can check a window's tag and search for a particular tag in the window tree; this makes tags useful for identifying components in shared option sheets and menus.
tap	A pen down event followed by a pen up, with no significant motion in between.
task	Generic term for a thread of control executing code in PenPoint; includes software tasks and hardware tasks.
task family	A process and all its subtasks.
task ID	Hexadecimal identifier of a task in DB.
TOC	Table of Contents—The browser page at the beginning of a notebook or section that shows its contents.
toolkit table	Workhorse class in the UI Toolkit for a tabular collection of other components; its descendants include choices, option tables, menus, tab bars, and command bars. You can define toolkit tables statically, so they form a simple user interface specification language.
translator	An object that when hooked up to a handwriting window receives captured scribbles and translates them into ASCII characters or gestures.
UI component	Any window implemented by one of the UI Toolkit's many classes.
UI Toolkit	PenPoint's User Interface Toolkit provides many different kinds of window subclasses to support a wide variety of on-screen controls, such as labels, buttons, menus, frames, option sheets, and so forth.
UID	Unique Identifier—A 32-bit number that is the handle on an object. When you send a message to an object, you send it to the object's UID.
UUID	Universal Unique Identifier—A 64-bit number that is guaranteed to be unique across all PenPoint computers, usually used to identify resources in resource files.
view	A window that presents a user interface and observes a data object; when the data change, the data object notifies its observers and the view updates its display of the object.
view-data model	An approach to designing applications and components that divides the presentation and storage of state into separate view and data objects.
volume	A physical medium or a network entity that supports a file system.

well-known

(1) An object is well known when its UID is statically defined for all PenPoint computers. Access may still not be possible if the object is not correctly installed on a particular PenPoint computer. Most PenPoint classes and globally accessible objects (such as theScreen or theWorkingDir) have well-known UID's. (2) Well-known resource IDs identify data and object resources that can be used by any client.

window tree

The hierarchy of windows formed by a window, its child windows, their child windows, and so on. The on-screen window tree starts with a root window on a windowing device.

windowing device

A pixel device that supports multiple overlapping windows. All windows are associated with some windowing device, even if the window is not currently inserted in the window tree on that device.

Index